Gender Issues in Jewish Law

Studies in Progressive Halakhah
General Editor: Walter Jacob, published in association with the Solomon B. Freehof Institute of Progressive Halakhah, Pittsburgh and Tel Aviv

Dynamic Jewish Law
Progressive Halakhah—Essence and Application
Edited by Walter Jacob and Moshe Zemer

Rabbinic-Lay Relations in Jewish Law
Edited by Walter Jacob and Moshe Zemer

Conversion to Judaism in Jewish Law
Essays and Responsa
Edited by Walter Jacob and Moshe Zemer

Death and Euthanasia in Jewish Law
Essays and Responsa
Edited by Walter Jacob and Moshe Zemer

The Fetus and Fertility in Jewish Law
Essays and Responsa
Edited by Walter Jacob and Moshe Zemer

Israel and the Diaspora in Jewish Law
Essays and Responsa
Edited by Walter Jacob and Moshe Zemer

Aging and the Aged in Jewish Law
Essays and Responsa
Edited by Walter Jacob and Moshe Zemer

Marriage and Its Obstacles in Jewish Law
Essays and Responsa
Edited by Walter Jacob and Moshe Zemer

Crime and Punishment in Jewish Law
Essays and Responsa
Edited by Walter Jacob and Moshe Zemer

GENDER ISSUES IN JEWISH LAW

❖ ❖ ❖

Essays and Responsa

Edited by
Walter Jacob *and* Moshe Zemer

Berghahn Books
New York • Oxford

First published in 2001 by
Berghahn Books

© 2001 Walter Jacob and Moshe Zemer

All rights reserved.
No part of this publication may be reproduced
in any form or by any means
without the written permission of Berghahn Books.

ISBN 1-57181-239-3 paperback

Printed in the United States on acid-free paper.

Contents

Acknowledgments   vii

Introduction   viii

Part I
Essays

Chapter 1
Innovation and Authority: A feminist Reading of the "Women's Minyan" Responsum
    Rachel Adler   3

Chapter 2
Gender Issue in Jewish Divorce
    John D. Rayner   33

Chapter 3
Gender, Halakhah, and Women's Suffrage: Responsa of the First Three Chief Rabbis on the Public Role of Women in the Jewish State
    David Ellenson and ***Michael Rosen***   58

Chapter 4
Custom Drives Jewish Law on Women
    Elliot N. Dorff   82

Chapter 5
Halakhah, Minhag, and Gender
    Richard Rosenthal   107

Chapter 6
The Woman in Reform Judaism:
Facing or Avoiding the Issues
    Walter Jacob   130

Chapter 7
Progressive Halakhah and Homosexual
Marriage
    Moshe Zemer   151

Chapter 8
Reform Judaism and Same-Sex Marriage:
A Halakhic Inquiry
    Peter S. Knobel   169

Part 2
Selected Reform Responsa

Reform Judaism and Divorce	187
A Reform *Get*	191
Agunot	195
Ordination of Women	198
Women Wearing a *Talit*	219
Marriage after a Sex-Change Operation	222
Homosexual Convert	226
Lesbians and Their Children	228
Contributors	229

Acknowledgements

We continue to be grateful to the Rodef Shalom Congregation for supporting the Freehof Institute of Progressive Halakhah and for assisting in technical matters connected with the publication of this volume.

Our thanks also go to Nancy Berkowitz who has carefully helped to edit this and some previous volumes of the series. We wish to thank Barbara Bailey for her efforts with the typescript.

Introduction

Biblical Judaism is clear when it deals with matters of gender in law or story. The role of men and women is either understood or defined. We may see this initially in the story of creation and the tales of the patriarchs, and subsequently in the historical books as well as the legal material. Men and women—whether single, married, homosexual, or in various other possible states—were given a definite status or were rejected.

Individuals in the long biblical history did not fit into these prescribed patterns; some rejected them dramatically, others quietly. Either way, such individuals were the exception, for most it was impossible to step out of their assigned positions, as the gender roles were well delineated.

Subsequent centuries brought changes, but rarely were they spectacular. The position of women changed slightly, usually in a positive direction, at other times, not. Additional rights were provided eventually, but within set limits. The most celebrated example was the ban on polygamy in the Ashkenazic world ascribed to R. Gershom a thousand years ago. It reflected, as did so much else, a reaction to the changes in northern and central Europe, the world in which these Jews lived. It did not, however, influence the Sephardic communities in their Islamic surroundings.

Radical changes in our understanding of gender began only in the nineteenth century and moved rapidly in the twentieth. Judaism had to react to these changes and did so through the liberal movements—Reform, Conservative, and Reconstructionist—that have slowly influenced the remaining Jewish world.

These changes, sometimes reluctantly made, at other times bold and revolutionary, have influenced the basic concepts of

Judaism, our family structure, our liturgy, our thoughts about leadership, and our halakhah. The changes are still occurring rapidly around us as the discussions within the responsa and liturgy committees of each movement reflect clearly.

What was static for many centuries or subject only to refinement has in the last half-century seen radical changes and a vast amount of experimentation. Perhaps in the area of gender more than any other, modern Judaism has seen itself redefined. This volume discusses some of those changes and new definitions and how they continue to be reflected in the developing Reform halakhah.

Part One

Essays

Chapter 1

❖ ❖ ❖

Innovation and Authority
A Feminist Reading of the "Women's Minyan" Responsum

Rachel Adler

On 13 Kislev 5745 (December 13, 1984), five faculty members of Rabbi Yitzhak Elhanan Seminary at Yeshiva University issued a brief proclamation on a subject unprecedented in Jewish legal history.[1] The proclamation announced that it was forbidden for women to participate in separate gatherings for prayer, for Torah reading, for reading the Book of Esther, or for Simhat Torah processions. Lacking both documentation and argument, the proclamation departed radically from the conventions governing classical responsa, but subsequently one signatory, Rabbi Zvi Schachter, buttressed its halakhic conclusions in an extensive and heavily documented essay published in Yeshiva University's halakhah journal, *Bet Yitzhak*.[2] The first responsum, as many of its critics noted, cannot really be analyzed, since it is more of a ukase than a responsum, offering neither argument nor evidence.[3] This paper is concerned, therefore, with the content and implications of Rabbi Schachter's responsum, which has been widely circulated and much quoted, both in subsequent decisions in

---
Notes for this section begin on page 27.

the United States and in the recent legal cases before the Israeli Supreme Court involving the prayer group Women at the Wall and their right to pray communally at the Western Wall in Jerusalem.

The responsum is interesting for several reasons. First, as a responsum, it confronts a singular challenge: to render a halakhic decision on a phenomenon for which halakhah has neither law nor precedent, data nor categories, and which involves behaviors in which classical halakhah had no interest. Hence, both Schachter's responsum and the activity it seeks to suppress raise questions about the location and the limits of halakhic authority and of communal creativity. These questions are not new. There is a sizable literature in the philosophy of halakhah about whether halakhah is an inclusive and self-sufficient system of behavioral norms or a code confined to particular concerns that allows room for supplementary ethical systems.[4] Similarly, there is both philosophical and historical literature concerning how customs originate and take root, and how Torah authorities respond to these new religious developments.[5] But it is interesting to trace the implications of particular answers to these theoretical questions in a work whose purpose is quite practical: to forbid a religious expression it views as subversive and to dismantle the institution that embodies it.

There is a second point of interest. Information exists about this responsum that is rarely available. Had Schacter's responsum been written five hundred years ago, we might now have only his legal argument, his precedents, and the counter arguments of opposing authorities from which to infer a complex social reality. The reasoning and motives of the innovators themselves would be refracted obliquely through the only perspectives referenced in responsa literature: those of the jurisprudential elite who control the discourse.

In contrast to law whose authors are specifically cited in the literature, custom is attributed to groups or communities rather than individuals.[6] In the case of women's prayer groups, however, indisputable evidence exists that identifiable leaders created and popularized the controversial legal and liturgical vision under discussion. We have their writings. We know their names. Yet the voices of women and the impact of women's actions on their social and religious environments are as subtextual in recent legal writings as they might have been five hundred years ago. The male elite who claim responsa literature as their domain continue to converse only with one another and to render anonymous the outsiders whose acts provide the content for the elite conversation. Hence, Rabbi Abraham Weiss in his book opposing Schachter's opinion, is hardly less reticent than Schachter about the social reality that occasioned its composition, nor does Weiss cite the women who created this new religious institution.[7] There is a "gentlemen's agreement" to converse *about* rather than *with* these mothers of inventions so that their accomplishments may be reframed for the purposes of the responsa literature as problems detected by one rabbi and referred to another for solution. The problem is framed either as an upsurge of antinomian rebellion against halakhah and its legitimate interpreters which the decisor must put down or as an inchoate longing felt by anonymous women for which the compassionate decisor will offer a remedy: the prayer group. Suppressing the social history of the prayer group, then, is a distortion designed to reinforce a rabbinic monopoly on authority.

Although the creators of responsa have excluded this social history as legally irrelevant, the student of responsa literature need not ignore it. As David Ellenson's pioneering work in this area demonstrates, applying sociological and historical methods to the study of responsa greatly enriches our understanding of the responsa themselves.[8] The Schachter responsum is a prime candidate for just such an analysis. It offers an unprecedented diversity of extralegal sources. We have observers' descriptions of women's prayer group services and discussions of related concerns in the innovators' own words, as well as news articles from the Jewish press that reveal political agreements and rabbinic motives unacknowledged by the responsum. A wealth of primary and secondary sources chronicle and analyze secular and Jewish feminist movements in whose contexts women's prayer groups were conceived. Once these extralegal sources are consulted and the responsum's author no longer exclusively controls information about the issue, the author's representation of the phenomenon that occasioned the responsum and his account of the legal facts about which he will reason, are revealed to us as a perspective on reality, rather than reality unmediated.

These concerns about the impact of context and perspective on legal decision making are fundamental to feminist jurisprudence. Feminists argue that law rests upon narratives and is composed of narratives.[9] Narratives are not abstract and general but concrete and sharply specific.[10] By dropping crucial contextual elements, a jurist may distort the nature of a case. A feminist approach to law demands an expanded notion of legal relevance that renders admissible more richly particularized accounts and wider temporal boundaries than classical legal argumentation would admit.[11] Feminist legal scholars argue that admitting more data about the actual circumstances and concerns of women into the legal process enables a better fit between cases and the legal principles applied to them.[12] In contrast to formalist legal approaches, this approach is implicitly historicist. It seeks out data about personal and social experience that abstract paradigms would exclude.

A second principle of feminist jurisprudence germane to the study of responsa concerning women is the hermeneutics of suspicion with which feminist legal theorists approach the ostensibly ungendered language and categories of law and social policy.[13] Discourse and principles may present themselves as universal and gender-free and yet harbor hidden androcentric presumptions or reflect exclusively androcentric narratives or perspectives. Feminist jurisprudence presumes that no unitary account of human nature and no universal enunciation of norms can ensure justice. Rather, justice demands an account of human difference and norms that reflects gendered existences.[14] To this end, feminist jurisprudence uses the social sciences to provide richer descriptions of human psychology and of human environments.[15]

In this article I have combined the principles of feminist jurisprudence with Ellenson's sociohistorical methodology for reading responsa to produce a feminist reading of the Schachter responsum. This methodology allows me to retrieve and interpret the narratives at issue: the narrative implicit in the responsum and the counter narrative the responsum seeks to repress. It peoples these narratives with real, complexly motivated human beings and situates them historically. Thus, it provides a social and historical frame within which to examine the form, function, and argument of the responsum. The article is organized as follows: First, I will situate the development of prayer groups within the context of the social history of the Jewish feminist movement and offer a description and analysis of prayer groups based on the testimony of members and observers. Next, I will recount the circumstances under which the Schachter responsum was elicited and place it in its larger social and ideological context. Third, I will analyze the content of the responsum. Finally, I will suggest implications and conclusions.

Prayer Groups and the Social History of American Jewish Feminism

The 1970s saw the burgeoning of Jewish feminism, an outgrowth of the second great wave of American feminist thought and practice that began in the mid-1960s. Although Jewish feminists borrowed theory from major feminist thinkers such as Simone De Beauvoir and practices such as consciousness raising from secular feminist praxis, distinctive Jewish concerns remained addressable only by a home-grown Jewish feminism. Central among these concerns were issues concerning halakhah and participation in Jewish ritual.[16] The mothers of Jewish feminism were thoroughly acculturated, highly educated, American Jews. They identified halakhah as a source of stigma and unequal treatment. Halakhah accounted for painful dissonances between secular and religious experience. As severely as sexism affected the secular lives of middle-class Jewish women, it was seldom as concrete and overt as the exclusion and disempowerment these women experienced when they attended synagogue or sought a Jewish divorce. From no field of secular knowledge were they excluded as comprehensively and openly as they were excluded from the knowledge of halakhah and its sources, nor did any other system of authority demand their obedience while explicitly denying them representation in the power structure that governed them. Secular sexism was an undercurrent, concealing and dissembling its menaces and biases beneath an ideology of merit. This ideology declared that all had equal opportunities to become corporate executives, senators, or scientists, and the best "men" won. Halakhah, in contrast, unequivocally stated that the status of woman disqualified them from full participation in the public life of the Jewish community.

Judged by the liberal civic values inculcated in American Jews, such a system could be regarded only as unjust. As American citizens and good liberals, Jewish women were taught that all people were entitled to equal rights; that communities should be structured democratically, with no one excluded from participation; and that privileges ought to be awarded fairly on the basis of merit. Where reality fell short of the ideal, the model of the Civil Rights movement and the assertion of Black Power demonstrated how a disenfranchised group can confront a discriminatory system and force it to change.

The critique of halakhah and the efforts both to mend it where it harmed or excluded women and to supplement it where it did not address women are among the earliest themes of feminist Judaism.[17] The activists on this issue were modern Orthodox and learned Conservative women. I wrote the much reprinted essay "The Jew Who Wasn't There," as an Orthodox woman in 1971.[18] The first Jewish women's group to place feminist themes on the American Jewish agenda, *Ezrat Nashim*, was an offshoot of the New York *Havurah* and had many Conservative Jewish members. Its members lobbied at the 1972 national meeting of the Rabbinical Assembly of the Conservative movement and distributed a manifesto calling for equal participation in Jewish life and ritual. They also provided the first nationally known model of a Jewish women's community at prayer.

Early in 1973, under the sponsorship of the North American Network of Jewish Students, a national Jewish women's conference was held in New York. Five hundred women attended, among them a number of Orthodox women, including the keynote speaker, Blu Greenberg. One of the most electrifying experiences of the conference was Shabbat worship for women only, led by members of *Ezrat Nashim*. Most of the attendees had never before heard women lead prayers or chant from the Torah or seen women wear a *tallit*, nor had they had ever experienced themselves as full participants in the service. Women who had never touched a Torah scroll before were called up for their first *aliyot*. They wept, and the congregation wept with them.

Participation was revelatory on many levels. Women experienced new spiritual dimensions in communal worship. They emerged with an enhanced sense of Jewish competence, a hunger to learn more, and a newly awakened determination to replicate their experience in their home communities. These themes are apparent in Blu Greenberg's recollection of lifting the Torah at the Network Shabbat service.

> Choose someone else, I pleaded. They persisted gently but firmly. It was only good breeding that propelled me down the aisle. Then something happened that was to make me think for a long time about the value of practiced skills. I had seen *hagba'ah* performed at least a thousand times in my life. Yet, as I stood there, I had to ask the women standing next to me, "What do I do now?" Also, to my surprise, caught as I was with my defenses down, I found it an exhilarating moment. It was the first time I had ever held a Torah scroll.[19]

In subsequent years, women's minyanim became an option at institutes and conferences. In some communities continuing women's minyanim were established. At first, Orthodox women participated without constraints in these minyanim, relying on unpublished decisions such as that of Rav Shlomo Goren, the Ashkenazic Chief Rabbi of Israel.[20] This opinion was explicitly withdrawn in December 1989. Well before that time, however, most of the rabbis upon whom American Orthodox feminists relied were telling them that women were not permitted to say the distinguishing prayers of a minyan, *devarim she-be-qedusha*, including *barekhu, qaddish,* and *qedusha*, citing *B. Berakhot* 45b and the accompanying *Tosafot* and *Shulhan Arukh Orah Hayyim* 55:1. Although permissions were unpublished and came to the women concerned only by word of mouth, relayed from rabbi to rabbi, interdictions were published early on.

The very project of an Orthodox feminism came under attack while still in its formative stages in a famous responsum in 1976 by R. Moshe Feinstein (*Igrot Moshe Orah Hayyim* 4:49): *Ha-Nashim Ha- Sha'anot Ve-Ha-Hashuvot* (Concerning the new movement of smug and important women.[21] In this responsum R. Moshe labels the feminists "heretics" (*kofrim*), a code word for Conservative Jews, and forbids their taking on mitzvot from which they are exempt, not because he regards this as categorically forbidden but because "the desire comes out of a rebellion against God and his Torah." The responsum clearly registers the political significance of the women's ritual behavior and sees *minhag* as the battleground.[22] The tone of the responsum is ambivalent, divided between a condemnation of feminism and an apologetic defense of the respected status of women in Judaism and arguing that "there is no reason to be angry." In conclusion, R. Moshe exhorts the rabbi who has submitted the question to "prevent these women ... from changing any sacred customs of Israel."[23]

No text and no precedent explicitly forbid women to pray in the company of other women, and that was an implicit permission upon which Orthodox feminists seized. In contrast to nontraditional feminists, who demanded that discriminatory laws be changed or simply defied such rules in spite of the rabbis, Orthodox feminists pursued two different strategies: first, they took on certain observances that were in practice performed exclusively by men but from which women were exempted rather than explicitly barred and second, they made innovations in areas unaddressed by halakhah. The prayer group may be regarded as a union of these strategies.[24]

In the late 1970s, Orthodox women began to organize worship communities that they called prayer groups rather than minyanim, to emphasize their compliance with the prohibition on *devarim she-be- qedusha,* in their liturgies.[25] By the mid-1980s, prayer groups dotted the East Coast as far north as Toronto and as far south as Baltimore. They were subsequently augmented by a few West Coast groups, and groups in England, Australia, and Israel. The ecumenical prayer group of Jerusalem, Women at the Wall, in which women from all branches of Judaism pray together omitting *davar she-be-qedusha,* takes much of its group culture from American prayer group worship. An umbrella organization, the Women's *Tefillah* Network, links the international web of prayer groups and distributes a newsletter.[26]

One of the organization's founders, Rivkeh Haut, describes the prayer group's distinctive ritual practices and ambiance in this way:

> *Halakhic* women's prayer groups enable Jewish women to commemorate important events in their lives in a synagogue setting. Women receive *aliyot* in order to celebrate engagements, marriages, receiving degrees, buying homes, getting new jobs. Women are able to nurse their babies in shul. *Bat Mitzvah* girls are able to actively participate in the prayer service by reading the Torah, reciting the

haftarah, delivering a *d'var torah*. Women can recite the *mi shebeyrach* prayer for people who are ill. Orthodox women have, through prayer groups developed a mode whereby women no longer have to vicariously experience religious expression in the synagogue through fathers or husbands; they can participate actively and directly in all aspects of synagogue services, and they can do so in an *halakhically* acceptable way.[27]

Haut's defense of the prayer groups emphasizes their function as communities where women's joys and achievements are given public religious acknowledgment. The values of prayer group worship appear strikingly similar to those of the *havurah*. Both appropriate the communality and active participation that characterize traditional worship but also demand that worship be personally relevant and expressive of experience.[28]

Significantly, when Haut speaks of what she values most in the prayer group, the Torah service comes immediately to mind. The Torah service, which is at the core of prayer group worship, is its most halakhically controversial feature. The Torah service is a solemn and elaborated liturgical metaphor for the group members' appropriation of the Torah as their own. In procession they carry the Torah, and reverently touch and kiss it, direct *access* denied to women in nearly all Orthodox synagogues, where women witness in their separate section a procession they can never join. Here, in contrast, women read to women, proclaiming performatively a Torah that addresses women and seeks their attention as auditors. Reading with cantillation, a skill traditionally unavailable to women, announces that competence with the Torah is no longer reserved for men. Finally and most daringly, there are *aliyot*. Individuals are called up by name for the sections into which the reading is divided. These honors are traditionally withheld from women, not because they are ineligible but because of *kavod ha-zibur*, the honor of the congregation.[29] Here, where women *are* the congregation, the *aliyot* declare their capacity to honor the Torah and be honored by it. The nature of these *aliyot* vary in different prayer groups, depending on the ruling followed regarding women saying *devarim she-be-qedusha*.[30] Thus, in some, the entire Torah blessing is recited; in others, the Torah blessings are not recited in *birkot ha-shahar*, and then each woman called to the Torah makes her blessing at that time omitting *barehu*; and in still others a creative prayer that does not technically constitute a blessing is substituted for the Torah blessing.

In short, through the institution of the prayer group, Orthodox women succeeded impressively in filling the halakhic vacuum. Without departing definitively from halakhic norms, they created a formidable liturgical statement that Orthodox authorities would be reluctant to endorse and a vigorous new institution that Orthodox authority had no precedents for controlling. Yet, ironically, although they expressly designed the prayer group to avoid confrontations with halakhah, it has been a principal focus of halakhic attack, both as an impermissible incursion into men's praxis and as an unprecedented innovation.[31]

Prayer Groups Under Attack: The Context of the Schachter Responsum

In 1984, Rabbi Gilbert Klapperman concluded his term as president of the centrist Orthodox Rabbinical Association of America by recommending that the organization "confront the needs of women to find some form of rewarding participation in the synagogue."[32] He urged his successor to create a commission (of male rabbis) to establish for congregations desiring them halakhic guidelines for "membership for women on synagogue boards, women's *hakafot* [Simhat Torah processions with the Torah], women's *davening* [prayer] groups, Torah study, bat mitzvahs, etc."[33] His successor, Rabbi Louis Bernstein, not only rejected this strategy of accommodation to feminist rumblings, but formed his own strategy of aggressive opposition. Citing the evidence of newspaper interviews, prominent Modern Orthodox Jews accused Bernstein of soliciting a responsum from five faculty members of Rabbi Yitzhak Elhanan Seminary (RIETS) of Yeshiva University. David Singer, editor of the American Jewish Yearbook, charged;

> The *teshuvah* [responsum] of the "RIETS five" was hatched as part of a plot. It was the brainchild of Rabbi Louis Bernstein, current president of the Rabbinical Association of America and staunch opponent of women's minya*nim*. Rabbi Bernstein went "shopping" for some *posekim* [decisors] who would back his position, and hit

upon the "RIETS five." Rabbi Bernstein openly admits that he "discussed the issue informally" with the learned gentlemen before asking them to prepare a written response. "I did have an idea of their position," he states.[34]

The resulting responsum affronted learned readers with its deviations from the traditional formal requirements, as Rabbi Michael Chernick's reaction makes clear: "The fact that the so called responsum ... contained no documentation for its position gives the impression of a lack of scholarship, or alternatively, a patronizing and tyrannical attitude toward the community."[35]

The simplest reason for issuing a ukase rather than a responsum, however, is that there was no legal precedent for forbidding women from sharing their private devotions with one another. It is rabbinically established that women have an obligation to pray, because prayer is supplication for mercy (*B. Berakhot* 20b) and thus, as Rashi explains, is needed by every creature.[36] As long as women's prayers are directed toward the God of Israel, however, rather than some other deity, and as long as they eschew the formulae that distinguish men's communal prayer, neither talmudic nor post-talmudic texts evince any interest in the content or form of women's prayers. Such prayers affect no halakhic categories, and hence, the tradition accumulates no information about them. From the perspective of the tradition, they are "non-data."[37] The fundamental problem facing contemporary decisors is how to exert authority over an issue that classical tradition does not address but that threatens the stability of Orthodox life and opinion. This dilemma shapes the document to which we are about to turn.

Authored by Rabbi Zvi Schachter, one of the signers of the RIETS Five responsum, *"Ze'i Lakh B'iqvei Ha-Zon"* superficially resembles a classical responsum, since it contains an argument buttressed with citations from classical sources.[38] But it is even more reminiscent of the polemical responsa against the nineteenth century Reformers. Polemical responsa attest that something is happening among Jews that is beyond the control of the legal decisor but that he wishes to label as deviant behavior for those obedient to his authority. In that sense polemical responsa are policy statements. As David Ellenson demonstrates, modern polemical responsa have a boundary-maintaining function that Durkheimian deviance theory effectively describes.[39] In his classic work on deviance, Kai Erikson emphasizes that deviant behavior is not merely different; it is different behavior that is not tolerated.[40] The function of intolerance is to rigidify group boundaries to exclude those that most resemble the group but who, it is feared, may compromise its identity. This fear surfaces, Erikson argues, when group identity has become unclear. Such crises occur periodically in Orthodox Judaism around issues of acculturation. By labeling this behavior deviant, Schachter hopes to arrest the synthesis of feminism with Orthodox practice that threatens to transform gender roles and gender relations and hence alter the distribution of power and authority.

Authority, in any case is, hotly contested among Orthodox decisors. The voluntary nature of modern Judaism creates a free marketplace of halakhic decisions in which, as David Singer accuses, interested parties may shop. Moreover, since warring factions compete for a share of the market, decisors undercut one another's decisions and credibility more often than they support them. One modern consequence has been a reluctance on the part of Orthodox rabbis either to assume responsibility for halakhic decision making or to publicize the decisions they do make. In these shark-infested waters two modern styles of responsa publication are common. One is the statement signed by a number of decisors pooling their prestige and spheres of influence for greater impact and circulated as a broadside or poster, or published in newspapers. The other is the scholarly article published in the format of a professional periodical devoted to issues of practical halakhah. Such periodicals cultivate a certain ambiguity about whether their contents are to be regarded as theoretical discussions or binding legal decisions. This hybridization with the scholarly article accounts for some ambiguity about whether Schachter's piece is indeed a responsum. Some who discuss it do not use the term, yet it has been invoked as a responsum in later practical arguments.[41]

Analysis of the Responsum: The Title

Schachter titles his piece with a literary allusion from Song of Songs 1:8: *"Ze'i Lakh B'iqvei Ha-Zon"* (Go follow the tracks of the sheep)." The woman asks where her lover's flock is resting and is advised: "If you do not know, O fairest of women / Go follow the tracks of the sheep / and graze your kids / by the tents of the shepherds." The title uses the feminine imperative, as if the responsum were addressing the deviants directly. Schachter has selected the eroticized shepherdess of the Song to deliver an admonition to women to follow rather than to lead as the rebels are doing. Nine pages into the response, Schachter cites Seforno's exegesis on this exhortation. It is obviously this text Schachter had in mind when he chose his title:

> *Go follow the tracks of the sheep.* When the *halakhah* vacillates in your hand, follow the *minhag. And graze your kids,* ... the students who will teach in the future. *By the tents of the shepherds.* By the interpretations of the scholars of the generation, according to their reasoning, and they will consider what to approve.[42]

Seforno appears to be quoting *Y. Maaser Sheni* 5:56b: "If the law vacillates (*roffefet*) in the courts and you do not know what its nature is, see what the people do." Schachter understands this passage to mean that halakhic uncertainty is best resolved by following prevailing custom, but rather than seeing what the people are doing as the Palestinian Talmud recommends, Schachter's reading of Seforno proposes that even *minhag* is contingent on the approval of the scholars of the generation, among whom he implicitly numbers himself. The allusion in the title, then, is more to Seforno than to Song of Songs directly. It betrays Schachter's admission that the case he is deciding is halakhically uncertain and that custom is at issue. Lacking hard halakhic evidence (which is why he has had recourse to an exegesis on Song of Songs in a legal argument), Schachter will base the core of his argument on an assertion that *poskim*, decisors, are the arbiters of custom.

The Introductory Statement

The responsum opens with a brief statement of the issue: some Orthodox congregations have permitted separate women's *hakafot, megillah* readings, and minyanim. In using the term minyan to describe the prayer groups, Schachter makes no distinction between the minyanim of liberal feminists and the prayer groups of Orthodox women that do not say *devarim she-be-qedush*. His equation of the Orthodox women with outright violators distorts a crucial fact about the case. There is another departure from classical form. Whereas classical responsa generally reserve their conclusion until the issues have been defined, Schachter's conclusion appears in his initial section: "It is clearly apparent that all such customs are forbidden for a number of reasons."[43] .

This opening section has a subtext of which its elite audience would be aware. The epistolary introduction to a classical responsum names the rabbi that requested it. This responsum lacks an epistolary introduction, but because of the publicity surrounding the RIETS Five responsum, readers know that this too is not the unsolicited responsum it purports to be. The circumstances surrounding its solicitation have been left unstated because authority was relocated in an aberrant manner. Rather than being handed up from a lower level of hierarchy, authority has been handed down. A powerful person representing a national constituency has delegated others to render the decisions he has commissioned. The reader's foreknowledge of these circumstances compromises the impartiality of the responsum *ab initio*, and exposes it, to use Ronald Dworkin's terminology, as a policy statement masquerading as a principle.[44] Ironically, the responsum relativizes halakhah in the eyes of adherents who were previously naive about its possibilities as a tool for social manipulation and had thought that halakhic decision making was "objective."

The Body of the Responsum

The body of the work, unlike classical, nonpolemical responsa and unlike scholarly articles, offers no arguments pro and con, no possible objections or contrary perspectives. It consists simply of a list of twelve reasons why women's communal worship is out of the question. Like other polemical responsa, the document consists not of, an introductory statement of the problem, a body of text debating it, and a conclusion rendering a decision, but of one massive conclusion. With the exception of the sections dealing with *minhag*, the argument does not build incrementally from section to section. Most of the twelve sections are self-enclosed, and some arguments even contradict the premises of others. The arguments fall into three general categories: (1) arguments for women's attendance at male-led services rather than their own groups; (2) arguments for denying women the authority to innovate; and (3) arguments that women's activism is forbidden because it imitates the behavior of non-Jews. I will analyze a selection of these arguments.

Arguments for Synagogue Attendance: Commandments Incompletely Fulfilled[45]

This section rests upon two contentions: First, that if women optionally assume commandments not obligatory for them, they must fulfill them "completely," according to Schachter's criteria. Second, completely fulfilling the commandments of prayer is not in women's power without dependence on a male minyan. Schachter is on firm ground reiterating the classical post-talmudic precedents excluding women from the structures of communal prayer: women are ineligible for minyan and thus may not say *devarim she-be-qedusha* (*Orah Hayyim* 55:1). Because there is no explicit talmudic statement excluding women from minyan for daily prayer, Schachter quotes *Berakhot 45b*, which in the context of the requirement of three for *mezuman* for *birkat ha-mazon* declares that a hundred women are like (that is, as inadequate as) two men; that is, women possess a qualitative lack that renders the presence of any number of them equally insignificant for the purpose of the quorum. The Tosafot to this passage extends the ruling to include any communal prayer situation and any *davar she-be-qedusha*. Thus, to hear or say a *davar she be-qedusha*, women are dependent on a minyan of men.[46]

The organizational premise of the prayer groups is that by forgoing *devarim she-be-qedusha*, women at prayer can make themselves independent of the male minyan. Schachter seeks to break the back of this independence by proving that women are unable to pray acceptably without men to pray for them. His first attack is directed toward the heart of prayer group ritual: the Torah service, which symbolizes direct access to Judaism and its sancta. Schachter argues that it is forbidden to read the Torah without the blessings, which women may not say. His argument rests on minority opinions and *hiddushim* (novelli). He cites an opinion that he says J. B. Soloveitchik attributed to his uncle, R. Velvele, an opinion for which there is no written source—that fulfillment of the obligation of Torah reading is incomplete without the blessings. He then cites a *hiddush* of the *Magen Avraham*,[47] who contends, based on the commandment of *hakhel* (assembly to hear the book of the law described in Deut. 31), that women are required to hear the Torah read. Schachter, however, has omitted the second part of the citation. The complete citation reads: "It is written in *Massekhet Sofrim*: Women are obligated to hear the reading of the scroll as men are, and one is obligated to translate for them so that they understand. But here the women are accustomed to go outside." The commentator contrasts the law of *hakhel* with the antithetical *minhag ha-makom*, but he does not condemn nor seek to eradicate the *minhag ha-makom*.

Schachter, on the other hand, concludes that women must hear the Torah read with its blessings. To reach this conclusion he places the condition attributed to R. Velvele upon the requirement of the Magen Avraham's, piling one minority opinion atop another. But in an implicit concession that this evidence will be less than universally convincing, he argues that even those who disagree that women are so obligated would have to agree that the commandment is fulfilled fully in a male minyan, whereas "by themselves [women] have only a facsimile and a vestige (*dugma ve-zekher*)" of the real thing.

Similarly, Schachter seeks to argue that the reading of *Megillat Esther* is another commandment that can be fulfilled completely only by attendance at what he calls "a regular, [that is, male] minyan." Without citing the explicit statement of *B. Megillah* 4a that women are obligated in *Megillah* reading, he moves immediately to the dispute among the *Rishonim* as to whether women counted in the *Megillah* minyan. Citing the *Shulhan Arukh* and the *Rema*, he argues that without a minyan one may not say the concluding blessing. This is Schachter's only acknowledgment that there is a body of opinion contending that the obligation of *Megillah* may be fulfilled without a minyan. For neither the issue of women counting in a minyan for *Megillah* nor for the question of whether a minyan is required for the final blessing does

Schachter lay out or weigh the conflicting arguments. He draws his conclusions by piling uncertainty upon uncertainty: it is uncertain whether women are obligated in *Megillah* and hence whether they count in the minyan for its reading. It is uncertain whether the concluding blessing requires a minyan (gender unspecified). So, on the apparent assumption that the most stringent opinion from every dispute must be applied, he combines the minyan dispute with the blessing dispute and concludes that women can fulfill the commandment completely only by dependence on a minyan of males.

Aside from the questions raised by this mode of legal calculus, Schachter's argument contains another basic flaw. There is no evidence that persons who assume commandments optionally are limited in the manner in which they choose to do so. Whether they pray in congregation or at home, they are still credited as non-obligated persons who fulfilled a commandment. Whether they do so according to one legal opinion or another is as much a matter of personal preference as whether they undertake the commandment in the first place. Even the tradition of whether men have an obligation to pray in a minyan is disputed, for while authorities are unanimous that *devarim she-be-qedusha* cannot be said without a minyan, they disagree about whether there is an obligation to say *devarim she-be- qedusha*.[48] There is not, as Schachter seeks to posit, a recognized legal category of incomplete fulfillment of commandments. The underlying point of the section seems to be that women are legally constructed to be incomplete, and consequently, their deportment and their religious expressions should properly be characterized by passivity, receptivity, and dependence on men . This view echoes a long-standing tradition in Western philosophy stemming from Aristotle that views women as maimed or deformed men who have "only a facsimile and a vestige" of what defines male superiority and justifies masculine privilege.[49]

Misrepresentation of the Torah

Schachter objects that the prayer groups misrepresent the Torah by fostering the impression that women are equal in status to men and hence appropriate for inclusion in a minyan.[50] Some of Schachter's critics counter this charge by pointing out that Schachter distorts the facts; prayer groups explicitly differentiate themselves from minyanim.[51] Schachter's objection, however, is more fundamental. As his previous section makes clear, Schachter regards women as incapable of fully effective prayer independent of men. His underlying assumption is that, by conferring on men the capacity to address God with a communal voice, the Torah renders them spiritually superior to women. Consequently, the Torah is misrepresented as soon as women pray together as though they constituted an entity to which God would listen. Schachter's category "misrepresentation of the Torah" is based upon a metaphoric and hortatory use of the prohibition on misrepresentation by the *Yam Shel Shlomo,* the sixteenth century authority Rabbi Solomon Luria. As Schachter himself must acknowledge, misrepresentation (*zi'uf*) applies legally only to monetary fraud. Neither Schachter's source nor his use of it qualifies as a legal argument.

The King is Honored by Multitudes[52]

This third objection is at best, quasi-halakhic.[53] The Talmud uses it to justify a worship aesthetic in which the largest possible number of persons participate, even though ritual efficacy does not depend upon their participation.[54] Having demonstrated that women are not part of the community, Schachter now forbids them to separate from an entity they did not belong to in the first place. The bulk of this section is a sermon based on Rashi's commentary on Korah's rebellion (Num. 16), which depicts the prayer groups as competing power structures that challenge normative authority by disrupting the alleged monolithic solidarity of Orthodox institutions. The prayer group is depicted as a forbidden attempt to circumvent the status of nonentitlement.[55]

These three sections are followed by an argument categorizing women's synagogue attendance as a mitzvah, preferably performed by those able to beautify it: the male minyan, its Torah reader, and its prayer leader.[56] In these sections, Schachter depicts the modern Orthodox synagogue as a place where men occupy center stage, controlling and mediating religious expression for an encircling audience of dependent women. The vision is a distinctively modern one because women are essential to it, in contrast to earlier notions that the presence of women at services is inconsequential or even, as the Vilna Gaon admonishes his daughters, bad for their characters.[57] Nevertheless, Schachter's modern vision is reactionary, since it seeks to reinforce precisely the subordination and powerlessness of women that a secular culture is eroding. This secular empowerment of women is the ultimate target of Schachter's wrath, as the concluding sections of the responsum will indicate.

Arguments Concerning Innovation of *Minhag*

As I have noted, a major strategy of Orthodox women has been to innovate in areas where there is no halakhah. Schachter consequently moves to close off these free areas to the feminists. He concedes that neither law nor *minhag* is static. But although changes may be made, he argues that women are ineligible to make them. Accordingly, Schachter cites Tosafot on *Pesahim 40b* reconciling two conflicting texts concerning Torah study that is not for the sake of heaven, and concludes that new *minhagim* may be created only for the sake of heaven.[58] There are two criteria for evaluating this: the character of the innovators and the attachment of the *minhag* to preexistent law. Schachter declares the *minhagim* created by prayer groups unacceptable on both counts. He charges their leaders with an unseemly desire for public recognition and accuses them of innovating so that they can publish. Since the customs they establish are not connected to the fulfillment of any Torah or rabbinic law to which they are obligated, these customs can have no standing.

The women are, in any case, ineligible to innovate, since in order to ensure that innovation is in the spirit of the halakhah, it can be made only by *vatikin*, experienced Torah scholars, "who do everything for the sake of heaven." To supplement this ahistorical account of the origins of *minhagim*, Schachter quotes the midrashic statement that everything a *vatik* will innovate was revealed to Moses at Sinai (*Y. Peah* 2:6). Since innovation is presumed to derive from the system and process of Torah study, its sources are handed down from teacher to student.

Schachter's description of the origins and criteria for legitimate *minhagim* excludes women in two ways. First, women can always be accused of ulterior motives because in a system where Torah study and communal prayer are gender-specific, status-conferring obligations, women's very desire to study and pray can be interpreted as desire for superior status. Yet even if women do study, since they are excluded from the yeshiva system in which learning, and with it authority, are passed from teacher to student, women can never qualify as *vatikin* . They are categorically denied access to the network through which divine revelation is said to flow.

Innovation that deviates from the teachings of the innovator's rabbi is rebellion, which immediately disqualifies the innovator on the grounds of flawed character. This ruling, Schachter maintains, applies to those students of J.B. Soloveitchik who have supported the prayer groups, for Schachter maintains that R. Soloveitchik, like R. Moshe Feinstein opposes all the women's customs at issue. Soloveitchik's concurrence is disputed by Abraham Weiss, who maintains that Soloveitchik not only told Saul Berman and Shlomo Riskin that women's prayer groups were halakhically permissible but suggested substitute texts for the forbidden *devarim she-be-qedusha*.[59] Moreover, even R. Feinstein's position is more moderate than Schachter's. A one page responsum by R. Feinstein's son-in-law, R. Moshe Tendler, written on R. Feinstein's stationery and circulated at the Women's Tefillah Network Conference of June 1983, permits "pious women whose considerations are solely for the sake of heaven" (that is, who remain doctrinally Orthodox) to pray together as long as they refrain from *devarim she-be-qedusha*.[60] This is the first overt indication in the responsum that the prayer group issue is implicated in a larger struggle between R. Soloveitchik's conservative and liberal disciples. The struggle is complicated by the fact that most of R. Soloveitchik's opinions were communicated orally and are difficult to verify. The latest scholars to offer an account of R. Soloveitchik's attitudes toward women's group prayer, the brothers Aryeh and Dov Frimer, represent Soloveitchik as having been convinced that women's group prayer is halakhically permissible, nevertheless, the brothers Frimer point out that Soloveitchk was gravely concerned that the groups were at odds with prudent public policy and erosive of a proper Orthodox world view.[61]

Schachter's second contention, that a *minhag* must be linked to a preexistent traditional obligation, employed previous exclusions of women's customs and concerns, and legal precedent for further exclusions. Elsewhere I have explained how women's concerns that do not fit the androcentric categories of halakhah are rejected by the system as non-data.[62] Since the categories determine future questions, huge bodies of precedent are amassed on some issues whereas other issues cannot be addressed because the system has no information with which to address them. This process eventually seals halakhah against the intrusion of non-data. Here, Schachter attempts to seal off *minhag* as well. It is in this context that he quotes Seforno on pursuing the existing *minhag*. Schachter further argues that the fact that something has never been done constitutes per se, a universal custom that can be preserved only by continuing not to do it. Eliezer Berkovits reduces this argument to absurdity, citing the halakhic principle *lo ra'inu eino ra'ayah*, that not having seen a practice is not a proof that the practice is forbidden:

> [The norm is that in the cases quoted] to show that *lo ra'inu* is *ra'aya* (proof), there are always two opinions, one for the practice and one against it. In all these cases, the nonpractice is a rejection of an opposing ruling. Where, however, there is no opposing ruling the nonpractice of an activity does not establish it as a *minhag* that must not be changed. ... During the Torah reading, writes the Magen Avraham, women would leave the synagogue. Shall we now argue that because it was not customary for women to attend the Torah reading, it is now not permitted for them to violate the *minhag* and listen to the Torah reading![63]

Schachter's position on innovation runs so far counter to everyday attitudes that he is forced to acknowledge the inherent contradiction in a modern Orthodox worldview. Orthodox rabbis are not Amish. They presume that progress—scientific and technological progress in particular—is largely good. That God has given a static Torah to a historical world is affirmed as a mysterious paradox. Schachter's defense for his extreme position on innovation is to portray himself as protecting an infinitely fragile system in which the slightest change may provoke an avalanche that inundates the tradition. Hence, even justifiable changes, such as reading *Megillah* in the vernacular to women who do not speak Hebrew or allowing daughters to recite *qaddish*, must be viewed in terms of the larger danger they pose.[64] The argument, ironically, calls for a broader concept of legal relevance. Schachter wants the effect on the entire system to be considered over and above the merits of the particular case. But whereas feminist jurisprudence seeks an extended definition of legal relevance to admit more data about the actual circumstances and concerns of women into the legal process, Schachter's concern is the protection of the system, even at the cost of injuring those whom it disadvantages.

Schachter's most astonishing piece of legal evidence that nothing may be changed is an absolutized and decontextualized citation from one of the most celebrated modernist authorities, R. Yehiel Yaakov Weinberg. Weinberg rules that an infant may not be anesthetized for circumcision because it is contrary to Jewish practice. A more apposite Weinberg responsum Schachter does *not* quote permits women to participate in mixed singing in Jewish youth groups.[65] In that responsum Weinberg gives priority to the context that demands such a ruling. He also observes that women accustomed to joining in would feel hurt by their exclusion, a consideration Schachter never raises in his halakhic decisionmaking. In this section, Schachter presents an idealized revisionist account of *minhag* that conflates custom and law and defines both as enactments handed down by an authoritative elite. A special power is attributed to communal *minhag*, from which it is forbidden to deviate. Not only is it forbidden to deviate from present local custom, Schachter argues, but from the customs of all the communities of the past. Given the temporal and cultural range of Jewish communities, it is impossible to imagine how anyone could fulfill such an obligation.

Arguments Regarding Imitation of Non-Jews

In the final section of the responsum, Schachter charges that the customs of the prayer groups are unacceptable because they are syncretistic.[66] He does not really mean to suggest that women's Torah readings or *hakafot* borrow from the practices of New-Age goddess-worshippers or Christians. Instead, this category codes Schachter's concern that Orthodox feminists have much less rigid boundaries with their non-Orthodox counterparts than he and his constituency approve. As Erikson emphasizes, a group stigmatizes as deviant those within or upon its boundaries from whom it is anxious to distinguish itself. Conservative Jews, especially the learned Conservative elite, are more like Orthodox Jews than any other group. Hence Orthodox authorities vigilantly reinforce the boundary with Conservatism. But the Orthodox feminists who fashioned the prayer groups participate in many undertakings with non-Orthodox feminists: conferences, periodicals, research centers, and study groups, where they rub elbows with their smart-mouthed peers from "Shechter's seminary."[67] These permeable boundaries expose Orthodox feminists to the ideas and influences that have caused massive changes in Conservative Judaism and in the broader society. Through the medium of the prayer groups, these ideas and influences percolate through Orthodoxy.

Here, Schachter recycles the common arguments of nineteenth century Orthodoxy's battle to preserve its distinctness from Reform and to control the processes of acculturation. He goes on to attack feminism itself for "licentiousness," by which he means the eradication of many gender distinctions, causing fewer differences between women and men. Some of the accusations are bizarre and salacious: for example that "women's lib" leads women to shave their pubic hair. The underlying concern, however is not about sexual license but about the effect of gender equality in secular society on the system of gender complementarity that constructs and justifies different roles and statuses for men and women in Orthodoxy.[68] Gender distinctions and gender discrimination were among the few plausibility structures left in modernity that continued to mirror, however partially or irregularly, the naturalness of Orthodoxy's gender distinctions.[69] Apologists argue that because complementarity ensures Orthodox women distinctive roles and necessary social functions, feminism is unnecessary for them. The treason of the prayer groups is to uphold Orthodoxy while belying this claim. The very existence of Orthodox feminism declares that gender complementarity no longer suffices to keep Orthodox women from desiring fulfilling and privileged masculine roles.

Conclusions and Implications

The final quintessentially modern feature of the prayer group controversy is that, like the other conflicts between traditionalists and modernists in the last two centuries, it focuses on synagogue decorum. As Riv-Ellen Prell maintains, because the secularization of modern society privatized and fragmented the everyday praxis of Judaism, the synagogue became the major institution where Jewish identity is rehearsed, authenticated, and replicated.[70] Because this is as true for Orthodox as non-Orthodox Jews, synagogue practice is the great Jewish battleground of modernity. The entrance of Orthodox women into the fray means that the Orthodox home no longer provides them an adequate rehearsal of Jewish identity. Orhtodox women also need a synagogue, and, like members of the *havurot* Prell studied, they have shaped it to meet the cultural aesthetic of third generation American Judaism, with its emphases on nonhierarchical structures, participation, and self-expression.

As a piece of legal argumentation, the Schachter responsum is third-rate, poor in legal evidence, lacking in balanced argument, and tortuously reasoned. What is remarkable is that a horde of elite male halakhists are spawning mountains of halakhic verbiage about an issue concerning which the tradition had no interest and hence accumulated no information. The latest of these productions is part one of an article by the brothers Frimer (part two is yet to come) consisting of 49 pages of argument, 20 pages of addenda, and 50 pages of footnotes. Paradoxically, these documents would be infinitely briefer if the classical tradition offered any specific data on the issue. Amid this din of pettifogging and pontification, only Eliezer Berkovits *z"l* has simply maintained that how women pray when they are not in the presence of men is a question on which tradition has neither data nor policy nor perspective but, rather is "a complete vacuum," that may be filled now that the need has arisen.[71] But for others engaged in prayer group legal polemics—both the defenders of the women graciously adducing permissions and their censorious opponents amassing prohibitions and stringencies—the notion of a halakhic vacuum in which women are free of any authority but their own seems the most intolerable possibility of all.

Notes

1. Abba Bronspiegel, *"Minyan Mehuhadim le'Nashim,"* Hadarom 54 (Sivan 5745), 51-53.
2. Zvi Schachter, *"Ze'i Lakh B'Iqvei Ha-Zon,"* Bet Yitzhak 17 (5745) 118-134.
3. For example, David Singer, "A Failure of halakhic 'Objectivity,'" *Sh'ma* 15 (May 17, 1985), 110; and Michael Chernick, "In Support of Women's Prayer Groups," *Sh'ma* 15 (May 17, 1985), 105
4. The literature on this point is too extensive to cite. For a sampling of differing contemporary perspectives on the issue see: Aaron Lichtenstein, "Does Jewish Tradition Recognize an Ethic Independent of Halakhah?" in *Contemporary Jewish Ethics*. Menachem Mark Kellner, ed., New York, 1978, 112-123. Shubert Spero, *Morality,* Halakhah *and the Jewish Tradition* New York, 1983, Chapter 6. Yeshayahu Leibowitz, "The Religious and Moral Significance of the Redemption of Israel" in *Contemporary Jewish Theology,* Elliot N. Dorff and Louis E. Newman, eds., Oxford, 1999, 453-464. Eliezer Berkovits, *Not in Heaven: The Nature and Function of Halakhah,* New York, 1983, 19.
5. See Menachem Elon, "Minhag" in Menachem Elon, ed. *The Principles of Jewish Law*, Jerusalem, 1975, 91-110. For discussions by liberal halakhists see Elliot N. Dorff and Arthur Rosett, *A Living Tree: The Roots and Growth of Jewish Law*, Albany, 1988, 421-434 and Louis Jacobs, *A Tree of Life: Diversity, Flexibility and Creativity in Jewish Law*, Oxford, 1984, 221-235.
6. For an early example involving women, see *b. Berakhot* 31a, where a custom concerning extra-menstrual spotting attributed to "the daughters of Israel" is cited as an example of halakhah *pesukah.*
7. Abraham Weiss, *Women at Prayer: A Halakhic Analysis of Women's Prayer Groups* Hoboken, NJ, 1990.
8. Singer, Op. Cit., 110 and Chernick, Op. Cit., 105.
9. Although agreement among feminists about the importance of narrative is widespread, some feminists characterize women's decision-making as narratively based and oppose this to legal rule making See Carol Gilligan, *In a Different Voice* Cambridge, MA, 1982 , 24-63. I base my own work on that of Robert Cover, who argued that all law is narratively based. Robert M. Cover, "The Supreme Court 1986 Term: Forward: *Nomos* and Narrative," *Harvard Law Review* 97, no. 4 (November, 1983): 4-68.

10. Narrative and contextuality are also distinguishing themes of critical legal studies. See Roberto Mangabeira Unger, *Passion: An Essay on Personality,* New York, 1984, 5-15.
11. For an extended discussion of Jewish law, see Rachel Adler, *Engendering Judaism: An Inclusive Theology and Ethics* , Philadelphia, 1998, 37-44. For specific articles regarding secular jurisprudence, see: Kenneth Karst, "A Woman's Constitution," *Duke Law Journal* , no. 3 (1984): 447-508, especially 499-500, and Robin J. West, "Jurisprudence and Gender" *University of Chicago Law Review* 55 (Winter 1988): 1-71.
12. Robin J. West, "The Difference in Women's Hedonic Lives: A Phenomenological Critique of Feminist Legal Theory," in *At the Boundaries of Law: Feminism and Legal Theory,* Martha Albertson Fineman and Nancy Sweet Thomadsen, eds., New York, 1991, 115-34.
13. Seyla Benhabib, "The Generalized and Concrete Other: The Kohlberg-Gilligan Controversy and Moral Theory," *Women and Moral Theory,* Eva Feder Kittay and Diana T. Meyers, eds., Totowa, NJ, 1987, 154-177. Another version of this essay can be found in Seyla Benhabib, *Situating the Self: Gender, Community and Postmodernism in Contemporary Ethics,* New York, 1992, 148-177.
14. Martha Minow, "The Supreme Court 1986 Term: Forward: Justice Engendered," *Harvard Law Review* 101, no. 4, November 1987, especially 31-70. Martha Minow, *Making All the Difference: Inclusion, Exclusion and American Law,* Ithaca, N.Y. and London, 1990.
15. Jean Bethke Elshtain, "Feminist Discourse and Its Discontents: Language, Power, and Meaning," in *Feminist Theory: A Critique of Ideology,* Nannerl O. Keohane, Michelle A. Rosaldo and Barbara Gelpi, eds., Chicago, 1982, 127-45. See also Robin J. West, "Authority, Autonomy and Choice: The Role of Consent in the Moral and Political Visions of Franz Kafka and Richard Posner," *Harvard Law Review* 99 (December 1985): 384-428.
16. These concerns distinguishing Jewish feminism from other religious feminisms are noted by Carol P. Christ and Judith Plaskow, eds., *WomanSpirit Rising,* New York, 1979, 134.
17. On this issue see the articles of Paula Hyman, Esther Ticktin, and Saul Berman in *The Jewish Woman: New Perspectives,* Elizabeth Koltun, ed., New York, 1976, as well as the articles of Rachel Adler, Blu Greenberg, Cynthia Ozick and Judith Plaskow in *On Being a Jewish Feminist,* Susannah Heschel, ed., New York, 1983, and Blu Greenberg, *On Women and Judaism: a View From Tradition* , Philadelphia, 1981.
18. Rachel Adler, "The Jew Who Wasn't There: Halakhah and the Jewish Woman" *Davka* (Summer, 1971), reprinted in *On Being a Jewish Feminist,* 12-18.
19. Blu Greenberg, *On Women and Judaism,* 33.
20. Weiss, *Women at Prayer,* 110-111n. In note 38, Weiss summarizes the argument of this responsum. Goren relates the question of whether women may say *devarim she-be-qedusha* to the right to recite *berakhot* on commandments from which one is legally exempt. In other instances, Ashkenazic practice on this matter follows Rabbenu Tam, who permits women to recite blessings on positive time-bound commandments such as holiday observances, and, indicates that this was the communal practice in his time. Goren reaffirmed this opinion in a conversation with Weiss in Spring 1989, but in a letter to the Sefardic

Chief Rabbi dated 1 Tevet 5750 (Dec. 29, 1989) Goren says that women are not permitted to say *devarim she-be- qedusha* when they pray together and characterizes his previous opinion as a purely theoretical exercise.

21. R. Moshe Feinstein, *Igrot Moshe Orah Hayyim,* 4:49.
22. Ibid., 4:49.
23. The term *hashuvot* is important, see Norma Baumel Joseph, who points out that the term has a halakhic history indicating women who are to be treated with special respect because they are learned ,wealthy, or powerful. She argues that the women referred to are clearly insiders and notes two passages unusual in a responsum: (1) the lengthy theological section that reiterates the credo that the Torah, written and oral is divinely ordained and may not be questioned, followed by a biological determinist justification of gender roles: and (2) the apologetic exaltation of women's status. I would add that the content of these passages, a rehearsal of ideology that the elite submitter of the responsum would regard as common knowledge, indicates that the responsum is designed to be "overheard" by the learned rebels under discussion. Norma Baumel Joseph, " 'Those Overconfident Women': Heretical Insiders in Rabbi Moshe Feinstein's Responsa" (unpublished manuscript, 1998).
24. For a study of women who support these strategies by participating in prayer groups, see Ailene Cohen Nusbacher, "Efforts at Change in a Traditional Denomination: The Case of Orthodox Women's Prayer Groups," *Nashim: A Journal of Jewish Women's Studies and Gender Issues,* no 2, (Spring 1999): 95- 113.
25. Compliance with the prohibition on *devarim she-be-qedusha* is neither uniform nor consistent. In a communication with R. Aryeh A. Frimer dated July 25, 1997, Ms. Haut confirms that the Flatbush prayer group, basing itself on the repudiated responsum of R. Goren cited here in note 20, still permits women to recite mourner's qaddish, a policy the Frimers condemn as "halakhically improper, unfounded and indefensible." (80) Aryeh A. Frimer and Dov I. Frimer, "Women's Prayer Services—Theory and Practice: Part 1:Theory." *Tradition* 32:2 (Winter, 1998): 5-118.
26. Women of the Wall (WOW) has its own organization, The International Committee for Women of the Wall, which raises funds for its legal expenses. WOW has e-mail and a web page. See "Haim Shapiro, "Women at the Wall," *Jerusalem Post* (March 30, 1989); Deborah Brin, "Up Against the Wall" *The Reconstructionist* 54 (June 1989) 13-17; Deborah Budner, "Facing the Wall: The Politics of Women and Prayer," *New Outlook* (June/July 1989): 25–26; Bonna Devora Haberman, "Women Beyond the Wall: From Text to Praxis," *Journal of Feminist Studies in Religion* 13:1 (Spring 1997) 5-34.
27. Rivkeh Haut, "From Women: Piety, Not Rebellion," *Sh'ma* 15 (May 17, 1985), 110. See also Rivka Haut, "Women's Prayer Groups and the Orthodox Synagogue" and Yonina Penkower, "Bat Mitzvah: Coming of Age in Brooklyn" both in Rivka Haut and Susan Grossman, eds., *Daughters of the King,* Philadelphia, 1992), 135-158 and 265-70.
28. Compare Riv-Ellen Prell, *Prayer and Community: The Havurah in American Judaism,* Detroit, 1989: 159-202.

29. *B. Megillah* 23a. However see *Tosefta Megillah* 3:5, which omits the phrase *kavod ha-zibu*r but says, "we do not bring a woman out to read in public." Weiss offers several explanations. Quoting Ritva to *B. Megillah* 4a and Rabbi Jacob Emden (Yavez, *Haggahot ve-Hiddushim* to *Megillah* 23a) he notes their assumption that a woman would not be asked to perform this act when there were men competent to do so. Hence, although her act is legally efficacious, the public display of female knowledge and competence with the Torah presumes male ignorance and incompetence, and therefore shames the (male) congregation. An alternative explanation is that modesty demands that women not be visible or audible in public. Weiss, *Women At Prayer*, 68–69.

The first explanation would seem to apply only in contexts where men are expected to be more Jewishly educated than women. If a single standard applied across gender lines, female competence and knowledge would not be experienced as offensive. The second explanation rests on the dual assumptions that men experience women primarily as sexual objects and that men's religious experience and behavior are of more value and concern than that of women. "Modesty" means women's acquiescence to their erasure from the "homosocial" public sphere where cultural norms are enacted and recreated and power and privilege are exercised and their relegation to a private sphere in which sexual and enabling functions define and circumscribe women's roles. See Eve Kosovsky Sedgewick, *Between Men: English Literature and Male Homosocial Desire,* New York, Columbia University Press, 1985: 1-27.

30. Personal communications from Bonna Haberman, Brandeis University, Norma Baumel Joseph, University of Toronto, and Chaia Beckerman, Women of the Wall, Jerusalem.

31. While it is clear in primary sources that women may assume mitzvot from which they are exempt, some later commentators complicate legal decision making by raising objections that would render women ineligible, and authorities opposed to feminism have assiduously collected such precedents. The major source for the question of whether it is permissible for women to assume commandments from which they are exempt is a discussion in *B. Eruvin* 96a-b, addressing whether women may optionally don *tefilin,* lay hands on a sacrifice in order to designate it, or blow the *shofar.* Regarding *tefilin B. Eruvin* 96a says that Saul's daughter Mikhal put on *tefilin* and the rabbis did not protest. However Tosafot s.v. *Mikhal* objects that women do not have the requisite *guf naki,* clean body, which is forbidden in *tefilin. Guf naki* is variously understood to mean that women are more flatulent than men or that the uncleanliness referred to is menstruation. See the discussion in Getzel Elinson *Ha- Isha ve-ha-Mizvot,* Jerusalem, Histadrut Ha-Zionit Ha-Olamit, 1975: 55-56. Moshe Isserles (Rema) gloss to *Shulhan Arukh, Orah Hayyim* 38:3 says, "we do protest [women's wearing *tefilin*]." See also the *makhloket* between Maimonides, *Mishneh Torah Hilkhot Zizit* 3:9 and Rabbenu Tam (*B. RH* 33a *Tosafot* s.v. *Ha*) concerning whether women may make a blessing on mitzvot from which they are exempt. Examples of books designed to nip Orthodox feminist observance in the bud by cataloguing authorities against women taking on practices from which they are

exempt are Moshe Meiselman, *The Jewish Woman in Jewish Law,* New York, 1979, and the aforementioned Getzel Elinson, *Ha-Isha ve-ha-Mizvot.*
32. Rabbi Gilbert Klapperman, Presidential Address, May 30, 1984 in Lancaster, PA, quoted in Weiss, *Women at Prayer,* xv.
33. Ibid.
34. David Singer, "A Failure of Halakhic 'Objectivit,'" *Sh'ma* 15 (May 17, 1985), 110. Singer derives his quotes from *The Long Island Jewish World* (Feb. 15, 1985).
35. Michael Chernick, Op. Cit., 105.
36. *B. Berakhot* 20a s.v. Rashi *Tefillah d'rahamei ninhu.*
37. See Rachel Adler, *Engendering Judaism,* 28-29 for the halakhic critique that explains how some data cannot be admitted to the system and is thus considered nondata. For a brief review of how classical liturgy rendered women's ritual non-data see Lawrence Hoffman, *Covenant of Blood: Circumcision and Gender in Rabbinic Judaism,* Chicago, 1996, 173-189.
38. Zvi Schachter, "Ze'i Lakh B'Iqvei Ha-Zon" *Bet Yitzhak* 17 (5745) 118-134.
39. David Ellenson, *Tradition in Transition: Orthodoxy,* Halakhah *and the Boundaries of Modern Jewish Identity,* Lanham, MD, 1989, 33-57.
40. Kai Erikson, *Wayward Puritans: A Study in the Sociology of Deviance,* New York, 1968.
41. Abraham Weiss *Women at Prayer,* xvi n.
42. Seforno on Song of Songs 1:8.
43. Schachter, 118.
44. Ronald Dworkin, *Taking Rights Seriously*, Cambridge, 1977, 1978: 22-28. Dworkin says, "I call a 'policy' that kind of standard that sets out a goal to be reached, generally an improvements in some economic, political, or social feature of the community (though some goals are negative in that they stipulate that some present feature is to be protected from adverse change). I call a 'principle' a standard that is to be observed, not because it will advance or secure an economic, political, or social situation deemed desirable, but because it is a requirement of justice or fairness or some other dimension of morality." (22)
45. The discussion below covers Schachter, 118-119.
46. For a critical analysis of the issue and its adjudication see Judith Hauptman, "Women and Prayer: An Attempt to Dispel Some Fallacies" *Judaism* 42:1 (Winter 1993): 94-103 and Michael J. Broyde, Joel B. Wolowelsky and Judith Hauptman, "Further on Women as Prayer Leaders and Their Role in Communal Prayer: An Exchange" *Judaism* 42:4 (Fall 1993): 38-413.
47. R. Avraham Gumbiner (Magen Avraham) gloss to *Shulhan Arukh OH* 282:3.
48. Although there are many statements encouraging men to attend synagogue and rebuking those who do not (see for example *B. Berakhot* 7b-8a), the Talmud enunciates no specific mitzvah of praying with a minyan. Weiss, *Women at Prayer,* 40–41 summarizes the controversy on this point in post-talmudic tradition, citing an overview by Yitzhak Yaakov Fuchs, *Ha-Tefillah Be-Zibur,* Jerusalem, 1978: 30-37.
49. Catherine Keller, *From a Broken Web,* Boston, 1986: 47-92.
50. The following discussion concerns Schachter,119-120.
51. Singer, 109, Haut, 110-111, Chernick, 107.

52. The scriptural source of the statement is Proverbs 14:28.
53. Schachter, 119-120.
54. See for example, *B. Berakhot* 53a, *B. Pesahim* 64b, and *B. Sukkah* 52b.
55. Schachter, 120. "For us there is only one synagogue and one prayer leader, and it is forbidden for those who are not suitable to be a prayer leader or bless the Torah to separate from the community and make a minyan for themselves."
56. Schachter, 121-122.
57. Israel Abrahams, *Hebrew Ethical Wills*, Philadelphia, 1976: 315-316. Reprint of original 1926 edition. According to the Gaon, synagogue attendance encourages women to gossip.
58. Schachter, 122-127.
59. Abraham Weiss, *Women at Prayer*, 107n.
60. Chernick, 107.
61. Aryeh A. Frimer and Dov I Frimer, "Women's Prayer Services—Theory and Practice: Part 1:Theory," *Tradition* 32:2 (Winter,1998): 40-47.
62. Rachel Adler, *Engendering Judaism*, 28-29.
63. Eliezer Berkovits, *Jewish Women in Time and Torah*, Hoboken, NJ, 1990, 78- 79.
64. Schachter, 128-129.
65. R. Yehiel Yaakov Weinberg, *Seridei Esh* 2, no. 8.
66. Schachter, 13 34.
67. Schachter, 127.
68. For a discussion of gender complementarity see Rosemary Ruether, "Women's Difference and Equal Rights in the Church" in Anne Carr and Elisabeth Schussler-Fiorenza, eds., *The Special Nature of Women?* London, 1991: 11- 18.
69. This is the terminology of Peter Berger, *The Sacred Canopy* , New York, 1969.
70. Riv-Ellen Prell, *Prayer and Community*. Detroit, 1989.
71. Eliezer Berkovits, *Jewish Women in Time and Torah*, 81.

Chapter 2

❖   ❖   ❖

THE GENDER ISSUE IN JEWISH DIVORCE

John D. Rayner

Traditional Jewish marriage law is predicated on a fundamental disparity of status between men and women that has been mitigated in the course of the ages but, except in one branch of modern Judaism, never fully rectified. This paper will sketch the history of that disparity, with special reference to divorce, then discuss various attempts to remedy it.

History

Biblical Times

Biblical matrimonial law was polygamous. More precisely, it allowed a man to have several wives (polygyny) but regarded the reverse (polyandry) as unthinkable. This is reflected in the process of marriage, which was unilateral. That applies both to the act of betrothal, for which the verb *aras* was used, and to the marriage proper, for which the usual verb was *lakah* meaning "to take" and to buy."

Notes for this section begin on page 56.

That very point is made at the beginning of Tractate *Kiddushin*, which opens with the Mishnah statement, *ha-isha nakita beshalosh d'rakhim*, that "a wife can be acquired in three ways," the first and most usual being *bakesef*, "with money." Then the *Gemara* comments that the same verb, *lakah*, which is used in the story of the Machpelah, when Abraham offers Ephron the purchase price for the field, saying *kah mimeni*, "Take it from me" (Gen. 23:13), is used in Deuteronomy about marriage when it says (22:13), *ki yikah ish ishah* "If a man takes a wife" (*Kid*. 2a). The bridegroom, essentially, therefore, "bought" the bride from her father.

The same inequality is reflected in divorce, which was likewise unilateral, when only the husband having the right to dissolve the marriage.

Information about Biblical divorce is, admittedly, sparse. Virtually the only relevant passage is Deuteronomy 24:1- 4, and that is an oblique reference, for it really deals with remarriage: that of a man to his former wife, whom he has divorced, an act permitted only if she has not been married to another man during the interim. Nevertheless, it shows clearly enough that the procedure was unilateral. The key phrase is: *vekatav lah sefer keritut venatan beyadah veshalhah mibeit*,—the husband "writes her a bill of divorce, hands it to her, and sends her away from his house" (v.1).

A husband's right to divorce his wife was unrestricted except if he had falsely accused her of premarital unchastity (Deut. 22:13 -19) or if he had raped her before marriage (Deut. 22: 28f); in both these cases *lo yukhal leshalhah kol yameha*, "he may not divorce her as long as she lives." It is not known how the biblical bill of divorce was worded, but it is likely that it would have included some such *ki hi lo ishti ve-anokhi lo ishah*, 'She is no longer my wife and I am no longer her husband' (Hos. 2:4).

There is no reason to suppose that divorce was common, or viewed with approval. Malachi makes God say *ki sane shalah*, 'I hate sending away' (2:16), where, incidentally, the same verb is used as in the key Deuteronomy passage. Above all, it follows from the frequent prophetic use of marriage as a metaphor for the Covenant between God and Israel (in for example, Isa.54:5, Jer. 31:30-33, Ezek. 16:8, Hos. 2:21f) that marriage was regarded as *ideally* permanent.

Second Temple Times

It seems that women enjoyed greater rights in the fifth-century B. C. E. Jewish military colony at Elephantine in southern Egypt. The Aramaic papyrus manuscripts found there include three marriage contracts; two of these stipulate that the husband may not marry a second wife,[1] and one indicates that the wife could take the initiative in ending her marriage, for it states: *mahar veyom aharon tikom miftahiah be-edah vatomer sanet le-ehsor ba-ali*, "tomorrow or another day, if Miftachiah should stand up in the congregation and say, 'I divorce Aschor my husband …'"[2]

According to Josephus, Queen Salome divorced her husband Costobarus, but, as he explains, her action "was not in accordance with Jewish law. For it is (only) the man who is permitted by us to do this. … Salome, however, did not choose to follow her country's law but acted on her own authority."[3]

Pharisaic sources concede no such right to the wife but do seek to discourage hasty divorce and show concern for a divorced woman's economic security. Hence the *ketubbah* (marriage contract) was instituted by Simeon ben Shetach in the first century B. C. E. *kdei shelo t'hei kalah be-enav lehotziah* "so that a husband may not regard it as a light matter to divorce his wife" (*Tos.Ket.*12:1; *J. Ket.*8:11). It entitled the wife to financial compensation from her husband's estate if he should divorce or predecease her. (*Ket.* 8:11; *Ket.* 4a).

Tannaitic Times

Polygamy was still permitted in Tannaitic times and marriage remained unilateral. A *baraita* emphasizes that the Torah says *ki yikah ish ishah*, "When a man takes a wife" (Deut. 22:13), not *ki tilakeh ishah ish*, "When a wife is taken to a man' (*Kid.* 2b), because he alone is permitted to take the initiative. A third possibility, that the Torah might have said, *ki tikah ishah ish*, "When a woman takes a husband," is not even contemplated.

The verb *aras*, now spelled with a *sameh* instead of a *sin*, continued to be used for "to betroth," referring to the first stage of the process of getting married, and gave rise to the noun *erusin* for "betrothal." It was often replaced by the verb *kidesh*, meaning "to set apart" or "consecrate," which yielded the alternative noun *kidushin* for "betrothal" and gave its name to the Mishnah tractate on that subject.

For the second stage, the marriage proper, in addition to *lakah*, the verb *nasa*, which means "to lift," "to carry" and "to take," was also used. It is found already in late Biblical passages, as in Ezra 9:2, *ki nasu mibnoteihem lahem velivnehem*, "for they have taken of their daughters for themselves and for their sons," a passage that gave rise to the noun *nisuin* for "wedding." Yet another verb is *kanah*, "to acquire," or "to buy;" it is used, as we have seen, in the opening statement of *Mishnah Kiddushin*: *Ha-ishah niknet beshalosh derakhim*, that "a wife is acquired in one of three ways." All three terms clearly indicate an act of acquisition by the husband.

Similarly, divorce remained unilateral: *eino domeh ha-ish le-ishah hamegaresh le-ishah hamitgareshet sheha-ishah yotzah lirtzonah ushelo lirtzona, vehaish eino motzi ela lirtzono*, "The husband who divorces is not like the wife who is divorced, for she is divorced with or without her consent while he divorces her only if he wants to" (*Yev.* 14:1).

Again we notice a change in terminology. Whereas in the Bible the verb for "to divorce" was *shile-ah* "to send away" or "dismiss," in rabbinic literature it is usually *garesh*, "to expel," or *hotzi*, "to cause to go out."

Divorce, though permitted, was looked upon as regrettable. On the Malachi verse, *ki saneh shileah*, that God hates divorce (2:16), Rabbi Eleazar ben Azariah made the famous comment, *kol hamegaresh ishto rishonah afilu mizbe-ah morid alav dimot*, "Whenever a man divorces his first wife, the very altar weeps over him"(*Git.* 90b).

In addition to the biblical restrictions we have noted, a husband was no longer allowed to divorce his wife if she became insane (*Yev.* 14:1) or if she was taken captive (*Ket.* 4:9). Conversely, although the right to effect a divorce continued to be vested exclusively in the husband, nevertheless, in certain situations a wife could sue for divorce, in the sense of asking the court to bring pressure on the husband to release her. Such grounds included refusal of conjugal rights (*Ket.* 5:6), impotence (*Ned.* 11:12), and unreasonable restriction of freedom (*Ket.* 7:2-5).

Moreover, an attempt was made to restrict the husband's right to divorce his wife so that he would be able to do so only if she had committed a matrimonial offence. What constitutes such an offense was disputed between Bet Hilled and Bet Shammas according to their divergent interpretations of the key phrase *ervat davar* in Deut. 24:1. The former understood it very broadly, the latter as referring only to adultery, which was also the view of Jesus according to one Gospel tradition (Matt. 5:32, 19:19). Rabbi Akiva, however, on the basis of the phrase, *im lo timtza hen be-enav*, "If she does not find favour in his eyes," (Deut. 24:1) would allow a husband to divorce his wife even in the absence of a matrimonial offense, *afilu matza aheret neah heimenah*, "If he had fallen in love with another woman" (*Git.* 9:10).The biblical *sefer keritut* for "bill of divorce" was now called *get*, an Aramaic word for a legal document, apparently derived from a Sumerian term meaning "oblong object,"[4] or, more fully *get ishah*, "woman's document."

As for its wording, an anonymous Mishnah states that its essential formula was *harei at muteret lekhol adam*, "You are free to remarry" (*Git.* 9:3), and this was codified. But the Mishnah adds a minority opinion from the same mishnaic passage, in the name of Rabbi Judah ben El'ai, that the correct formula is an Aramaic one that reads: *Vedin dihavai lekhi minai sefer terukhin ve-igeret shivukin veget piturin, limhekh lhitnasva lekhol geverdetatzvayin*, "Let this be to you from me a document of release, a letter of dismissal of and a bill of divorce, so that you may go and marry any other man you wish."In the subsequent development of the text, both phrases were included.

Regarding the language of the *get*, the Mishnah makes it clear that it may be written in Hebrew or Greek (*Git.* 9:8), which was taken to mean that it may be written *bekhol lashon*, in any language (*Git.* 19b).

The Mishnah also raises the question whether divorce documents executed in a Gentile registry, *he-olim be-arkhot shel goyim*, are valid; 'no' was the majority view, but Rabbi Simeon ben Yochai thought "yes", *af al pi shehotmeihem goyim*, even if the signatories were non-Jews (*Git.* 9.8).

Amoraic Times

Polygamy was still permitted in Amoraic times, but viewed with disfavor. Marriage remained unilateral. Admittedly, however, the bride's consent was now considered mandatory. As the Talmud puts it, *midatehah, ein, shelo midatehah, lo,* "With her consent it is valid; without her consent it is not valid." (*Kid.* 2b) Nevertheless, the bride's role in the marriage ceremony was passive, as it remains in Orthodox Judaism to this day.

Divorce likewise remained unilateral. But the feeling persisted that it was a serious matter. Accordingly, divorce proceedings were made increasingly elaborate, necessitating expert supervision, and it became a principle that *kol sheino yodeah bativ gitin ukedushin lo y- he lo asak imahem,* "Anyone who does not understand the nature of divorce documents and betrothals should have nothing to do with them." (*Kid.* 6a)

The greatest precision was required for the process of writing witnessing and delivering; the writing materials; the *toref* (that is, the "variables" as the date, the place, the names of the parties, and the signatures of the witnesses); and the *tofes,* (i.e. the "constants," which were now in Aramaic, with only the essential phrase stipulated by the Mishnah in Hebrew.

This process of elaboration took place principally in the Babylonian academies throughout the Amoraic period. Details of wording and even of spelling were still debated between Babylonian rabbis of the fourth and fifth centuries (see *Git.* 82a—88b).

The wife could still take the initiative in asking the rabbinic court to coerce the husband to divorce her if she had objective grounds for complaint, which now included his refusal to support her (*Ket.* 77a). Indeed, she could apparently do so even in the absence of such grounds, if he had become repulsive to her, provided that she was willing to forgo part of her alimony; for the Palestinian Talmud (*Ket.* 7:7) cites a *ketubah* clause to that effect, similar to the Elephantine one quoted above.[5]

Gaonic Age

The wife's right in certain circumstances to sue for a divorce was maintained throughout the Gaonic period and, as we shall see, beyond. This is confirmed by a tenth-century *ketubah* found among the manuscripts of the Cairo Genizah, which again includes a clause similar to the Elephantine one.[6] But, of course, the husband alone could instruct that the *get* to be written.

Although all the necessary prescriptions and ingredients are already present, if somewhat scattered, in the Talmud, the full text of the *get* is first found in the attempts to codify talmudic law that began during the Gaonic Age. The most important early work of that genre is *Halakhot Gedolot* (Great Laws) commonly attributed to Simeon Kayyara but of disputed authorship, probably compiled in Babylonia in the eighth or ninth century. It gives a text of the *get* that is virtually identical with that subsequently found in the medieval law codes.[7]

Middle Ages

Several important developments took place during the Middle Ages. First, by a decree attributed to Rabbenu Gershom ben Judah (tenth-eleventh centuries) polygamy was forbidden (*Shulhan Arukh., Even Haezer* 1:10). Ze'ev W. Falk, however, has shown that the attribution is incorrect and that the decree actually dates from the twelfth century.[8] Moreover, it was not immediately accepted by all communities, and there were various views as to whether it admitted of exceptions and whether it remained in force only until the end of the fifth millennium, which was the year 1240 (*Even Haezer*, 1:10). In any case, prohibition is not the same as abolition. Thus, a man's bigamous marriage, though forbidden, remained valid ex post facto (*bedi-avad*), and any children resulting from it were unblemished (*kasher*), whereas a woman's bigamous marriage was considered void (*ein kidushin tofsin*), and the children of such a union were illegitimate (*mamzerim*)—which remains the position in Orthodox Judaism to this day.

Secondly, contrary to the Mishnah statement quoted above (*Yev.* 14:1), a husband was no longer allowed to divorce his wife without her consent. This decree was also attributed to Rabbenu Gershom (*Shulhan Arukh, Even Haezer* 119:6); but it, too, has been shown to date from the twelfth century.[9]

Thirdly, "divorce was no longer a private act by the husband, for it was subject to public supervision by a tribunal, or by representatives of the community."[10] Indeed, the tendency was to require the *get* to be authorized, not only by the individual *Bet Din*, but by larger communal authorities. Rabbi Jacob Moellin (the Maharil, fourteenth-fifteenth centuries) reports: "The custom of the three communities of the Rhineland [Speyer, Worms, and Mainz] was ... when they intended to give a *get* in one of these communities they would first obtain the agreement of the other two, so that the *get* might be given with their authorization" (*Sefer Maharil*, 68a).

Thus Jewish divorce was now mainly by mutual consent, but not reciprocal, for it was still the husband who initiated it by instructing a scribe (*sofer*) to write the *get* before a rabbinic court (*Bet Din*) in the presence of witnesses (*edei hatimah*). The delivery, too, took place before the court and in the presence of witnesses (*edei mesirah*). However, on the principle that "a person's agent is like himself" (*sheluho shel adam kemoto*, Ned. 72b), the husband could appoint an agent to deliver the *get* (*sheli-ah leholakhah*) and the wife could appoint an agent to receive it (*sheli-ah lekabalah*).

There were, however, some exceptions to the principle of mutual consent. If, for instance, either party wished to condone adultery or apostasy on the part of the other, or if the marriage had been contracted in contravention of the so-called "negative prohibitions" (*issurei lavin*), as when a Kohen (man of putative priestly descent) married a divorcee—in all these cases the *Bet Din* could, in theory, "enforce" a divorce by bringing pressure on the husband to give the *get* to his wife against the wishes of either or even of both parties.

As for the wife's right to petition for a divorce, that too continued, at least until the twelfth century, when Rabbi Jacob ben Meir, known as Rabbenu Tam, argued against the practice of rabbinic courts' coercing husbands to divorce their wives; and his influence was so great that he "single-handedly changed the course of the *halakhic* attitude."[11]

The wording of the *get* became standardized, with only minor variations, chiefly between the Sefardi and Ashkenazi traditions. Following the pattern of the Gaonic *Halakhot Gedolot*, which we have already mentioned, it can be found in medieval law codes such as the *Halakhot* of Isaac Alfasi (1013—1103; *Git.* 89a) and the *Mishneh Torah* of Moses Maimonides (1135—1204; *Hilkhot Gerushin* 4:12). The *Shulhan Arukh* of Joseph Caro (1488-1575) devotes a whole appendix to the rules and regulations pertaining to the writing of a *get* (*Seder ha-Get*, appended to chapter 154 of *Yoreh Deah*). Here, according to the standard Ashkenazi text, are the key phrases, the man apostrophising the woman:

I, of my own free will and without being under any constraint, ... release, dismiss and divorce you, my wife ... who have been my wife hitherto I dismiss, release and divorce you, so that you may have permission and authority over yourself to go and marry any man you wish, and no person may prevent you from this day and for ever, and you are free to marry any man, and this shall be to you from me, a document of release, a letter of dismissal, and a bill of divorce, according to the law of Moses and Israel.[12]

A final point to be noted is that after the delivery of the *get* to the wife or her agent it was returned to the *Bet Din*, which defaced it by cutting it crosswise and stored it away. Instead, the wife or her agent received a certificate *(te-udat gerushin* or *patur)* to the effect that the *get* had been executed.

The Modern Situation

The Emancipation changed the situation in several respects. First, the affected Jewish communities lost their juridical autonomy. Second, the secularization of Christian countries led in most of them to the institution of civil divorce of which Jews could now avail themselves without *necessarily* obtaining a Jewish divorce as well. Thirdly, there occurred a steady and in the end massive increase in marriage breakdown and divorce among Jews, as among non-Jews. Fourth, since many of those concerned divorced civilly only, this resulted in a corresponding increase in the number of Jewish women who remarried without a *get*, with serious consequences for the status of any subsequent children.

These developments have brought into prominence a twofold problem that always existed in Rabbinic Law but now occurred on a vastly increased scale: that of the *Agunah* and that of the *Mamzer*.

The Agony of the Agunah

The term *Agunah* derives from a verb that occurs only once in the Bible, when Naomi advises her widowed daughters-in-law to go home rather than wait in vain for her to bear more sons for them to marry, for, as she says, *halahen te-agenah levilti heyot la-ish*, "Should you on their account debar yourselves from marriage?" (Ruth 1:13). Since the key verb is a *hapax legomenon*, it is impossible to know precisely what it meant, but in rabbinic Hebrew it meant "to tie down," so that an *Agunah* may be said to be a "tied" or "chained" woman.

In the case of Orpah and Ruth, the disability would have been a self-imposed commitment to marry Naomi's hypothetical future sons, a wildly extravagant feature of the story that was no doubt meant to be humorous. But in the real world the status of *iggun* (cf. *Git.* 3a) results from any one of three quite different causes.

The first is the disappearance of the husband in circumstances that leave room for doubt whether he is alive or dead. He may have deserted his wife or gone abroad, or he may have died, but evidence is unsufficient to prove it. Such cases are relatively rare in normal times but tend to become numerous in times of war or persecution.

A second possible case is that of a widow whose husband has died without issue. According to the biblical law (Deut. 25:5—10), her brother-in-law is then obligated to marry her *velo yimaheh shemo meyisra-el* , "that his name may not be blotted out from Israel," such a levirate marriage being known as *yibbum,* or else he must obtain release from that obligation through the ceremony of *halitzah* ("taking off the shoe"). Until *yibbun* or *halitzah* has been performed, the widow is said to be *zekukah*, bound to her brother-in-law. But if he refuses both *yibbum* and *halitzah,* then she is, additionally, an *Agunah.*

The third and commonest cause of *iggun* is the case of the "recalcitrant husband," who refuses to free his wife to remarry by giving her a *get.*

Indeed the converse problem also exists, of the "recalcitrant wife," who refuses to free her husband to remarry by accepting a *get* from him. According to one estimate, as many as one-third of all cases of disbarment from remarriage are caused by the wife's refusal to co-operate in the matter of the *get.*[13] But if the husband nevertheless remarries (civilly), then, as we have previously observed, his second marriage is valid ex post facto, since polygamy was only forbidden, not abolished, by the twelfth-century decree, and any children resulting from it are unblemished (*kasher*). Whereas, if the civilly divorced woman remarries without a *get*, her second marriage is void (*ein kidushin tofsin*) and any children resulting from it are branded *Mamzerim.*

The Misery of the Mamzer

The relevant verse occurs in Deuteronomy and says that a *Mamzer* may not enter the congregation of the Eternal One "even in the tenth generation" (23:3). The meaning of the word, *Mamzer*, however, is uncertain.[14]

The very next verse, which uses the identical formula about an Ammonite and a Moabite, suggests that it might have been the name of a pagan tribe, a conjecture that can draw some support from the fact that in the only other occurrence of the word in the entire Bible (Zech. 9:6) it is associated with a geographical region, that of Ashdod. Indeed, the exact meaning of the word was still disputed in Rabbinic times (see, for example, *Yev.* 49a—b), but it was eventually defined as the offspring of an incestuous or adulterous union.

According to Rabbinic law, a *Mamzer*, so defined, is forbidden to marry a Jew not similarly tainted. Furthermore, since "even in the tenth generation" was taken to mean "forever," the disability perpetuates itself indefinitely, both in the male and in the female lines, on the principle that 'the child follows the more blemished parent' (*havelad holekh ahar hapegum*; *Yev.* 76b; *Shulhan Arukh, Even Haezer* 8:4).

The tragedy of the *Agunah*, therefore, is not only that, in Orthodox Judaism, she is forbidden to remarry, but that if she remarries in a non-Orthodox way, her subsequent children and children's children (*ad sof kol hadorot*) until the end of all generations, are burdened with the stigma and disability of *Mamzerut*. It is worth reiterating that this twofold problem stems from two quite separate causes: (1) the inferior status of women in Rabbinic matrimonial law, which preserves the ex post facto validity of male polygamy, even though it is no longer permitted and makes the procedures of marriage and divorce unilateral; and (2) the law of the *Mamzer*.

We shall now look at various attempts to solve or alleviate this twofold problem, within the parameters of rabbinic Judaism.

Remedies

Purification of the Mamzer

If it were possible to remove the stigma and disability of *Mamzerut*, although that would not *solve* the problem of the *Agunah*, it would take the sting out of it. Already in the Tannaitic period Rabbi Tarfon made an ingenious suggestion to that end that the *Mamzer* should be advised to marry a slave-girl, whose children would then be slaves rather than *Mamzerim* and, if subsequently converted to Judaism, would be as unblemished as any other proselyte (*Kid*. 3:13). But such a circumvention of the law became unavailable when slavery ceased.

Another way out, not mentioned in the sources but allegedly practised in various times and places, is for the rabbinic authorities to turn a blind eye to the problem by allowing the *Mamzer* to go and merge into another community where the circumstances of his birth are unknown. Such a policy would be humane but hardly honest.

The only other way of dealing with *Mamzerut* is the drastic one of retroactively annulling the woman's first marriage so that her subsequent marriage will not, after all, have been adulterous, and therefore any children born from it will not, after all, be *Mamzerim*.

Retroactive Annulment of Marriage

Such annulment of marriage is called *hafka-at hakidushin* and is based on the statement in the Talmud, *kol hamekadesh edata derabanan mekadesh ve-afkinehu rabanan lekidushin minehah*—"When a man marries, he does so under rabbinic authority; therefore the rabbis may annul such a marriage" (*Ket*. 3a, *Git*. 33a, 73a). But in the Talmud the principle is invoked only in precisely defined and unusual circumstances, and in post-talmudic times there was a general reluctance to invoke it at all.[15]

It would in any case be inconsistent with any kind of integrity to annul retroactively a marriage except when there are genuine grounds for doubting its initial validity—for example, when there is reason to think that one of the parties was at the time insane or not Jewish, or that the marriage ceremony did not satisfy the indispensable requirements of Jewish law. As Louis Jacobs points out, this remedy, therefore, offers no solution "in those many cases in which the first marriage cannot really be questioned as to its complete validity."[16]

We may, however, ask: if a rabbinic court can in some instances retroactively annul a marriage, why can it not dissolve a marriage? Other legal systems do give such power to the courts, just as they empower them to declare a missing person dead. But rabbinic law is quite clear that nothing can terminate a marriage except either a *get* willingly given and received or the death of one party incontrovertibly attested.

Conditional Betrothal

Since to all intents and purposes, there is no cure either for the problem of the *Agunah* or for that of the *Mamzer*, rabbinic authorities have generally concentrated their efforts on prevention.

An early example of this is the "conditional betrothal," *kidushin al tenai*. This device was allegedly used in Alexandria in Second Temple times. To avoid the risk of a betrothed woman being "snatched-up" by another man before being married, the betrothal included a conditional clause in which the bridegroom said to the bride: *Tehe li le-anto kedat mosheh veyisra-el keshetikhnasi leveti*, "You shall become my wife according to the law of Moses and Israel when you enter my house" (*Tos. Ket.* 4:9; *BM* 104a).[17] A more sophisticated form of this conditional clause, known as *simpon* or "codicil" was subsequently introduced in Palestine and remained standard practice there throughout the Amoraic period. (*J. Kid.* 3:3} In Babylonia this was not done, but *Takkanot* (rabbinic decrees) were issued forbidding under pain of severe punishment, betrothal without a prior engagement and parental consent. (*Kid* 12b)[18]

A form of the Palestinian *simpon* was also used in pre- Expulsion Spain and, after 1492, in Palestine and Syria, usually to the effect that if the bridegroom did not claim the bride within one year, the betrothal would be retroactively voided. Of course, all this was before the two stages, *kiddushin* (betrothal) and *nissu'in* (wedding) were combined into a single ceremony, which proved in the end the most effective solution.[19]

Conditional Divorce

Ultimately, therefore, the most commonly proposed remedy was not the conditional betrothal but the conditional divorce, *get al tenai*. An early example of this is a passage in the Talmud that asserts that King David's soldiers, before they went into battle, would write out *get keritut*, a bill of divorce, so that, if they did not return, their wives would be free to remarry (*Ket.* 9b). The first known instance in modern times occurred in Algeria in 1812, when Rabbi Ben-Zion Alkalai, to overcome the problem of the recalcitrant husband, suggested that immediately before the betrothal benediction the bridegroom should make a deposition before two witnesses, authorizing the *dayanim* to have a *get* written and signed whenever it is required, from the time of any civil divorce onward.[20]

A similar suggestion was made by Rabbi Jacob Meir (1856 - 1939), Sefardi Chief Rabbi of Palestine during the Mandate, with the addition that the witnesses to the *get* should be appointed immediately after the marriage and that the husband remain responsible for his wife's maintenance until the *get* had been transacted (ibid.).

In 1925 Rabbi Joseph Elijah Henkin (1880—) of New York proposed a conference of Torah scholars in Jerusalem to consider various suggestions for the prevention of *Agunah* cases, including his own suggestion, which was, once again, that the bridegroom give instructions for the execution of the *get* at the time of the marriage.[21]

In 1930 Rabbi Judah Leib Epstein of Brooklyn made the novel suggestion that the bridegroom authorize the bride to write a *get* for herself if he should desert her, or fail to provide for her for three years or divorce her civilly.

In modern Britain, a form of *get al tenai*, as proposed by Dayan Yehezkel Abramsky at a conference of Jewish chaplains to the forces during the Second World War to protect the wives of serving men who might be killed in action in "missing, presumed dead" circumstances. (This was reported to me by the late Rabbi Leslie I. Edgar, who was a Jewish chaplain to the forces at the time.)

Thus, many suggestions have been made in the course of the ages to solve the *Agunah* problem, especially through the preventive measure of a conditional *get* at the time of the marriage. But they have encountered strong opposition, chiefly because it is extraordinarily difficult to formulate the condition in a way that would not cause the *get* to be *me-oseh*, "coerced," and therefore invalid.[22]

To these remedial measures should be added attempts that have also been made to facilitate the transaction of the *get*. For instance, Rabbi Solomon Kluger of Brody (1783—1869), in a famous responsum, ruled that, since a Gentile could act as "agent of transmission," *sheliah lholkhah*, it was permissible as the agent to designate the Post Office and hence to transact a *get* by mail.[23]

Prenuptial Agreement

The *Agunah* problem more recently has come into renewed focus through the huge increase that has taken place in the incidence of marriage breakdown and divorce, and more particularly of cases in which there is a civil divorce without a Jewish one. That, in turn, can happen if the couple are unaware of the need for a Jewish divorce, or reluctant to submit themselves to it, or, most commonly, if the husband, out of spite, refuses to cooperate or, out of greed, makes prior financial conditions that the wife considers unreasonable.

In Great Britain, through the initiative, first of Rabbi Berel Berkowits, then of Chief Rabbi Dr. Jonathan Sacks, this situation led to the consideration, over a period of some twelve years, of a pre-nuptial agreement" which was finally adopted by the major Orthodox synagogal bodies in 1996. Essentially, it is an undertaking by the bride and bridegroom, signed before the marriage, that, in the event of a matrimonial dispute, they will both attend the relevant *Bet Din* and comply with its instructions with respect to mediation and divorce. There is also a clause referring to arbitration by the *Bet Din*, but that was made optional in the United Synagogue.

The prenuptial agreement, it could be said, is an attempt to restore a little of the power of law enforcement that the rabbinic courts lost with the Emancipation by making Jewish marriage conditional on an undertaking to abide by its terms. How effective it will prove to be—depending on the willingness of Jewish couples to give, and abide by, such undertakings—remains to be seen.

The case for a form of prenuptial agreement, as a way of overcoming the problem of the recalcitrant husband has also been strongly argued by Rabbi Shlomo Riskin, chief rabbi of Efrat, Israel, and founding rabbi of Lincoln Square Synagogue in New York.[24]

Communal Sanctions

The idea of communal sanctions, that is., disciplinary measures against a husband who ought to give his wife a *get* but refuses to do so, is not new. In former times rabbinic courts could even order corporal punishment in such a case. As the phrase goes, *makin oto ad shyomar rotzeh ani*, "They flog him until he says: I am willing" (*Yad, Hilkhot Gerushin* 2;20). Such a procedure is not considered tantamount to coercion (!); consequently a *get* written under these circumstances is deemed to be valid (ibid.).

Similarly, Israeli courts have been known to send a recalcitrant husband to prison or to hold him liable for his wife's maintenance until a *get* has been transacted.

Such draconian measures are not available to diaspora courts. In Great Britain, however, the *Bet Din* of the Federation of Synagogues has been known to issue a *nidui* (a mild form of excommunication, renewable every thirty days) against a recalcitrant husband. Other measures that have been proposed include public announcements and the withholding of privileges (as distinct from rights) such as being called up to the Torah or elected to synagogue office.

Together with the prenuptial agreement, these communal sanctions, and the publicity attending them may do something to raise the level of "*get* consciousness" in the community and, to that extent, make it marginally more likely than hitherto that Jewish couples obtaining a civil divorce will seek to obtain, additionally, a Jewish divorce.

Enlisting the Civil Law

More effective than either the prenuptial agreement or the communal sanctions might be the enlistment of the civil courts to exercise a power of law enforcement that rabbinic courts no longer possess. That was the purpose of the "Jakobovits Amendment" to the Family Law Bill passed by the British Parliament in 1996. It will empower the civil courts in the United Kingdom to withhold or delay a civil divorce on the plea of either party that the other unreasonably refuses to cooperate in the matter of a religious divorce. How willing or reluctant the courts will be to exercise that power, remains to be seen.

Conservative Judaism

We have considered a number of attempts to deal with the *Agunah* and *Mamzer* problems while upholding the authority of rabbinic law and keeping within its parameters. In modern times that has been the approach of Orthodox Judaism. But Conservative Judaism, too, has sought to operate within these limitations. Thus, the *Summary Index of the Committee on Jewish Law and Standards of the Rabbinical Assembly*, 1995 edition, lists seven ways of dealing with the *Agunah* problem, of which, it says, three "are generally practised at the current time."

1. A *Bet Din* may use the principle of *kol dimekadesh adata derabanan mekadesh* [that Jewish marriages are valid by virtue of rabbinic law, *Git.* 33a] to annul a marriage in a case where a *get* cannot be obtained by any other means and the situation is considered appropriate.[25]
2. A *takkanah* [the "Lieberman clause"] is added to the *ketubah*, in which the couple recognize the authority of the *Bet Din* to counsel them in the light of Jewish tradition, to summon either party at the request of the other, and to impose terms of compensation as it sees fit for failure to respond to its summons or to carry out its decision.[26]
3. Marriages should be performed *al t'nai*, on the condition that if the husband does not give the wife a *get* within six months after a civil divorce, the *kiddushin* will have been null and void.[27] In practice, rabbis will remarry a woman based on evidence that the *t'nai* has not been fulfilled.'[28]

Progressive Judaism: The Traditionalist Tendency

In the history of Progressive Judaism, three distinct though overlapping tendencies are discernible, and each has taken a different approach to the problems of divorce and remarriage, as of other controversial aspects of Jewish tradition.

The first, which might be called traditionalist, differs little from the Conservative movement. It is represented in Britain and Israel by the Masorti movement and is also broadly characteristic of the more conservative constituents of the Progressive movement, including the RSGB and most of the Progressive communities of continental Europe and Israel.

Since it is the way of these movements to reform Judaism slowly, minimally and pragmatically, they have not tackled head-on the issues that are the subject of this paper. Thus, they have generally ignored in practice the problem of *Mamzerut* but have rarely, if ever, said explicitly that they reject the concept. Similarly, the RSGB has, since the establishment of its *Bet Din* in the aftermath of the Second World War, transacted the *get* in its traditional, unilateral, Aramaic form, while dealing with the case of the recalcitrant husband by issuing its own certificate (which admittedly cannot claim traditional halakhic validity) declaring the marriage to be dissolved.[29]

Progressive Judaism: The Radical Tendency

At the other extreme is the radical tendency, which goes back to Samuel Holdheim (1800—1860) and inspired, in a slightly less extreme form, the "Classical Reform" that dominated Progressive Judaism in the United States from its beginnings in the nineteenth century until the 1930s. It also influenced, through its first rabbi, Israel I. Mattuck, the ULPS in Britain and some other constituents of the World Union for Progressive Judaism. The radical tendency has always inclined toward antinomianism. Nevertheless, it has passed some resolutions of far-reaching *halakhic* importance. One of these must be mentioned here because it goes to the root of the inequality of the sexes in biblical and rabbinic marriage law.

In 1869 the Philadelphia conference declared: "Polygamy contradicts the idea of marriage. The marriage of a married man to a second woman can, therefore, neither take place nor claim religious validity, just as little as the marriage of a married woman to another man, but like this it is null and void from the beginning."[30]

On the specific subject of divorce, Samuel Holdheim argued that it should be regarded as a civil act only and that the *get* was therefore superfluous.[31]

The Philadelphia conference essentially endorsed Holdheim's position[32] and resolved:

> The dissolution of marriage is, on Mosaic and Rabbinical grounds, a civil act only, which never received religious consecration. It is to be recognised, therefore, as an act emanating altogether from the judicial authorities of the State. The so-called ritual *get* is in all cases declared null and void. The dissolution of marriage, pronounced by a civil court, is also fully valid in the eyes of Judaism, if it can be ascertained from the judicial documents that both parties consented to the divorce; where, however, the court issues a decree against one or the other party by constraint, Judaism recognises the validity of the divorce then only, if the cause assigned is sufficient in conformity with the spirit of the Jewish religion. It is recommended, however, that the officiating rabbi, in rendering a decision, obtain the concurrence of competent colleagues.[33]

Broadly speaking the ULPS has always followed the policy of the 1869 Philadelphia conference and of the CCAR in recognizing a civil divorce as effectively dissolving a Jewish marriage. In the days when English divorce law was based on the concept of the matrimonial offense, however, the "guilty" party of a civil divorce was required to satisfy the rabbi that he or she nevertheless had a responsible attitude toward marriage.[34]

In addition, a civilly but not Jewishly divorced man seeking remarriage within the ULPS has always been required, in appropriate cases to give, or offer to give, his former wife an (Orthodox) *get*, so that she may be free to remarry in an Orthodox synagogue and that any future children of hers may not be subject to the disabilities of *Mamzerut*.[35]

A civilly divorced woman whose former husband refuses to give her a *get* or makes unreasonable preconditions, however, has always been allowed to remarry in the ULPS without a *get*, after the consequences of such remarriage have been explained to her.

Thus, the general thrust of past ULPS policy has been threefold: (1) to recognize that a civilly dissolved marriage is no longer an existent marriage; (2) to protect individuals as far as possible from any disabilities in Orthodox Judaism; and (3) nevertheless to grant remarriage to civilly-only divorced persons in cases where, on grounds of humaneness, it would be unreasonable to refuse.

Progressive Judaism: The Intermediate Tendency

Broadly speaking, then, the traditionalist tendency has affirmed the halakhah and retained the *get*; the radical tendency has negated the halakhah and abolished the *get*.

But in addition to these, there has always been in Progressive Judaism an intermediate tendency. This may be said to go back to Abraham Geiger (1810—1874). In the later history of Progressive Judaism in Germany, it inspired rabbis like Caesar Seligmann and, through him, the 1912 *Richtlinien* (Guiding Principles) and the 1929 *Einheitsgebetbuch* (Union Prayerbook). In the United States the intermediate tendency produced the 1937 Columbus Platform, considerably modifying the radicalism of the 1885 Pittsburgh Platform.

More recently, in Britain (through both the RSGB and ULPS), the United States, and other countries, there has shown itself in a new desire to embrace the best of tradition and modernity, not one or the other but both. This can be seen most clearly in a new generation of prayerbooks, beginning with *Service of the Heart* (ULPS, 1967), that combine a notable return to tradition with innovative creativity.

What are the implications of this tendency for our subject? On the one hand, one would expect from it a clear affirmation of the principle of sexual equality, as well as an unequivocal repudiation of the law of the *Mamzer* as a manifest case of misinterpretation of the Divine Will.

But one would not expect it to be satisfied with a mere rejection of the *get*. After all, it makes perfectly good sense to say that a Jewishly inaugurated marriage should, when it has broken down irretrievably, be Jewishly terminated. That view has in fact been taken throughout Jewish history, and there is nothing wrong with it. It is only the antiquated, unilateral character of the traditional *get* that is objectionable from a principled Progressive point of view.

Therefore, just as the attitude of the intermediate tendency towards the halakhah in general is one neither of uncritical acceptance nor of outright rejection, but of appropriate modification, so one would have expected this tendency long ago to have produced a modified *get*, satisfying the principle of reciprocity.

Just such suggestions have in fact been made from time to time. Already at the Leipzig and Augsburg Synods of 1869 and 1871, Geiger and others submitted motions suggesting that the form of the *get* be revised, that it be written in the vernacular, and that the wife be allowed to remarry without it if the husband refused to give it. These matters were referred to a committee that was to report to the next Synod—which, however, never took place.

An interesting suggestion was made in Germany in 1910 by Rabbi Israel Goldschmidt. He proposed a reciprocal *get*, in modified language, to be transacted in the context of a religious ceremony stressing both the sadness of the breakdown and the need for healing. "The rabbi then should show that in this tragic moment there could be found a reconciling element which could silence the anger of the heart. Tragedy is a power which often is stronger than the human will. It must purify the heart and not poison it with hatred."[36]

In 1969 I wrote in the then quarterly journal of the ULPS: 'A respectable case can therefore be made for reintroducing the *get*, although in a modified form which would make it, formally and effectually, a reciprocal act.'[37]

In 1983 Rabbi Bernard H. Mehiman and Rabbi Rifat Sonsino published an article in the (American) *Journal of Reform Judaism* arguing for a modern *get* and suggesting an appropriate Hebrew and English text.[38] But nothing much came of any of these proposals, except that in 1988 the CCAR issued a new edition of its *Rabbis Manual* that includes two important innovations. The first was, a Ritual of Release, *seder peredah*, by which husband and wife, before a rabbi and in the presence of witnesses, declared their consent to the termination of their marriage (there is a modified version for when only one party is present). The second was a "Document of Separation" *(sefer keritut)*, which serves as a mutual release, in writing, "from the sacred bonds that held us together." "The rabbi," states the Manual, "will explain to the participants that this ceremony and the accompanying document do not constitute a *halakhic get*" (p. 97).

Finally, A Progressive Get

In 1996 the Rabbinic Conference of the ULPS accepted a proposal to introduce, on an optional basis, a truly progressive version of the traditional *get*, in Hebrew and English, to be known by its biblical name, *sefer keritut*, translated as "Document of Release," by which the parties release each other from their marriage vows and free each other to remarry. The considerations that persuaded the atendees of the conference to take this step can be summarised as follows:

1. Our marriages have both a civil and a religious aspect. In so far as they are civil, it is right that, when they have broken down irretrievably, they should be civilly terminated. But in so far as they are religious, it is, by the same token, appropriate that there should be a religious termination. This consideration is reinforced by the importance we attach to the vows of mutual love, respect, and loyalty made in the marriage service, which point to the need for a formal release from them (*hateret nedarim*).
2. Divorce is often a traumatic experience, not unlike bereavement, and those involved in it may benefit from pastoral counselling or communal support. This may help to reassure them that they are still valued as individuals and as members of their synagogue to fortify their self-respect, and, to make it more likely that they will remain associated with the community, and continue their children's religious education. Thus the availability of the proposed act of release would provide, for those who choose to take advantage of it, an occasion for a potentially beneficial contact with their rabbi and synagogue.
3. The proposed step would be a logical conclusion of a trend which, since the 1960's, has been manifest in the ULPS in other respects (that is, in its liturgy), to move from a radical towards an intermediate position and, in particular, from a negation of the halakhah towards a qualified affirmation and principled reconstruction of it. At the same time it may serve as an example to other

Progressive movements and thus prove to be a step towards reunifying the various branches of Progressive Judaism in an area in which their practices have hitherto diverged widely.

The ULPS Rabbinic Conference, in deciding to introduce its "Document of Release," was clear that it was unlikely to be recognised by the authorities of Orthodox Judaism, and was thus insistent that this fact and its implications always be meticulously explained to applicants; also that, in cases where serious consequences might otherwise ensue, they should still be advised, as hitherto, to take the precaution of obtaining an Orthodox *get* either in lieu of or in addition to the ULPS one.

Finally, the attendees of the Conference decided that in cases where one party of the former marriage cannot be traced or persuaded to cooperate, it would take upon itself the power to declare the marriage dissolved and issue an appropriate certificate, on request, to that effect.

The ULPS divorce certificate is in Hebrew and English, and in two parts identically worded except in gender, since by one the husband releases the wife, and by the other the wife releases the husband; the certificate is signed by both parties as well as two witnesses and the rabbi. The text incorporates both the Hosea verse (2:4) and the essential formula prescribed in *Gittin* 9:3, and thus satisfies the requirements of the Mishnah. Here are the key phrases of the wife-to-husband section:

> *Hineni beratzon nafshi materet otakh mikishrei hakidushin,* I hereby release you of my own free will from the marriage bonds *shebam hayinu keshurim mekodem lakhen,* which have hitherto united us, so that henceforth *umehayom vehalah atah lo ishi ve-anokhi lo ishtekha,* you are not my husband and I am not your wife, *veharei atah mutar lekhol isha,* and you are free to marry another woman. *Vezeh yihyehlkha mimeni sefer keritut veget piturin,* accordingly, I ask you to accept from me this document as a bill of separation and a certificate of divorce, *kedat mosheh veyisrael,* according to the law of Moses and Israel.

The introduction of this document may be said to complete the process by which the fundamental inequality of men and women under biblical and talmudic marriage-and-divorce law has been progressively—in both senses of that word!—rectified.

Notes

1. Reuven Yaron, *Introduction to the Law of the Aramaic Papyri,* Oxford, 1967, 60.
2. A. Cowley, *Aramaic Papyri of the Fifth Century B.C..,* Oxford, 1927, 45; Yaron, *Introduction,* 53f.
3. Josephus, *Jewish Antiquities,* Book XV, 7:10; Loeb Classical Library, Cambridge, MA, 1918, verses 259 f.
4. Jeffrey H.Tigay, *The JPS Torah Commentary, Deuteronomy,* New York, 1996, 221.
5. See Shlomo Riskin, *Women and Jewish Divorce,* New York, 1989, 31.
6. Ibid., 79 f.
7. Simeon Kayyara, (ed.) *Mekitzei Nirdamim, Hilhot Gittin,* 339.
8. Ze'ev Falk, *Jewish Matrimonial Law in the Middle Ages,* Oxford, 1966, 13-34.
9. Ibid., 119.
10. Ibid., 122 f.
11. Riskin, Op. Cit., 94, 134.
12. See, e.g., *Encyclopedia Judaica,* vol. 6, p. 131; *Encyclopedia Talmudit,* vol. 5, 656; Isaac Klein, *A Guide to Jewish Religious Practice,* New York, 1992, 479.
13. Lord Jakobovits, House of Lords, 23 January 1996; Hansard, 1004.
14. Louis Jacobs, *A Tree of Life,* Oxford, 1984, 257–65.
15. *Encyclopaedia Talmudit,* Jerusalem, 1952, vol.2, 137–140; Menachem Elon, *Jewish Law,* Jerusalem, 1978, vol.2, 631ff; Abraham Chayyim Freimann, Seder *Kiddushin v' Nissu'in,* Jerusalem, 1964, 285 f.
16. Louis Jacobs, Op. Cit., .274.
17. Freimann, Op. Cit., . 12.
18. Ibid., 12 f.
19. Freimann *Op. Cit.,* p 34, 61, 112, 119; Hayyim Schauss, *The Lifetime of a Jew,* Cincinnati, 1943, 160 f.
20. Freimann, *Op. Cit.,* 394.
21. Ibid., 394 f.
22. J. David Bleich, *Contemporary Halakhic Problems,* New York, 1977, vol. I, 150–176.
23. Solomon B. Freehof, *The Responsa Literature,* Philadelphia, 1955, 136-40.
24. Riskin, Op. Cit., 139-142.
25. David Aronson, *"Teshuvah,"Proceedings of the Rabbinic Assembly,* Philadelphia,1951, 120–140.
26. *Proceedings of the Rabbinic Assembly,* Philadelphia, 1954, 64–68.
27. *Proceedings of the Rabbinic Assembly,* New York, 1968, 229–241.
28. See also Abraham Klein, *A Guide to Jewish Religious Practice,* 498 f.
29. See Anne Kershen and Jonathan Romain, *Tradition and Change, A History of Reform Judaism in Britain (1840–1995),* London, 234, 238, 272 f.
30. Moses Mielziner, *The Jewish Law of Marriage and* Divorce, Cincinnati, 1884, 31; Sefton Temkin, *The New World of Reform,*Bridgeport, 1974, 58.
31. Samuel Holdheim, *Autonomie der Rabbinen,* Schwerin, 1843.
32. See Gunther Plaut, *The Rise of Reform Judaism,* New York, 1963, 222 f and Temkin, *The New World of Reform,* 84-87.

33. See Mielziner, *The Jewish Law of Marriage and Divorce,* 135. For a summary of the CCAR position and its history, see Walter Jacob's responsum in *American Reform Responsa, New York, 1983,* 511-14.
34. John D. Rayner, *The Practices of Liberal Judaism,* London, 1960, 53.
35. Israel I. Mattuck, *Marriage, Doctrine and Practice of Liberal Judaism*, ULPS pamphlet, London, 1950, 6 f.
36. Gunther Plaut, *The Growth of Reform Judaism,* New York, 1965, p. 263.
37. *Pointer*, London, (Autumn), 1969, p. 5.
38. Bernard Mehlman., "A Reform *get*: A Proposal," *CCAR Journal,* (Summer), 1983, pp. 31–36.

Chapter 3

❖ ❖ ❖

GENDER, HALAKHAH, AND WOMEN'S SUFFRAGE
Responsa of the First Three Chief Rabbis on the Public Role of Women in the Jewish State

David Ellenson and Michael Rosen

A modern notion of gender equality is foreign to classical rabbinic Judaism. The ancient Sages, like patriarchs in other cultures, assigned men and women distinct gender roles. In their view, Psalm 45:14, where it was written, "*Kol kevodah bat melekh penimah,* the King's daughter is all glorious within," consigned women to the domestic realm. Susan Grossman and Rivka Haut, in commenting upon this passage, have observed that it serves as the halakhic warrant for the position that a woman can play no role in public life. As they have pointed out:

> This verse has been cited as proof that, according to tradition, women have divinely ordained roles that preclude any public activity. Rabbis, throughout the ages, including our own, have cited this beautiful image to justify excluding women from public life, … and stressing that women's sole legitimate sphere of activity is *within* the home.[1]

Notes for this section begin on page 80.

During the past century, many Jews have expressed opposition to this traditional gender ideal and the socially constructed behavior patterns it has established for each sex. Among them were the non-religious Zionist *halutzim* that migrated to *Eretz Yisrael* at the turn of the century. These people were adamant in their conviction that traditional notions of gender roles were, at least in theory, outmoded. They believed that men and women should be equal participants in society, and they insisted that the role of women in the public life of the *yishuv* had to be broadened.[2]

For the Orthodox of *Eretz Yisrael*, it was another matter. Many religious members of the old *yishuv* promoted traditional gender-role notions and were determined to resist and protest any changes proposed. As late as 1946, this determination could be witnessed in the pages of *HaTzofeh*, the organ of the Orthodox National Religious Party. During that year, Golda Meir replaced Moshe Sharet as head of the Political Department of the Jewish Agency. Commenting upon her ascension to this post, *HaTzofeh* , on August 28, 1946, did not hesitate to employ Psalm 45:14 as a basis for opposition to her appointment.

Although the paper acknowledged that Meir was, without question, "understanding, industrious, ethical, a distinguished woman," she was, "all that notwithstanding—a woman!" This fact led *HaTzofeh* to the following conclusion. The paper wrote:

> It is hard to become accustomed to the fact that this people, which, for generations, has been guided by the formula, 'The king's daughter is all glorious *within*,' whose Torah has imposed commandments on the man and not the woman, [and which has denied women] the right to serve as judges, in administration, and as witnesses, which has established for her an honored place *within the tent*—that a woman stands at the head of the political department of this people. ... It is impossible to appoint her [to such a post]. This is a law like the laws of nature. This is eternal Jewish law. There are boundaries and borders, and each sex needs to know its limits ... [3]

At this source indicates, all Orthodox Jews recognized that the realities of their setting compelled them to grapple with the ideal of gender equality. While one faction remained determined to resist any concession to this notion, another group pragmatically contended that an Orthodox accommodation was demanded by the realities of the modern setting. Finally, some Orthodox

Jews had themselves internalized this western ethos and they held that Jewish law ought to embrace the position that men and women be full participants in the public life of society. *Eretz Yisrael* fast became an arena wherein conflict ensued among these camps of Orthodox Jews.

This paper will present and analyze selected responsa of three leading twentieth century Orthodox Israeli decisors—Rabbis Isaac Halevi Herzog (1888–1959), Avraham Yitzchak Hacohen Kuk (1865–1935), and Ben Zion Meir Hai Ouziel (1880–1953)—on the matter of women's suffrage and the related issue of women's participation in the public political life of Israeli society. In so doing, it will indicate how *Eretz Yisrael* served as a venue for Jewish legal struggles with issues of gender and how those struggles produced diverse halakhic responses in a place where Jewish law had to grapple with the demands of governance in a modern Jewish nation. After all, each of the men whose writings we will describe occupied the post of Chief Rabbi in *Eretz Yisrael*. Upon the formation of this position in 1921, Kuk ascended to the office and occupied it until his death in 1935. Herzog was elected as his successor in 1936 and assumed the post of Chief Ashkenazic Rabbi in 1937, remaining in office for over two decades. Ouziel, the son of the *av bet din* of the Sephardic rabbinic court of Jerusalem, was elected first Chief Sephardic Rabbi in 1939 and served until his death. In this essay, after outlining the historical and social contexts that prompted these writings, we will show how the rulings of these men on issues of women in the political order reflect the gamut of positions advanced by Orthodox Jews on these matters in the modern era.

Initially, we will consider the writings of Rav Kuk on the matter, as his thoughts were penned in 1920, when the issue of women's suffrage was still a matter of great debate in the *yishuv*. Following that analysis, we will take up the writings of Rabbi Ouziel. Although his opinions on this subject, as well as on the attendant issue of women's suitability for public office, were written at the time that the State of Israel was established, Ouziel employed the debates of the 1920s as the grounds for his discussion. Finally, Rabbi Herzog, like his Sephardic peer, also wrote on this matter as the fledgling Jewish state emerged in 1947–1948. Aware of the ferocious debates that had wracked the *yishuv* during the 1920s as well as the fact that the nascent Israeli government was about to enact laws that would govern elections for the Knesset, Herzog felt it imperative that he articulate the attitude of Jewish law on the question of female voting and eligibility for public office. Both Rabbis Ouziel and Herzog, as officers of the State, considered themselves obligated to express the position of the halakhah on matters of gender, as these attitudes were of signal import for Orthodox Jews as they coped with the challenge of adapting halakhah to the demands of a modern nation. In this sense, the rulings they issued on these matters of gender are part of a larger project that occupied all these men as they confronted the challenges that the modern situation posed.

In considering these writings, we, as Liberal Jews, not only uncover documents of history, but we measure our own attitudes towards gender over against the writings of these Orthodox authorities and clarify the principles that operate within our community. In so doing, we witness the vitality of the halakhic system and gain some understanding of the resources it might provide us as we in our movement strive to create an authentic Judaism capable of meeting the demands of the modern world.

Historical Background of the Responsa

After World War I, an occidental trend emerged that extended the right of suffrage to women. In 1918, Germany and Poland decided to grant women this right, as did England. One year later, Czechoslovakia offered voting rights to women, and the United States followed suit in 1920.[4] The prestate *yishuv* in *Eretz Yisrael* was destined to be part of this trend.

In 1917, the British Mandatory Government in Palestine decided to create *Knesset Yisrael* (Jewish Assembly) as the institutional structure that would govern the affairs of the Jewish community, and an Elected Assembly (*Asseifat ha-Nivharim*) was to be chosen. On December 28, 1917, the committee charged with responsibility for the First Elected Assembly, decided that the Elected Assembly should be chosen through direct elections based on proportional representation. The electorate was to comprise all Jews in the *yishuv* who did not explicitly deny membership in the organized Jewish community, and the committee maintained that suffrage should be granted to all men and women above the age of twenty.[5]

This last recommendation was vehemently opposed by ultra-Orthodox elements in the *yishuv hayashan*, which saw this advancement in the rights of women as an attack upon their efforts to preserve a traditional way of life in *Eretz Yisrael*. In contrast, the Zionists of the *yishuv hehadash* saw this proposal as an indispensable foundation for the creation of a modern nation. Over the next two years, stormy arguments ensued, and although one representative of the ultra-Orthodox party in 1918 contended that a compromise wherein women could vote might be acceptable, the notion that women could also be elected to office could never be countenanced by the Orthodox community. Progressive forces within the *yishuv*, however, would brook no compromise on this matter, and they prevailed in their insistence that full rights be granted women to vote and to serve in office. This led to a movement among *hareidi* elements in Jerusalem that called for nonparticipation in any election that would allow female participation. At this point, the more moderate Orthodox Mizrachi party dissented from the stance of the *hareidim* and elections—in which women would participate as the full equals of men—were ultimately set for April 19, 1920. The ultra-Orthodox, fearing that nonparticipation in the elections would be against their self-interest, ultimately chose to vote, though they did insist on special polling places where women could not appear.[6]

Even after the elections for the *Asseifat ha-Nivharim* in 1920, however, the *hareidi* factions in the *yishuv* refused to surrender on this issue, and the debate over women's suffrage did not abate. The right wing Agudah minority anxiously strove to rescind this right, though their efforts were to no avail, as the overwhelming secular majority of the community opposed any surrender on this point. The Mizrachi sought to effect a compromise on this issue, and they called for a public referendum on the matter. When the Agudah issued a ban of *herem* upon participation in the referendum, the Mizrachi ceased its efforts, as its leadership felt nothing could be done to pacify the *hareidi* elements within the *yishuv*. At this point, the Agudah withdrew from the larger community and adopted a sectarian posture, whereas Mizrachi joined the communal polity that was to govern the Jewish inhabitants of the land. On December 6, 1925, votes were cast for the second Elected Assembly, and the debate over women's suffrage came to an end. It is against this background that we are now able to turn to the writings of Kuk, Ouziel, and Herzog on these issues.[7]

The Stance of Rav Kuk—Unequivocal Rejection

On May 28, 1920, a scant month after elections for the *Asseifat Hanivharim* had been held, a letter penned by Kuk was printed in *Ha-Ivri*, an organ of Mizrachi, on the question of whether women should be allowed to vote in elections for public office. In light of what was universally perceived as his positive attitude toward the Zionist enterprise, the modernist Orthodox members of Mizrachi fully expected Rav Kuk to take a lenient position on this issue and they anticipated his issuing a strong ruling that would favor the addition of women to the electorate.[8] To their great astonishment, however, Kuk unequivocally condemned such inclusion as a complete break with Jewish tradition and law.[9]

At the very outset of his piece, Kuk maintained that the entire weight of the tradition was opposed to such an innovation. He wrote, "The one voice that we hear from the Torah, the Prophets, and the Writings, from both *halakhah* and *aggadah*, asserts that the national spirit is entirely opposed to this modern innovation." It is the last part of this statement, his invocation of the "national spirit" that marks the Jewish people, that is most crucial to an understanding of why he ruled that suffrage not be extended to women. For, in looking at his position on this issue, Kuk did not put forth specific legal arguments, i.e., citations of Jewish legal precedents, against such extension. Instead, he composed a "meta-legal" argument that centered on what he perceived as the nature of the Jewish people and on the need for *Am Yisrael* to construct a nation that would be true to its authentic character and indigenous religious-national principles. Indeed, Kuk argued that the Jewish people possessed a unique national value system and he maintained that the imposition of this innovation would run counter to the Jewish national character.

Kuk continued by stating that the "national spirit" of the Jewish people was more refined than that of modern nations and maintained that the family unit animated this spirit. Indeed, the Jewish family served as the vortex of the nation. Furthermore, within the family, the wife was at the center. It was she who held the family together, and the attendant responsibility she possessed as wife and mother for the welfare and purity of the Jewish nation knew no bounds. Allowing women to vote could thus have only negative consequences, and Kuk cited two reasons for this belief. First, the wife might well bow to the will of her husband and vote as he instructed. If this were the case, it would constitute an "obsequiousness, *hanufah*" on her part that would compromise her "internal freedom, *hufshah ha-p'neemeet*." On the other hand, should she differ with her husband, the tranquillity of the home would be shattered and domestic discord would result. Either behavior would be inappropriate for a Jewish woman and the subsequent rent in the life of the family would only undermine the people, bringing shame to *Am Yisrael* in the eyes of the nations.

Kuk therefore called upon his "modern brothers" in the *yishuv* to "act beyond the letter of the law and surrender their novel demand." The extension of suffrage to women should not be forced on the Jewish nation, as it was completely alien to the national spirit that infuses Israel. Kuk recognized that the modern advocates of this position "claim that morality demands that what they call equal rights for women—their participation in the public realm in accord with the modern spirit—is a fine and acceptable thing." However, this is "not as it is with us." Instead, the Jewish spirit regards this innovation a "repulsive thing—*davar ka-ur*," and could not accept it. Every nation has the right to construct a state in keeping with its own character, to weigh that which is "good and bad, beautiful and repulsive, in accord with its own values." In refusing to acknowledge this change in gender roles for women as legitimate, Kuk contended that he was only asking that the Jewish people be allowed "to build our nation according to our own values."

In looking at Kuk's argument, we find it noteworthy that he did not cite a single halakhic precedent to support his position. After all, the novelty of female participation in the public life of liberal civil society may well be said to have no exact precedent in the Jewish past. Therefore, Rav Kuk, as stated at the outset of this section, was compelled to define what he regarded as the overarching ethos of Jewish tradition on appropriate gender-roles to guide his ruling on this matter. Nevertheless, there is no question that this decision was, in the final analysis, consistent with his weltanschauung. Throughout his writings Kuk was able to support the Zionist movement precisely because he regarded the Zionist endeavor as part of a divine plan that would allow the Jewish people to achieve their spiritual destiny. As such, he could support the Zionists and regard their work as "holy," even if they themselves did not recognize it as such. As Kuk wrote in his posthumously published book *Orot* (1942):

> "Many of the adherents of the present national revival maintain that they are secularists. If Jewish secular nationalism were really imaginable, then we would indeed, be in danger of falling so low as to be beyond redemption. But Jewish secular nationalism is a form of self-delusion: the spirit of Israel is so closely linked to the spirit of God that a Jewish nationalist, no matter how secularist his intention may be, must, despite himself, affirm the divine. An individual can sever the tie that binds him to life eternal, but the House of Israel as a whole cannot. All of its most cherished possessions—its land, language, history, and *customs*—are vessels of the spirit of the Lord."[10]

In this instance Kuk was convinced that this transformation in gender custom and role on the national soil of the Jewish homeland would undermine the Jewish soul. Consequently, he felt compelled to oppose those secular Zionists who favored granting suffrage to women. It was they, not the *hareidim*, who were required to compromise on this issue "for the greater good." Kuk's view of gender roles was absolute. He would brook no change. Rabbi Ouziel, as we shall see, was of a different halakhic opinion.

The Position of Rabbi Ouziel—Complete Approval

In 1948, at the time the State of Israel was founded, Rabbi Ouziel decided to publish a responsum on the topic, "Concerning the Participation of Women in Elections for Public Institutions." [11]

Although he asserted that he wrote this opinion during the 1920s, when the issues discussed in the responsum had not yet "been resolved," he did not publish his responsum at that time. Rather, he elected to do so two decades later, he claimed, "so that the greatness of Torah could be magnified."

There is no reason to doubt his sincerity on this point, but it is equally true that the moment he did decide to grant public expression to his views was decisive in Zionist history. The Jewish State had just been declared, and though the issue of female participation in the public life of the nascent nation no longer elicited the furor it had twenty years earlier among all sectors of the Orthodox world, debates over the proper role of women in the public life of *Medinat Yisrael* nevertheless persisted in Orthodox precincts.[12] As Sephardi Chief Rabbi, Ouziel's *p'sak* in this responsum had practical importance for informing the attitudes that marked many traditional Jews as they considered the roles women would play in the Jewish nation as both voters and officeholders. Furthermore, as the "public face" of Orthodox Judaism in Israel, his writings commanded the attention of the secular populace, and his views informed their attitudes toward Jewish religious traditionalism and its ability to adapt to the demands of a modern world. Ouziel understood all this, and his publication of the responsum at this moment should be regarded as a crucial policy statement on his part concerning the place of women in the public sphere.

In approaching this matter, Rabbi Ouziel noted that the 1920s were marked by the daily publication of circulars, pamphlets, warnings, and newspapers articles that prohibited women's participation in elections for the *Asseifat ha-Nivharim*. He observed that some rabbis asserted that the Torah itself prohibited extending suffrage to women, whereas others argued that the prohibition would serve as a hedge to guard morality and modesty. Still other authorities insisted that this prohibition would preserve peace in the family. All these men relied on the slogan popularized a century earlier by the Hatam Sofer (1768–1839), "All innovation is forbidden by the Torah itself." In this responsum Ouziel intended to respond to all these viewpoints, contending that the issue itself was divided into two parts: (1) May women vote, and (2) may women be permitted be elected to office?

At the outset of his discussion, Rabbi Ouziel asserted that there was no clear halakhic foundation that would prohibit women from voting. Indeed, elsewhere in his responsum Rabbi Ouziel did note that one rabbi had opposed extending the vote to women on the halakhic ground that women constituted neither an "*eidah,* community" or a "*kahal,* congregation." In response to this position, Ouziel wrote, "Let us assume that they do not constitute a 'congregation' or a 'community'. ... Nevertheless, are they not creatures created in God's image and possessed of intelligence!" Logic itself therefore rejected the idea that women should be denied this basic human right (*zechut ishit zot*). After all, through these elections, officials were granted power and authority to levy taxes and order public affairs. Women, no less than men, accepted the rule of those elected and obeyed their directives. In light of this, he felt it was wrong to thrust these decisions upon them on the one hand and deny them the right to vote on the other. Simple justice demanded that women be granted this right.

Ouziel then responded *seriatim* to the objections raised by those who would deny extending the vote to women. First, he noted that some opponents claimed that women were intellectually incapable of casting ballots. These opponents cited two talmudic passages to buttress their position. The first passage, found in two places (*Shabbat* 33b and *Kiddushin* 80b), stated, "Women are feeble-minded," and a second (*Yoma* 66b), "A woman's wisdom is only in the home," confined women to the domestic realm. Ouziel dismissed both these citations as mere rhetoric. Indeed, if one wanted to cite talmudic precedent to discover a warrant for how women ought to be regarded, he stated that *Niddah* 45b, "God gave extra understanding to women," more accurately described the ability and talent that characterized women. Educated women in the modern era, like those in the past, were fully as able as men. Their business skills, as well as their talents for organization and administration demonstrated this truth. Moreover, even if some women did lack intellectual ability, so did many men. If lack of intellectual acuity was to be put forth as a criterion for excluding women from voting, then Rabbi Ouziel bitingly asserted, "Let us also exclude from the electorate those men who are feeble-minded, of whom there has never been a lack in the land."

Ouziel then went on to consider the arguments of those who charged that sexual misconduct would result from the sexes mingling at polling places. He immediately dismissed such fears as absurd. After all, people go to the ballot box for the express purpose of casting a vote. If extending suffrage to women could be denied on the grounds that this might lead to sexual licentiousness, then no semblance of normal life could remain. Such logic would require that men and women be forbidden from walking together in the street, and would not countenance the joint presence of a man and woman in a store. Furthermore, men and women would also be prohibited from speaking with one another on business matters, as this would lead to proximity that, in turn, could surely foster sexual impropriety. Yet, no reasonable person, Rabbi Ouziel maintained, would entertain such notions.

Ouziel also condemned the notion that domestic tranquillity would be shattered if wives were given the right to vote. Indeed, he viewed such a claim as ridiculous. He pointed out that the Talmud (*Babba Metzia* 12b) compared women to adult sons who were still dependent on their fathers. Rabbi Ouziel therefore approvingly cited the words of the *Malki Ba-kodesh*, Rabbi Hayyim Hirschenson, "If this is so, then we would also deprive sons and daughters still living at home and dependent upon their father the right to vote," as a warrant for his own views on the matter of women's suffrage. Just as no one dared suggest that suffrage not be extended to adult dependent males on the grounds that their rejection of their fathers' position might create domestic discord, so no one should suggest that voting rights be denied women on this basis. After all, differences of opinion on such matters cannot be suppressed, and the strength of family bonds would surely prove more enduring than whatever ire might result from familial disagreements on political issues.

On the other hand, Ouziel, at the end of the entire responsum, took note of Rav Kuk's position and noted that some critics maintained that the vote should be denied women because it might lead to obsequious behavior on their part. That is, a wife might fear expressing her own will, and might simply vote for the party or candidate her husband favored. However, Ouziel was not distraught at such a prospect. Instead, he contended, if this were the case, it should simply be viewed as a "gift of instruction and love" that the husband shared with his wife. Indeed, said Rabbi Ouziel, "Who would not desire such an act, one wherein the wife would display such esteem for her husband that she would defer to him in this way?" In fact, this outcome might constitute the strongest possible argument for extending suffrage to women, for this would allow the wife to display her love for her husband in an active way, thereby increasing domestic peace among the Jewish people!

In concluding the first half of his responsum, Rabbi Ouziel turned to *Hagigah* 16b as a warrant for his position. There, the Talmud relates that R. Jose permitted women to lay their hands on a "peace-sacrifice" if they so desired. As the Talmud states, "Once we had a calf that was a peace sacrifice, and we brought it to the Women's Court, and women laid hands on it—not that the laying on of hands had to be done by the women, but in order to gratify them." One commentator, in explaining this passage, noted, "So that they should feel that they have a share, like men, in the sacrificial rites of their offering." Inasmuch as this was their offering, the women, like the men, were called upon to participate actively in the ritual. This precedent, claimed Ouziel, was relevant here. Women, he reasoned, should participate in elections just as men would, for their interests in this matter, like the interests of the women called upon to participate in the "peace-offering," were involved. In the case of voting, where there was no ground for prohibition, failure to grant them this right would constitute "an insult and an oppression, *elbon v'ho'na'ah*." Jewish law and equity demanded that suffrage be extended to women.

Having disposed of the question of whether voting rights should be granted women, Ouziel now turned to the second issue: can women serve in public office? Here he noted that some halakhic precedents seemingly opposed granting women this privilege. In *Sifrei* Deuteronomy 157, the Midrash, citing Deuteronomy 17:15, "Thou shalt in any wise set a king over thee," commented, "a king, but not a queen," and Maimonides, on this basis, ruled, in *Hilkhot Melachim* 1:5, that there was a prohibition against a woman serving in public office.

Ouziel took these sources seriously and addressed them directly. In analyzing them, Rabbi Ouziel observed that actually neither the Mishnah or Gemara prohibited women from holding public office. Furthermore, the Bible itself contradicted the sense of these rulings, for the story of the prophetess Deborah in Judges 4 surely indicated that Judaism allowed women to serve as public officials. The Sages themselves, in commenting on Judges 4:4, noted that Deborah officiated as a judge and that the Children of Israel "were compelled to obey her legal judgments." This precedent proved that the statement contained in *Sifrei* 157 did not prohibit women from all public service.

Rabbi Ouziel indicated that the scope of the rulings in both *Sifrei* and the Rambam was circumscribed, and he maintained that each ruling applied only to appointments made by the Sanhedrin. As he stated, "All prohibitions against the appointment of women to public office are confined to appointment by the Sanhedrin." In cases where the Sanhedrin was involved, women were indeed ineligible for office. In other instances, however, women are able to serve. Indeed, this was the case with Deborah, for she was not appointed by the Sanhedrin. Moreover, Rabbi Ouziel wrote that the people were not simply forced to accept her rule. Rather, basing himself on the classical talmudic commentary of Rabbenu Nissim on a passage in Shavuot, he asserted that the Children of Israel willingly accepted Deborah as their leader. In a modern state, wherein the polity, through direct elections, expresses "its opinion, its agreement, and its faith in those elected," present-day women can therefore surely serve in office. Should women be the choice of the electorate, they have the right to wield public authority and power, for their election would demonstrate that present-day *am yisrael* accepts them, just as *b'nei yisrael* received Deborah in the hoary past. Halakhah is clear: "From [the standpoint] of the *din*, [we] are also able to elect women."

In concluding his responsum, Rabbi Ouziel noted that the same objection concerning licentiousness lodged against extending suffrage to women might be applied to the question of their serving in office as well. Indeed, "from an ethical standpoint, as a hedge to modesty, perhaps there is a prohibition concerning this," he wrote. Yet, he dismissed this objection on this point just as he had rejected it when applied to the question of whether women should be allowed to vote. As Rabbi Ouziel commented, "Since we have learned that the Torah did not prohibit [women occupying public office] except by appointment of [the Sanhedrin], there is no justification for prohibiting [such occupation] on account of licentiousness, for if there was any justification for such prohibition on account of licentiousness, then the Torah would not have permitted Deborah [to serve as a judge]."

Echoing the position he had taken earlier, R. Ouziel observed that men and women had business transactions together every day. They constantly engaged one another in business negotiations, and there was no hint of untoward conduct in them. The rabbinic statement, "Do not speak overly much with women," (*Pirkei Avot* 1:5) applied only to idle talk. Matters of public import, however, were not included in this prohibition. Indeed, to even think such thoughts of Jewish men and women engaged in public affairs was insulting, and Rabbi Ouziel claimed that the people Israel were holy and should not be suspected of improper sexual conduct. He concluded this argument by asserting that *Sukkah* 51b, where the Sages ruled that men should sit downstairs while women should sit upstairs in the Temple courtyard during the time of the Sukkot water libation festival, did not apply to the current case, for the talmudic ruling dealt with a large gathering during a time of rejoicing when it was likely that the "evil inclination" might dominate. In the *Asseifat ha-Nivharim*, however, such misconduct was inconceivable. Behavior of this type "among the people Israel" in an Elected Assembly "could never be." He therefore concluded that just as women possessed a "meaningful obligation" to vote, so all women—elected as they would be with the approval and consent of the public—were eligible for political office. Traditional gender roles that confined women to the domestic realm while rendering them ineligible for participation in the political order had no Jewish legal basis, and Rabbi Ouziel considered them inapplicable in the modern Jewish state.

The Approach of Rabbi Herzog—Equivocating Acceptance

Rabbi Herzog wrote his response to these issues at the time of the creation of the Jewish State. The Israeli government was preparing to enact legislation that would define the process and procedures whereby the Knesset would be selected. At the very outset of his work, Rabbi Herzog stated that he supported a position that would permit women to vote as well as to be elected. He derived a Jewish legal precedent for this from the work of Rabbi David Zevi Hoffmann (1843–1921) of Berlin, who had ruled in a 1919 responsum that Jewish law allowed for the extension of suffrage to women. Although R. Hoffmann had not addressed the question of whether Jewish law permitted the election of women to public office, R. Herzog simply cited R. Hoffmann's ruling and indicated that he countenanced a public policy position that favored the admission of women into the body politic both as voters and as officeholders.[13] At the same time, he stated that he had grave personal reservations about these developments and that as an individual he was displeased that traditional gender roles had been so transformed in the present era that the extension of these rights to women in the modern nation-state was unavoidable. His subsequent exposition of the stance that he adopted on these questions is interesting and noteworthy precisely because it reflects the complex and ambiguous welter of pragmatic and legal considerations that informed his own thinking on the role that Jewish law permitted women in the modern political order.

In the first part of his responsum, R. Herzog took into account a number of pragmatic points that informed the decision he was about to render. Indeed, these considerations and the political realities of his day caused him to assert that Jewish law was sufficiently flexible to meet the challenges of an era in which radical innovations had taken place in the roles assigned men and women. Indeed, he noted that the United Nations was committed to a notion of gender equality and that the United Nations would demand that suffrage be extended to women as a precondition for recognition of Israel as a nation. Although he himself was personally opposed to granting women the vote, the necessity that the State of Israel be created overrode all other considerations, including this one.

Since the extension of suffrage to women was both unthinkable and unavoidable in the contemporary setting, R. Herzog was completely opposed to any Orthodox attempt to boycott the election as a mark of protest against this innovation. Indeed, R. Herzog wrote, "The rabbis will dissuade no one [14] from going to the ballot box," and an Orthodox refusal to cast ballots on this account would therefore constitute "an internal disaster" for the religious community, as "Orthodox Judaism would lose all its strength and influence" in the emerging State. He therefore bluntly concluded, "The matter does not depend upon my opinion, or the opinion of the rabbis at all." The classical model of a community responding to rabbinical rulings had no force in the modern world. To pretend that it did would only further weaken Orthodox interests. Indeed, he observed that a "great deal had already been lost" by the failure of the *Hareidi* community to participate during the 1920s in the elections for the *Asseifat ha-Nivharim*. Present-day Orthodox Jews ought not repeat their mistake. Instead, they should follow the example of Simeon ben Shetah, who participated in a Sanhedrin dominated by Sadducees so that Pharasaic interests could be championed.[15]

Having delineated these pragmatic considerations, R. Herzog now shifted his discourse to a discussion of the classical sources. Like R. Ouziel, R. Herzog argued that there was no precedent that would clearly prohibit women from participating either passively (voting) or actively (serving in office) in the modern democratic order. Although those opposed to female officeholders routinely cited *Hilkhot Melakhim* 1:5 as a warrant for their position, R. Herzog, like R. Ouziel, argued in this instance, that this law did not constitute a precedent. The Maimonidean ruling applied only in a case where a woman would occupy her position, as a king would, for life, and where she could transmit her post as a birthright, again as a king would, to her sons. Yet, these conditions clearly did not obtain to a seat in the Knesset, as these posts had fixed terms of three, perhaps five years, and were the result of election, not hereditary right. Hence, the *Mishneh Torah* passage did not constitute a prohibition against women serving in public office in *Medinat Yisrael*.

Furthermore, R. Herzog noted that despite this ruling that prohibited a woman from serving as sovereign, there was a precedent in the Talmud, in fact, that contravened the prohibition. After all, the Sages had countenanced the rule of Salome as Queen over Israel without even a hint of protest. Herzog said this was so because the Sages knew that Salome was faithful to the Oral Law and upheld it. Not a single halakhic source, therefore, raised an objection to her rule. This indicated that in an instance like this, where "the perpetuation of the faith, *kiyum ha-dat*, depended upon the queenship of a woman, the rule, as found in the *Sifrei* and the *Mishneh Torah*, could be set aside for the sake of the greater good. In adopting this stance Herzog was implicitly invoking a utilitarian calculus that had an halakhic source. In *Berakhot* 9:5, the Tannaim, in a wordplay on Psalm 119:126, "It is time to work (*Et la'asot*) for the Lord: they have made void Your Torah," reread the verse as, "They have made void Your Torah because it is a time to work for the Lord," and employed this as a warrant for uprooting a single commandment during a time of emergency so that the Law as a whole could be saved. Consequently, the Sages, as R. Herzog pointed out, suspended the prohibition that forbade the writing of the Oral Law, and they permitted its written composition so that the Torah would not be forgotten in Israel. The writing of the Oral Law, was of course, considered a defining act in rabbinic history. The Sages had assented to this, for the alternative would have been to consign the Tradition to death. Herzog drew upon this precedent precisely because it granted him tremendous flexibility to dislodge a single tradition while staunchly defending the Tradition as a whole. As a result of these considerations, R. Herzog concluded that the present-day Orthodox community, even if it felt that Jewish law prohibited women from participating in public life either as voters or as officeholders, had no right to boycott elections for the Knesset. By exercising their franchise and casting ballots, the Orthodox today, like their ancestors who displayed their commitments in the past, could affirm "the Torah in its entirety," for through the political power they would wield, they would "prevent the destruction of the faith in the Jewish State."

Having put forth this argument, Herzog completed this segment of his responsum by stating that one need not actually depend upon this extraordinary warrant to sanction Orthodox involvement in a modern political process where women would participate as equals. After all, there was no explicit halakhic prohibition that forbade women from voting. Nor, in light of the historical-legal precedent of Salome the Queen, was there a cause for maintaining that women could not hold office. Jewish law allowed for an interpretation that permitted women to participate as the equals of men in the present-day political order, and there was no doubt that such an interpretation, for all the reasons advanced above, was in the best interests of Orthodox Jews in the newly-established State of Israel.

R. Herzog then considered the opinion that Rabbi Salomon Spitzer of Hamburg had written on this matter. R. Spitzer forbade both the extension of suffrage to women and the right of women to hold public office on the grounds that each innovation violated the dictum contained in Leviticus 19:2, "You should not walk in their ways." R. Spitzer maintained that such practices constituted an imitation of Gentile ways, and he condemned female participation in the political process as unseemly for a Jewish woman. Indeed, he feared that these innovations would lead to sexual misconduct.

R. Herzog dismissed this objection as groundless, and pointed out that men and women already mingled together constantly both in the courts and in the marketplace. Like R. Ouziel, R. Herzog argued that if one defined such conduct as immodest, no semblance of normal life would be "left any human being." The appearance of women at the polls was the same as their presence in any other arena of public life. Nor would the existence of female members in the Kenneset lead to sexual transgression. The members of Kenneset were engaged in their work and had no time for these kinds of thoughts to get in the way of their work!

R. Herzog then went on to examine the nature of the prohibition concerning *hukat ha-goy* (imitation of the Gentiles), based on Leviticus 19:2. R. Spitzer had quoted R. Mordecai Benet, who, in the famed anti-Reform 1819 Orthodox polemic, *Eileh Divrei Habrit*, had stated that *any* custom or law that originated among the gentiles—not only an idolatrous one—was forbidden on the basis of Leviticus 19:2. R. Spitzer therefore reasoned that as the extension of suffrage to women fell under this category, it was forbidden. R. Herzog countered by condemning such reasoning as faulty. Indeed, if this logic were to hold, the State of Israel could not have an army, as other nations before Israel had established a military. He therefore stated, "It is as clear as the noonday sun that the prohibition of Leviticus 19:2, 'You shall not walk in their ways,' is a fence that the Torah erected as an obstacle to idolatry [only]." The role of women in the modern political order had no relationship to idolatry. It was simply the custom of civilized nations. As such, the concept of *hukkat ha-goy* did not apply here.

As a postscript to this point, R. Herzog observed that the extension of these political rights to women could not be defined as an imitation of gentile practices even in a general sense. After all, until modern times no one ever extended suffrage to women. Universal suffrage was a modern phenomenon, and women were granted these political privileges now only because of the social reality that marked the present era. Although these practices, he wrote, were "never observed among the people Israel, neither were they observed among the nations." These innovations "stemmed from a sociological change in the status of women [in western society]," and this resulted in the demand that the right of suffrage as well as the right to be elected be extended to women. R. Herzog maintained that Jewish law now, as in the past, possessed the flexibility and resources to countenance changed gender roles in a way that Jewish law could deem acceptable, and he cited medieval rabbinic precedent as a warrant for this assertion.

R. Herzog pointed out that the role of women in the realm of commerce had been altered during the Middle Ages and that the rabbis of that era had little trouble in interpreting Jewish law so as to cope with a transformed setting in which women played a visible role in the economic marketplace. The modern political phenomena of women casting ballots and holding office surely posed no greater challenge to present-day halakhic authorities than those business developments had presented medieval decisors. Medieval rabbis did not view these changes as threatening the foundations of Jewish law. Instead, these authorities recognized that these changed gender roles could be incorporated within the four ells of halakhah, and they accommodated the changes brought on by their era by plumbing the range of resources Jewish law provided them.[16] Modern rabbis should do no less. They should follow the example set by their medieval predecessors, and recognize that although social-political reality in these areas compelled Jewish law to respond, such responses could be positive, for these changes posed no danger to the authority of the halakhic system. Instead, R. Herzog observed that the expansion of roles played by women in these areas "removed a discrimination that had led to the denial of their rights as human beings," and that there was "no prohibition at all" against these changes from a halakhic perspective.

R. Herzog concluded his responsum by employing the legal convention of "accepted custom and usage" to support his stance. He noted that the pious Sephardic community of London had extended women the right to vote more than one hundred years earlier. He wrote:

> "The members of this *Kehillah* were observers of the Torah... and all of their actions were done by the authority of Sages... I do not claim that we should do so in our *kehillot*. Nevertheless, from this it is apparent that there is no absolute prohibition [against extending the right of suffrage to women]."

Given the weltanschauung that marked Herzog as an Orthodox rabbi and as the holder of a doctorate in literature from the University of Liverpool, the precedent supplied by the London Sephardic community was particularly crucial. After all, the London Sephardic *kehillah* was simultaneously western and observant. It constituted an apt model for the nascent Jewish state, and Herzog was clearly delighted that there was such precedent in the modern Jewish world for countenancing gender-role innovation.[17]

Conclusion

In comparing the stance that R. Kuk adopted concerning these issues with those advanced by Rabbis Ouziel and Herzog, we see that Rav Kuk viewed traditional gender roles as inviolable. Social reality might extend female gender-roles into the public sphere. Their assigned realm, however, remained a domestic one, and all change was to be resisted. Indeed, R. Kuk seems to have believed that transformations in this area threatened the very framework of traditional Judaism.

Rabbis Ouziel and Herzog adopted a different perspective. Both men rejected the classical legal category of kingship as appropriate for approaching these matters. Although they conceded that these innovations were driven by the unprecedented phenomenon of parliamentary democracy and universal suffrage, they believed that this reality no more challenged the viability of Jewish law in the twentieth century than the presence of women in the business world had challenged Jewish law during the Middle Ages. As such, the question of whether the halakhah could permit women to vote and stand for public office in the modern setting could be dealt with as the expansion of women into the economic sphere had been handled in a previous time. For these men these changes in the political realm were not revolutionary events. They were simply additional considerations that had to inform the rabbinic leaders of the community as they chartered a future course for Judaism and the Jewish people. Their view of gender was surely more elastic than was that of R. Kuk.

For us, as Liberal Jews, these responsa constitute interesting data for the analysis of the attitudes Jewish law permits concerning gender, but they reveal something more as well. In looking at the responsa of R. Ouziel and R. Herzog, there is much we applaud. Their writings reflect an ethical vision that "both men and women should be equal and full social participants."[18] It is a liberal vision that informs western culture. At the same time, we contend that our Jewish heritage contains this truth as well. Genesis 1:27 teaches us that women, as well as men, are created in the divine image. Precisely because women shared a common humanity with men, they could not be denied the basic right of full and equal participation in the modern political process.

Yet, R. Ouziel and R. Herzog compartmentalized this teaching of equality, and they sought to limit its application to the political realm. They were willing to extend the gender role assigned women in politics, but they would not, elsewhere in their writings, expand that role in the public realm of Jewish religious life. Neither rabbi drew what we would consider the logical conclusion that ought to have been derived from this teaching. If the humanity that marked women meant that they could not be denied their political rights as full and equal participants in the political domain, that same humanity ought to have led those rabbis to conclude that women be granted full and equal expression in the religious realm as well. Indeed, Reform, Reconstructionist, and Conservative Judaism have internalized this egalitarian vision and, as a result of the ethos that marks it, have celebrated female entry into the public religious life of the Jewish people.

In looking at R. Kuk's responsum, we see the classical rabbinic separation of women in sharper focus. Women are identified with the domestic realm; men are actors in the political sphere. We would reject this assignment of roles for men and women. At the same time, we acknowledge that R. Kuk was correct when he "warned" that the entry of women into the public domain of politics could not be confined there and that the ethos that sparked this innovation was destined to have revolutionary implications for Judaism as well. Rather than decrying these implications, however, we welcome them as a fulfillment of the moral challenges that face all Jews.

As Rachel Adler has indicated, in her pathbreaking book, *Engendering Judaism: An Inclusive Theology and Ethics*, Judaism confronts an "ethical task" as it begins "to reflect and address the questions, understandings, and obligations of both Jewish women and Jewish men. It is not yet fully attentive to the impact of gender and sexuality either on the classical texts or on *the lived experiences* of the people Israel."[19]

Our study has demonstrated that Jewish legal literature has approached "gender categories and distinctions" in diverse ways. Yet, despite our awareness of those categories and distinctions, this study, like others, does not tell us "what sorts of changes we ought to make in the future." That will unfold over time. We are confident, however, that changes inspired by these sensitivities will be "negotiated in conversations where participants invoke and reexamine the values and priorities enunciated in Jewish tradition in light of the current needs, injuries, or aspirations demanding to be addressed."[20] As such, their outcomes need not be feared. Instead, they should be celebrated, as Jewish women, along with Jewish men, seek to realize the messianic promise of truth and joy that lies at the heart of Jewish faith.

Notes

1. Susan Grossman and Rivka Haut, eds., *Daughters of the King: Women and the Synagogue*, Philadelphia and Jerusalem, 1992, pp. xxii–xxiii.
2. The gap between a theoretical commitment to gender equality on the part of the Zionist settlers that established the State and the reality of an Israeli society that never realized this commitment, has been well documented. In the voluminous literature on this topic, three books stand out. They are Deborah Bernstein, *The Struggle for Equality: Urban Woman Workers in Prestate Israeli Society*, New York: Praeger, 1987; Lesley Hazelton, *Israeli Women: The Reality Behind the Myths*, New York, 1977; and Natalie Rein, *Daughters of Rachel: Women in Israel*, Harmondsworth, England, 1979.
3. *HaTzofeh*, August 28, 1946.
4. Shulamit Aloni, *Nashim Kiv'nei Adam*, Jerusalem, 1976, p. 21.
5. The primary source for this information is Moshe Atias, *Kenesset Yisrael B'eretz yisrael: Yesodah V'irgunah*, Jerusalem, 1944, pp. 11ff. In addition, valuable material on this matter is contained in Dan Horowitz and Moshe Lissak, *Origins of the Israeli Polity: Palestine Under the Mandate*, Chicago and London, 1978, pp. 21ff.
6. All this information can be found in Atias, *Knesset Yisrael B'eretz Yisrael* , pp. 14–21.
7. Atias, Ibid., pp. 21–28. In addition, see S. Zalman Abramov, *Perpetual Dilemma: Jewish Religion in the Jewish State*, London,1976, pp. 108–109; as well as Menachem Friedman, *Society and Religion: The Non-Zionist Orthodox in Eretz- Israel 1918–1936*,(Hebrew), chapters 5 and 6.
8. See Friedman, *Society and Religion*, pp. 158–169, for a discussion of the relationship that obtained between Kuk and the Mizrachi on this matter.
9. *Ha-Ivri* 20 (May 28, 1920), pp. 11–13. Rav Kuk's writings on this and other halakhic topics have been treated in Michael Nehorai, "Remarks on the Rabbinic Rulings of Rav Kuk, *Tarbitz* 59 (1990), pp. 481–505. In addition, Zvi Zohar has analyzed the Kuk responsum, as well as the Ouziel responsum dealt with in this paper, in his insightful piece, "Traditional Flexibility and Modern Strictness: Two Halakhic Positions on Woman's Suffrage," in Harvey Goldberg, ed., *Sephardi and Middle Eastern Jewries*, Bloomington and Indianapolis, 1996, pp. 119-133. Nehorai, in his essay, focuses principally on the Jewish legal issues involved in the Kuk responsum, while Zohar concentrates on the poltical-social implications of these writings. While we speak of these issues as well in our paper, we provide a gender focus that distinguishes our paper from theirs, even in the treatment of these two figures.
10. A.I. Kook [sic.], "Lights for Rebirth," in Arthur Hertzberg, ed., *The Zionist Idea*, New York, 1959, p. 430. Italics ours.
11. *Mishpetei Uziel* , *Hoshen Mishpat* , no. 6.
12. Indeed, the last responsum we shall consider in this paper, issued by Rabbi Isaac Halevi Herzog, *Tehukah L'yisrael 'Al Pi Ha-torah* I, Jerusalem, pp. 95ff., indicates that this issue was still a controversial one among some Orthodox Jews. As a result, Ouziel's decision to publish his decision at this time was more than an intellectual exercise. It addressed what was still a vital public matter.

13. Hoffmann's responsum on this matter was originally published in two parts as *"Ein Gutachten ,"* in *Jeschurun* VI (1919), pp. 262–266 and 515–522. It has been republished in Hebrew translation in *Ha-kibbutz B'halakhah: Asseifat ma'amarim* (*Kevutzat Sha'alavim* 5744), pp. 286–290. Herzog did not actually have the Hoffmann responsum before him. He simply knew its holding and cited it as a warrant for his own position. This is unusual, as a halakhic decisor generally wants to examine the argument of the authority he has quoted. Herzog's use of the Hoffmann decision in this way testifies to the high regard Herzog had for Hoffmann.
14. That is, no non-Orthodox Jew.
15. See *Megillah Ta'anit* 10.
16. R. Herzog cited the commentaries of the *Ba'er Heitev* and *Pithei Teshuvah* on *Even ha-Ezer* 80 as examples of rabbinic authorities who had dealt with these novel developments in their interpretations of Jewish law.
17. On this change in the life of the London Sephardic community, see Albert M. Hyamson, *The Sepharadim of England: A History of the Spanish and Portuguese Community, 1492-1951,* London, 1951, p. 380.
18. This wording is taken from Rachel Adler, *Engendering Judaism: An Inclusive Theology and Ethics,* Philadelphia, 1998, p. xiv.
19. Ibid.
20. Ibid., pp. xiv–xv.

Chapter 4

❖   ❖   ❖

CUSTOM DRIVES JEWISH LAW ON WOMEN[*]

Elliot N. Dorff

The thesis of this article is that we err if we try to decide issues concerning the status of women in Jewish law on the basis of the texts and legal arguments that have come down to us because they were all post facto reflections of what was determined by custom in the first place. The Conservative Movement's commitment to be honest to the historical context of Jewish law in the past and present thus requires us, on the one hand, not to be too constrained by specific texts that limit the role of women, for they were only giving retroactive legal justification for what common practice was at the time. On the other hand, we must not take undue advantage of texts that might be interpreted as allowing for women as well as men to do certain things but that, in historical context, were undoubtedly never intended that way.

In our own day, then, we must pay much more attention to the continuing development of custom in these matters, allowing for diversity of expression without being too insistent on either the letter of Jewish law as it has come down to us on these issues or on the egalitarian agenda. We should instead, I pro-

Notes for this section begin on page 103.

pose, be flexible, allowing some people to hold on to old and familiar customs, giving others time and support in getting used to new ones that have evolved over the last fifty years in many of our congregations, and simultaneously allowing those in our movement who are so inclined to shape further, new customs that will enable women to function even more fully within our community.

The Role of Customs on Women's Status in Biblical and Talmudic Times

When one studies biblical and talmudic sources on the role of women, it becomes clear very quickly that the legal status of women was not equal to that of men. Given the role of women in other ancient cultures, that should not be surprising. At the same time, one also does not find delineated a clear status for women subservient to that of men in all respects. Instead, one finds a patchwork of laws, in some of which women are indeed equal to men, while in others they are clearly at a legal disadvantage.

Examples of this abound, but a few will suffice to make this clear. None of the biblical stories or laws depict a woman proposing marriage to a man or instituting a divorce, and later rabbinic law specifies that only a man may institute those procedures.[1] That would argue for women's subservience. On the other hand, women are specifically included in Deuteronomy's command that all Israelites are to hear the Torah read every seven years,[2] and the Torah's rules about accidental homicide, which specify that they apply to "a man or a woman," are used by the rabbis to extend all of the Torah's tort laws to women perpetrators and victims as well.[3] Thus in some ways, women had a lesser, and in some ways an equal, status *vis-à-vis* men.

Moreover, there is a discrepancy between what the law says and what we read in our sources' reports of our history. On the one hand, when interpreting Deuteronomy's discussion of appointing a king over the people, the rabbis limited eligibility for sovereignty to men.[4] Deborah, however, had long before been the political and military leader of her people, and in times close to what was probably the era of that rabbinic ruling, Shelomziyyon (Salome Alexandra), the Queen, ruled as well.[5] While our ancestors' political and military leaders were overwhelmingly men, these examples indicate that even in ancient times, women could serve in these very public and important roles, contrary to what Jewish law became. Conversely, a *baraita* permits women to be among the seven who go up to the Torah and read it in the synagogue on the Sabbath. While that was legally permissible for women to do, it was not open to them in practice, for, as the *baraita* itself explains, to have women read the Torah would dishonor the men in the congregation.[6] We certainly do not hear in later stories or rulings of many (any?) women who in fact read the Torah in the synagogue, despite the legal permission embedded in the sources for them to do so.[7]

These kinds of disparities between what the legal texts say and what the stories report become especially striking in the extended discussion in the tractate *Kiddushin* about the commandments from which women are exempt. The legal rationales for those exemptions are, to put it mildly, extremely suspect, for the very verses which are quoted to exempt women from given commandments could just as easily be read to include them. Most are dependent upon masculine forms of nouns or verbs which grammatically can just as easily include women as exclude them—a fact which the Rabbis surely knew as well as we do. One must conclude, then, that the choice of whether to use the masculine noun or verb in question to designate men alone or both men and women was not at all determined by the verses themselves but rather by what was pre-existing custom at the time.[8]

This discussion is based on the Mishnah's attempt to generalize over the commandments from which women are exempt. Its generalization, that women are exempt from positive, time-bound commandments, is very quickly challenged in the Talmud, which adduces quite a few practices which do not fit that rule. Women are obligated, for example, to light candles on Friday evening, even though that is a positive commandment which is most definitely tied to a specific time. On the other hand, women are freed from the commandment to wave the palm branch (*lulav*) on *Sukkot* even though that could be done at any time during the day—hardly much of a restriction on time.[8]

The Talmud's discussion and rulings, then, indicate clearly that neither a legal analysis of biblical verses nor even a rabbinic attempt to generalize over the practices of their time was the ground for determining what women may or may not do. That, instead, was decided on the basis of the multiple and inconsistent, but apparently well-established, customs of their community.

Medieval Texts vs. Practices Regarding Women

If custom ruled the day in governing the roles that women might have in society in biblical and rabbinic times, we should expect it to do so in medieval times as well, and it did. The clearest cases of this are in the laws governing the relationships between men and women. So, for example, although biblical, talmudic, and Muslim law all allow a man to marry more than one woman, Christian law does not, and so Ashkenazic Jewish men and women, who lived predominantly among Christians, were enjoined by Rabbeinu Gershom from polygyny while Sephardic Jews, who continued to live among Muslims, were not restricted in that way.[9] Similarly, Sephardic rabbis, living among Muslims who permitted and even encouraged husbands to beat their wives, generally allowed Jewish husbands to do so as well, whereas Ashkenazic rabbis, especially those in Germany who were influenced by both Christian and Jewish pietism, resoundingly condemned wife-beating.[10]

We do not, however, hear of women taking public roles in the synagogue, either among Ashkenazim or among Sephardim. That is important when we read medieval texts that say, for example, that "ten" are necessary for a prayer quorum, *minyan*, without specifying whether women may be counted toward that number.[12] It is certainly true that the authors of texts like that could have specified "ten men" if they meant to restrict those who count to males, but it is equally true that they could have specified "ten men or women" if they had meant that. It is a mistake, then, to read such texts as a justification for including women in the count, for that is reading the text totally divorced from the historical context from that it came and to that it undoubtedly referred. As a member of a Conservative synagogue that has been egalitarian for some twenty years, I, for one, am sorely tempted to read such texts in that way, but I must be honest in pointing out that would be playing fast and loose with the plain meaning of the text when it is read, as it should be, in its historical context.

The same argument applies to solitary texts that seem to report that in some places women actually did what we do not want to allow them to do. The medieval text used to indicate that even in those times women could be counted for a prayer quorum *minyan* is a good example of this. It is a comment of the Mordecai (thirteenth century), who, in turn, is reporting what he "found" in the writings of an earlier Rabbi Simhah, possibly the compiler of the *Mahzor Vitri*.[13] Even if such texts are to be credited, and even if they mean what we take them to mean, we surely must admit that they represent exceptions to the rule, that the overwhelming practice in the synagogues of our medieval and early modern ancestors was to permit only men to count for the quorum and to lead the services. To say otherwise is simply not being honest.

The Nature of Custom

The fact that custom determined the role of women in synagogue services, in witnessing, and in marriage and divorce means, for me, that if we are going to be true to that historical precedent, we must give custom a much larger role in determining our own practices as well. To stick to specific formulations of what was communal custom in these matters as if they were determined by legal analysis in the first place is, in my view, to ignore history in an excessive exercise of legal formalism.

Custom, however, is a slippery animal. Customs are not established at a specific time and place by recognized rabbinic authorities. Many times, in fact, customs are not even acknowledged by the rabbis, let alone validated by them. Because customs are not clearly stated in a rabbinic ruling, others, especially those living at a different time and place, often cannot understand its scope. The very genre of custom, coming as it does as a "fact on the ground" rather than a proposal to be considered, suggests that it is somehow illegitimate to evaluate its legal cogency. We are supposed to obey the custom just because that is the accepted practice. Customs are not, in a word, legally "neat," with explicit details specifying who and what is involved and with clearly stated rationales open to analysis, challenge, and change. Instead, custom emerges from the masses—in our case, from Schechter's "Catholic Israel." As such, its rationales, its demands, and the scope of the communities it governs are often unclear. Moreover, because it emerges from the populace in given times and places, it is likely to differ from one Jewish community to the next.

The ways in which custom remains or changes are also hard to grasp and even harder to control. Those customs that are never formalized in law but rather passed down in the form of "what we do around here" may become so entrenched that they cannot be uprooted despite compelling reasons to do so. Rabbis sometimes try, denouncing certain customs as stupid or foolhardy *(minhag shtut)*, but rabbinic opposition, even if unanimous and forcefully expressed, does not always succeed in uprooting objectionable customs. Indeed, in their time and place, customs may become every bit as binding as statutory laws or rabbinic rulings—so much so that after awhile rabbinic rulings may officially recognize a given custom and enforce it. Before a given custom becomes well established, however, practices will differ, and judges that have to base their rulings on what the parties could legitimately have expected will want to tear out their hair. This is especially problematic because customs can pass out of existence just as quickly and inexplicably as they appear.

Custom as a legal genre, then, is definitely not for the anal compulsive. It requires one to ride with the waves, as it were, being flexible enough to adjust to ill-defined and changing practices and expectations. In that way, it is like living languages as opposed to dead ones; the dead ones have the advantage of being set and determined, but the living ones, that can drive you crazy with their ever-changing words, nuances, and phrases, nevertheless have the distinct advantage of being alive.[14]

Lest I be misunderstood, I am *not* saying, à la Mordecai Kaplan, that custom should replace law in our time. Law, whether in the form of legislation or judicial rulings, carries with it distinct advantages for any society. It specifies clearly what is expected of everyone. This enables people to live together. It also contributes a sense of security to all citizens: I know that for that I can hold others responsible and, in turn, that for that I myself can be called to account. Law thereby saves me from the threat of Kafkaesque trials, where I know neither the charges against me, nor the rules for determining my guilt or innocence, nor the penalties for my guilt. Law also enables society to articulate its sense of justice in concrete terms, thus giving a moral quality to social norms. Moreover, because law is open to public scrutiny, it enables people to criticize and improve the rules by that they live. Finally, because laws generally change less rapidly than popular tastes do, law contributes to society a sense of continuity and rootedness. Jews, who are spread out all over the world, need these aspects of law even more than more geographically concentrated societies do, and so I would be the last to argue for understanding Judaism in our day in ways that deprive it of its traditional footing in law.[15] For those who also believe that there is a divine component to Jewish law, as I do, the obligatory nature of it goes well beyond these prudential concerns. Even without that theological component, however, the benefits of law to any society should make anyone think twice before abandoning law for custom alone.

Living legal systems, though, incorporate not only law, but custom, and each exercises a claim on the members of the society. Sometimes these dual claims pose no problems. On the contrary, law and custom can actually reinforce one another, as, for example, when customs augment and even beautify observance of the law. Another type of symbiotic interaction between law and custom occurs when they complement one another by filling in gaps in the norm of a community where the other is absent.

Sometimes, however, custom and law oppose each other, and then the question of which one takes precedence over the other is not always clear. This is true not only in Jewish law, with its application to widespread communities and its lack of one central authority, but in virtually any living legal system. American law, for example, that governs a clearly identified group of people in a relatively coherent land mass (even counting Alaska and Hawaii) with a clear chain of legal authority, nevertheless is subject to modification and even to veto by popular custom.

As a result, one must come to understand that the content of the law itself is always a product of the interaction between the dictates of those entrusted with interpreting and applying the law and the actual practices of those governed by it. Law and custom, *din* and *minhag,* may pull in opposite directions, but they ultimately must take account of one another because neither automatically supersedes the other. In the paragraphs below I will use American law to illustrate these multifaceted interactions so it is clear that custom has authority of its own and affects law even in fully functional and enforced legal systems.

Sometimes law overrules customs or creates new ones. In American law, one example of that process was *Brown v. Board of Education* (1954) and the subsequent Civil Rights Act of 1964. That Supreme Court decision and Congressional legislation not only changed many state laws and local ordinances, but also changed some of the social and commercial customs based on segregation. So, for example, before that time advertisements almost never depicted blacks and whites enjoying a given product together, but by the 1960s such pictures began to appear.

On the other hand, custom can undermine law and change it. The clearest example in American law is Prohibition. Most Americans—probably some eighty-five or ninety percent—abided by the law, but the refusal of the remainder to do so made it impossible to enforce even a law with the status of a constitutional amendment.

Conversely, custom can be the source of new laws. One clear example in American law is the Uniform Commercial Code, a version of that forty-nine states ultimately passed. This code specifically invokes the "usage of trade" as a criterion for judging cases.[16] A parallel development in Jewish law is the case of wine merchants putting their marker on kegs of wine, which, according to the Talmud, does not normally effect a legal transfer *(kinyan)*, but it does do so if that is the custom among merchants.[17]

Periodically, every legal system has to catch up to the actual practices of the people it seeks to govern. Sometimes, as we have seen, the legal authorities will seek to uproot a custom that has emerged, and sometimes they will instead confirm it in law.

Sometimes, they will do neither, letting varying customs in different regions determine what the practice will be. The United States is probably more sensitive than most other nations to the need to allow local custom to govern, for the federalist system embodied in its constitution establishes the rights of states to determine many, many matters, ranging from education to welfare to zoning to criminal penalties.

In Jewish law, custom has interacted with law in all the same ways. Indeed, in light of the widespread nature of the Jewish people, one would expect custom to have an even greater effect in shaping the practices of the Jewish people than it has had in other communities. Because of the divine status ascribed to the Torah, however, rabbis have not allowed custom to countermand a prohibition of the Torah, especially in ritual matters *(issur v'heter)*, but even there one first has to define what is a rule with Torah status and what is instead rabbinic level of authority in order to decide whether this restriction applies. Most often, the Torah cannot be claimed as the basis for a custom, and rabbis must confront the custom on its merits, deciding whether to wage war with it, confirm it, or just let it remain as the custom of some but not necessarily of all.

Conservative Judaism

One thing that has characterized the Conservative Movement from its early history in North America is its evolving practices with regard to the role of women. Mixed seating in worship was established totally by the customs of the people affiliated with Conservative congregations; to my knowledge, that practice has never been justified and confirmed in a rabbinic ruling, but it is overwhelmingly accepted within our movement.[18] Bat mitzvah ceremonies, initiated first by Mordecai M. Kaplan in 1922,[19] varied widely in degree of acceptance and in form through the 1960s, with some congregations having girls do exactly what boys did for their Bar Mitzvah, and with others, at the other end of the spectrum, restricting the girls' ceremonies to Friday nights and to parts of the service not *halakhically* required. Here again custom ruled the day.

Custom and law, as I have mentioned, continually interact and affect each other. It should be no surprise, then, that some steps in this evolution of the status of women were initiated by rabbis, or, at least, confirmed by them in very early stages of the emergence of the practice. Specifically, calling women to the Torah was officially permitted by the committee on Jewish Law and Standards in 1954,[20] but it did not become widespread until the late 1970s or 1980s. Similarly, counting women for a *minyan* was approved as a majority decision of the Committee in June 1973, but that, too, did not become widespread until the 1980s and 1990s. The next year, a minority opinion approved by six members of the committee permitted women to serve as witnesses.[21] Only three votes were required under the committee's rules then to represent a valid option within the Conservative movement; the six votes in favor of permitting women to serve as witnesses would even satisfy the more stringent requirements enacted in 1985 for that status. Even so, women did not serve as witnesses in any significant numbers until the 1980s, and it is probably still not the practice among the majority of rabbis and congregations to permit women to do so.

In what was probably the most public forum for deciding an issue, the Rabbinical Assembly asked the chancellor of the seminary to form a special commission to decide on the permissibility of ordaining women as rabbis. That commission voted in favor of women's ordination, leading ultimately to the first ordination of a woman by the seminary in 1985.[22] That decision was never officially confirmed by the committee, but several members of that committee now are themselves women rabbis, and so custom has ruled there as well! It has taken some time, however, for women rabbis to be eligible for appointment to congregational posts on an equal footing with men, and there is still some way to go in that regard. The existence of women rabbis in the various settings and capacities in that they now serve, though, has created a whole panoply of new customs, not only in creative, new rituals but also in the ways in that rabbis and lay Jews understand each other and interact with each other.

Other customs regarding women have emerged, or are emerging, from the masses, just as one would expect for this genre of legal norms. So, for example, some women put on *tefillin*, others don only a *tallit,* and others use neither in their worship. Some women wear head covering during worship and study (or always), and some do not. Some congregations insert the matriarchs in the opening blessing of the *amidah,* some do not, and some make it a prerogative of the one leading services to decide.

Women Witnesses

This variation, I think, is even true for what is emerging as the most difficult issue in this area, namely, women witnesses. The *Sifre,* both Talmuds, and Maimonides all maintain that only men may serve as witnesses as a matter of biblical law.[23] That, however, is founded on reading the masculine plural word for witnesses (*edim*) in either Deuteronomy 19:15 or Deuteronomy 17:6 as exclusively male in reference, even though the text of the Torah itself can just as easily be read to include women as to exclude them, and even though the *Sifrei* itself interprets the masculine plural words for the litigants in these verses to include women. If historical records are to be believed, however, in the large majority of cases it was indeed only men who have, over the ages, served as witnesses.[24] The power of the practice of restricting witnesses to men, then, is not really the Torah or even the rabbis' interpretation of it, but rather the ongoing custom of Jewish communities over the centuries. This is Solomon Schechter's doctrine of Catholic Israel at its clearest and most compelling.

The customary roots of restricting witnessing to men do not automatically justify permitting women in our own time to serve as witnesses, for custom, as we have seen, has a continuity and an authority of its own, sometimes even surpassing that of law. Custom, though, is not changed as much by argumentation as it is by the emergence of new customs. Sometimes new customs can be motivated by a conscious need to address new situations, for example, the new level of Jewish education open to women in our society, but most often, it should be remembered, customs either endure or change as a result of the practice of the concerned Jewish community.

In the case of witnesses, if we look at the matter on its merits, although I myself would want some distinction of the roles of men and women in synagogue and home rituals, as I will explain below, I simply cannot understand the grounds on that women should be denied the right to sign as witnesses. Rabbi Ben Zion Bergman has suggested that the traditional restriction of testimony to men was not based on a blanket devaluation of women or on an assessment of women as incorrigible liars, but rather on two specific factors that would undermine the accuracy of a women's testimony, namely, that women's lack of experience in the world at large would taint their understanding and memory of events in that world, and second, that women were generally dependent upon their fathers or husbands and therefore were too likely to be influenced by them for their testimony to be trusted as their own independent witnessing of the event. Rabbi Bergman then suggests that since these factors do not apply to the women of contemporary times, the restriction on women's testimony should be reversed.[25] Rabbis Joel Roth and Mayer Rabinowitz have argued in similar ways. Because I have deep respect for the law and the legal process, I am glad that several members of the Committee on Jewish Law and Standards are now doing research to see whether there are additional legal grounds to permit women to be witnesses. In addition to the changed perception and role of women in our time, the warrant for doing so will probably be based on a showing that the exclusion of women was not as categorical as it should have been if the source was really biblical. Even those who advance such arguments, though, will inevitably differ on the extent to that we can rely on them to overturn longstanding practice, as the conclusions of Rabbis Bergman, Rabinowitz, and Roth demonstrate.[26]

I would guess, then, that any changes in this matter will arise not primarily from legal argumentation but simply by an increasing number of rabbis recognizing women as valid witnesses in practice. This will occur when male rabbis agree to be part of a court *(bet din)* with female rabbis in matters of conversion or divorce, and it will occur more pervasively when rabbis increasingly permit couples they marry to have significant women in their lives sign their wedding contracts, if they so choose.

Such acts, of course, will officially not be in keeping with the law as it has come down to us. A minority opinion of the Committee on Jewish Law and Standards approves of permitting women to be witnesses, but it was not justified with a formal paper.[27] It is therefore important to note that, contrary to the claim that legal formalists might make, allowing women to serve as witnesses in practice is *not* civil disobedience or, worse, an abandonment of the law. It is, instead, a use of one of the sources of the law, namely custom, to lead the way. That source may not have the advantages of law delineated above, but it has reciprocal advantages, as also described above. Moreover, custom is a historically authentic source of the law and, in this case, the very one that produced the law on witnesses as it is in the first place. It thus seems to me to be exactly appropriate that this law, generated by custom, that limits witnessing to males, should ultimately be changed by custom as well.

Implications For Our Own Day

This sets the stage for my recommendations about how we should treat the status of women generally. All in all, we have a veritable patchwork of practices with regard to women within our movement. Some Conservative professionals and laypeople would advocate that we as a movement become egalitarian by fiat, enacting a *takanah* to make women fully equal to men in all privileges and obligations of Jewish law. On the other end of the spectrum, others regret the extent to that we have already gone, claiming that we have lost our claim to legitimacy as a *halakhic* movement by taking steps to enfranchise women without careful and closely reasoned rabbinic rulings justifying such action. Such people often feel downright attacked by any step to equalize women's status. In the meantime, some people have left the movement, either because we have moved too slowly and too narrowly on these issues or because we have moved too far and too fast.

I would suggest that we have all talked about these matters in the wrong way, although in practice we have done exactly what we should do. The task to be accomplished in justifying new roles for women in Jewish life, we have thought, is to find warrant in the codes and responsa literature for doing what we want to do.

That has led, frankly, to forced readings of texts and to conclusions that either ignore or distort what historically happened in Jewish communities and what motivates us today to act differently.

Some that have acknowledged this have argued that if we were really honest, we would institute a *takanah,* once and for all making women equal to men in all matters of Jewish law. There is even some precedent for that in the *takanah* enacted by the Chief Rabbinate of the Jewish community in Israel in 1943, which made daughters inherit equally with sons. Even without that specific ruling, Jewish legal history offers us the vehicle of *takanah* to make significant changes that cannot be made through less disruptive techniques.[28]

Until recently, I myself thought we should enact a *takanah* to equalize the status of women and men in Jewish law. I have had to face the fact, though, that more than a few women object to wearing *tefillin* because it seems to them to be a man's garment. More broadly, I have come to recognize that we all must take more seriously the clear unwillingness of some of our most observant women to take on the responsibilities of Jewish law from that they are traditionally exempt. More broadly still, we dare not just brush aside as antiquarian or reactionary the feelings of those men and women within our movement who object to the changes egalitarianism has brought. I myself will advance an argument below for maintaining at least some distinctions between males and females in our liturgy and law while yet affirming their equal status. Even that, though, may be much too intellectual a statement of the issue. For, in my view, many of the problems we are having in defining new liturgical and legal roles for men and women emerge from the differing levels of tolerance we individually have for trying out new customs as we also gain meaning and rootedness from the ones that shaped our past. Objections to new egalitarian practices on the part of religiously committed Jews of both genders make even more sense when we remember that Jewish laws differentiating women from men are rooted in the customs of the times in that they were formulated in the first place; they therefore are not open to change through rational analysis alone but must rather he replaced, if at all, by new customs that often seem strange at first but that gradually become acceptable and eventually even cherished.

Consequently, although we should certainly probe legal sources to discover what our ancestors actually did in these matters, we should recognize that the real foundation for the laws that have come down to us on the roles of women was custom and that therefore the most appropriate vehicle for changing those laws will also be custom. We therefore need to take a four-pronged approach:

(1) Some customs have led to laws that indisputably harm women. These include wife-beating (at least in some Jewish communities), legal institutions that chain a woman in Jewish law to a man from whom she has already been civilly divorced, and the exclusion of women from Jewish education. Such bad customs we must annul altogether, and the Conservative movement has already done so.[29] We should similarly declare both morally reprehensible and legally null and void the kind of extortion now going on in part of the Orthodox world in Israel in that fathers marry off their minor daughters to men they refuse to identify as a ploy to force their wives either to stay with them in marriage or to give them money or custody rights in divorce. In these and other cases where the harm to women engendered by Jewish law is undisputed, we have already done, and should continue to do, what we must to rid ourselves of such bad customs.

(2) Most of the customs that have come down to us are appreciated by some and opposed by others. In such cases, I would argue for tolerance on all sides. That is, we should allow a diversity of customs to take hold and develop as they may. That will require tolerance for diversity in these matters, but such diversity is in the very nature of custom.

Thus, even though I myself am an egalitarian in these matters, I would plead with my fellow egalitarians to respect the will of some synagogues, or some *minyanim* within those synagogues, to restrict some roles to men, and perhaps others to women. Conversely, those that want to maintain the traditional role differentiation in services should recognize the deep roots these matters have in communal custom, even those that ultimately found their way into codes or responsa, and that consequently, in our own day, citing a text to justify exclusion of women from a give role will generally not suffice. We will instead need to confront the custom head-on, evaluating it in terms of its role in our community now.

That will not be easy. In 1984, I wrote an article for the University of Judaism's *University Papers* series in that I suggested that the proper stance was "equal but distinct."[30] That is, I would want to recognize that men and women as classes are equal in their legal status, and in their theological status as creatures of God are created in the divine image, but I would also want to have our rituals express the fact that men and women differ from one another in important ways linked to their respective genders. Some of these differences, of course, are socially engendered (if not determined), and then one must ask whether such differentiations are justifiable or desirable. Increasingly over the last fifteen years, though, we have discovered that a number of the factors that differentiate men and women are biologically based, including most recently, the study based on functional magnetic resonance imaging (MRI) of the brains of men and women as they respond to the same questions; this study demonstrated that men and women do think with different parts of their brains.[31] In any case, whether the result of nature or nurture or both, men and women are now demonstrably different from each other in the way they think, talk, reason morally, and respond to life in general, as indicated by studies carried out largely by women such as Carol Gilligan, Deborah Tannen, and Nel Noddings.[32] Moreover, as it has become politically acceptable to acknowledge these distinctions, men and women have dared to explore in women's and men's groups the meaning of their engendered states of being, as well as, and in denigration of, their common humanity and, in our case, their common Jewish identity.

I, for one, then, would like to repeat the suggestion that I made in 1984, but now with much more evidence. Specifically, I think that Jewish ritual life should incorporate many leadership roles are open to people of both genders. On the other hand, though, there should be, in my view, some elements of worship and rituals that specifically are performed by women, and others that are restricted to men. That would acknowledge in graphic, ritual terms that we are at once equal and different. If the slogan "separate but equal" had not had such bad press in American history because of its abuse in justifying situations that were definitely not equal, I might use that to summarize my position. Perhaps the phrase I used, "equality with distinction," or as Rabbi Zion Bergman suggested to me, "equal but vive la difference!"captures the position better while simultaneously avoiding any association with applications of its policy that do not preserve both factors in their entirety.

My favorite example to justify this position is, appropriately, one based on custom. By law, both men and women are obligated to light Sabbath candles and to recite the kiddush on Friday nights.[33] When Jews of both genders are not present, then, indeed, people of only one gender are supposed to do both things. When Jews of both genders are in attendance, however, then, by custom, women generally light the candles and men recite the kiddush. The distinction retains equality because family members pay roughly the same amount of attention to both. When they do not, the factors that lead them to pay more attention to the one or the other vary according to the family custom, the age of the children, and so on; they are not a function of an inherently unequal degree of significance in the two ceremonies. This can serve as a good example, then, of how customs can emerge or even consciously be created to enable us to be equal but different in our religious life as Jews.

In that example, the choice of that would normally be done by men and that by women was not determined by anything inherently male in saying kiddush in the home or anything inherently female in lighting candles there. The choice evolved as common practice, but, from a rational or even a symbolic point of view, it was largely arbitrary. That, too, is something to note as we make our way into the new customs that are evolving. Although we should certainly seek to differentiate the roles of men and women in meaningful, symbolic ways if we can, that will not always be possible. In such circumstances, we may choose to let men and women serve on an equal basis, or, at least in some cases, we may decide to differentiate their roles arbitrarily. So, for example, individual congregations might designate one *Shabbat* a month in that only women will serve as cantors and another *Shabbat* in that only men do so, with the remaining ones open to members of both genders. That frankly seems forced to me, and I probably would opt for leaving that open to both genders at all times on a totally random basis. I can imagine, though, that if designating specific Sabbaths each month in the way I described were the practice in my synagogue, I would not only get used to it, but actually prize it after awhile as a further way of distinguishing men and women without impugning their equality. Alternatively, a synagogue might designate one Sabbath a month in that there would be, at least as an option, separate minyanim for men and women in order to accomplish the same purpose.

(3) Along with this toleration of varying degrees of adaptation of the customs of our past, I hope that we will develop new customs now that express both the equality and the distinctiveness that I, for one, seek. We have already begun, whether intentionally or not, to do this. This is especially evident in our emerging life-cycle rites.

Parents justifiably feel that their joy is no less for having a girl than it would be if they had had a boy, and the community's joy ought not be any less either. Traditionally, the birth of a girl is marked by an *aliyah* for the father (and now often the mother), accompanied by a blessing for the mother's health and naming the newborn girl. Even if these ceremonies are done nicely and even if a festive kiddush is held in celebration of the newborn afterward, modern couples have increasingly felt that these rites are not enough. They have consequently created new ceremonies that usually take place at their home, just as a boy's *brit milah* (ritual circumcision) often does.

Sometimes the ceremony is called *brit banot*, "the covenant of the daughters," thereby emphasizing the parallelism between the new ceremonies for girls with the traditional one for boys. Sometimes they are called *simhat bat*, "the joy of a daughter," thereby indicating the differences between this rite and the one for boys. Under either title, the ceremony itself may incorporate some of the same elements and language as the one for boys and may even be scheduled for the eighth day after birth as a boy's circumcision would be; or it may veer markedly from the ritual for boys. The point is that both the equal significance and the distinctiveness of having a girl are being symbolized by these new ceremonies.

Similar experimentation is happening with bat mitzvah ceremonies—again, some emphasizing the sameness of the event marked by a bar mitzvah for boys and some stressing the differences—and with weddings are increasingly involving both the bride and the groom in a more active role in both planning the rite and in participating in it. So, for example, if the groom is going to be called to the Torah in honor of his forthcoming wedding in the synagogue in that he grew up (his *aufruf*), the bride should be likewise called up for that honor in her home synagogue, assuming that that synagogue calls women to the Torah. In each case, if the person having the *aufruf* normally gives a homily *(devar Torah)* as well, that should be true for both the bride and the groom. Alternatively, at the wedding itself it could be not only the groom who gives a word of Torah in advance of the ceremony (the *hatan's tisch*, the groom's table), but the bride could do so as well. Similarly, if the bride follows the custom of walking around the groom, the groom might then walk around his bride (usually three times each)—and then, for the seventh circuit, both together might walk around the wedding canopy, which symbolizes their new home.

Jewish rites of death and mourning are already egalitarian, in that there is only one thing that we do for men that we do not do for women; namely, we traditionally bury a man's cut *tallit* (prayer shawl) with him. Perhaps some ritual object connected with the deceased woman could be buried with her, such as the head covering or the candlesticks she used for lighting Sabbath candles. That men prepare a man's body for burial and women prepare a woman's is not only important for reasons of modesty, but also to symbolize the embodied and engendered nature of the deceased. The genders are equal but different even in death. I would also encourage women to say kaddish during the year after a parent's death; a daughter's relationship with her parents may be different from a son's, but it is no less close, and the law demands honor of parents from daughters just as much as it does from sons.[34]

As we continue to experiment with new customs, we must allow some to retain traditional practices without being attacked as somehow anti-women or reactionary, while we simultaneously permit others to try various forms of egalitarianism. The latter may include, as I advocate, some role differentiation together with other roles open to both genders. This will require tolerance and good will on all sides as we feel our way into appropriate expressions of our new (and old) understandings of who we are as men and women, as Jews, and as people of the modern world.[35]

Although all the ferment in our time about the changing definitions of male and female roles has clearly generated much anxiety and even social upheaval, one distinctly positive result has been that both men and women are thinking much more carefully about Jewish liturgy and law. Rabbis working with families in preparing for a life-cycle ceremony should take advantage of that new consciousness. In addition to explaining the traditional rituals and their meanings, rabbis should point out that some families in our time are adding to those rituals or doing them in new ways. As Conservative Jews, we will insist that those elements of the ceremonies that are legally required be done, but we should at least inform families of the possibility of using some of the new rituals that have been developed to accompany the traditional ones—and of creating new rituals of their own. Some families will not want to take an active role in shaping the rituals of their life-cycle event, but some will, and all will minimally learn that these rituals are intended to express both what the Jewish tradition and what they themselves feel and hope for on this day. Some of the new rituals will, of course, succeed wonderfully, and some will fall flat; that is the nature of creativity. Ultimately, though, we will all be the richer as new customs emerge for any or all of us to use.

(4) Finally, cognizant as I am of the continual interaction between law and custom, I would urge that we continue to probe our legal sources for legitimation of our new practices, but only where that is honest to the historical context of the sources as well as their language. I am, after all, deeply interested in the continuity, the authority, and the rootedness that grounding in legal sources can supply. Where history must be ignored, though, or even where the practice in question was only practiced by a small minority of Jews in the past, I would prefer that we be honest in asserting that we are creating new practices in

response to the new sensitivities we have on these matters vis-à-vis the relation between the genders. In doing so, we should call attention to the factors that differentiate our age from times past in these matters—especially the new Jewish and general educational opportunities open to women—in order to explain our deviation from previous practices. We should also point out, as I have maintained in this paper, that many of the practices and laws of the past were themselves based on the customs of their times, that law and custom always influence each other, and that in our day, as well, the law must catch up to the new customs emerging in our communities.

At this time, though, we should *not* institute an amendment (*takkanah*) totally equalizing the status of the two genders. This should happen only in some future time, if ever, for it would be justified only if and when the customs of our community have totally, or at least overwhelmingly, become egalitarian. Delaying the institution of such an amendment will enable people of both genders to have some time to get used to women donning *tefillin*, for example, without prejudging the case from the outset to say that they must. We need to feel our way gradually into our new understandings of what it means to be a man or woman and how we are going to express those meanings in ritual and legal forms, and we must do this with mutual respect both for those of us who want to go more slowly in this process and for those of us who want to proceed more quickly.

When Israel stood at Sinai, the rabbis tell us, each Jew heard God's voice according to his or her own sensitivities and abilities.[36] That did not preclude our tradition from having laws that governed everyone, but it did establish the theological basis for a diversity of practice among our ancestors, at least within certain bounds. These practices sometimes served as the source of the law, as they did with regard to most matters concerning the legal distinctions between men and women. In our own day we must let custom evolve and determine these matters as it did in the past.

Notes

* Reprinted from *Conservative Judaism*, Spring 1997, vol. 49.3. Copyright by The Rabbinical Assembly, 1997. Reprinted by permission of the Rabbinical Assembly.

1. Deuteronomy 24:1–4; *M. Yevamot* 14:1; *B. Yevamot* I 12b; B. *Gittin* 49b; *Yad, Hil. Gittin* 1:1–2; *Shulhan Arukh, Even Haezer,* 120:1; *Be'er Ha-golah,* there and 134:1–3.
2. Deuteronomy 31:12.
3. Numbers 5:6; *Mekhilta, Nezikin*, Ch. 6 on Exodus 21:18; *M. B. K.* 8:4; *Yad, Hil. Nezikin,* 4:21; *Shulhan Arukh, Hoshen Mishpat,* 424:9.
4. Deuteronomy 17:15; *Sifrei Deuteronomy, par.* 157 (Ed. Louis Finkelstein) New York, 1939, 208); *B. Berakhot* 49a.; *Yad, Hil. Melakhim* 1:5.
5. Deborah: Judges 4–5; Shelomziyyon was the wife of Aristobulus I and AlexanderYanai, upon whose death she alone ruled the Hasmonean kingdom during the years 76-67 B. C. E. See "Salome Alexandra," *Encyclopedia Judaica* 14:691-3.
6. B. Megillah 232; *Yad Hil. Tefilah* 12:17; *Tur, Shulhan Arukh Orah, Hayim* 282:3) that follow that version of the *baraita*. Note that *Megillah* 3:5 does not mention the honor of the community but rather says two separate, and apparently, contradictory things: (1) "Anyone may ascend for the seven honors, even a minor, even a woman; (2) One may not appoint (literally, bring) a woman to read in public." Maimonides, as is his style, tries to iron out the inconsistency; he says: "A woman may not read in public because of the honor of the community. A minor who can read and knows to Whom prayer is addressed may ascend." Alfas (1013–1103) the *Tur* (Jacob ben Asher, died before 1340), and the *Shulhan Arukh* (Joseph Karo, 1488–1575), however, retain the inconsistency in the original sources. Isserles, following the Ran and Rivash, says "They may be counted among the seven, but all of them may not be women or minors."
7. Even Rabbi Aaaron Blumenfeld, who in 1955 wrote a responsum to permit women to be called to the Torah, admits that "there is no recorded instance of a woman called to the Torah either in the Talmud or in the Gaonic literature. However, there is a medieval decision that *seems* (my italics) to be practical halachah." He then cites a responsum of Rabbi Meir of Rothenburg (1220–1293), who says this: "In a city whose men are all Kohanim and there is not even one Israelite among them, it *seems* (my italics) to me that one Kohen takes the first two *aliyot* and then women are to be called, for 'All may ascend …'" This is hardly, though, a clear indication of an actual case or of accepted practice. Rabbi Meir's very words indicate that he is thinking through a logical conundrum in the law rather than recording what his community actually did. Aaron Blumenthal, "An Aliyah for Women," *Proceedings of the Rabbinical Assembly*, 55:168–181; reprinted in Seymour Siegel, ed. *Conservative Judaism and Jewish Law*, New York, 1977, 266–280; the citation is on 275.
8. *M. Kiddushin* 1:7, *B.Kiddushin* 33b–36a; Rachel Biale interprets these texts in the same way, indicating that the general rule that in fact characterizes the

division between what women were required to do and what they were not is the home/community distinction—namely, that women were required to do everything that takes place in the home, but not that that takes place in the community, because the place of the woman was construed to be at home. Rachel Biale, *Women and Jewish Law*, New York, 1984, 17.

9. In the Bible, Abraham, Jacob, and a number of kings have more than one wife. The Talmud permits a man to marry more than one wife, provided that he fulfills all his obligations, including his sexual ones, to each of them: B. *Yevamot* 44a (where the recommended maximum is four!); B. *Kiddushin* 7a. Here again, though, there was apparently a discrepency between what the law allowed and what custom dictated, for no case is recorded in the Talmud of a rabbi or a plaintiff in a case who had more than one wife. See Biale, *Women and Jewish Law*, 49–51..

10. See Avraham Grossman, "Medieval Rabbinic Views on Wife Beating, 800–1300," *Jewish History*, 5:1,Spring 1991, 53–62, esp. pp. 57 and 59–60. I discuss these precedents and how we should read and apply them in our day at some length in my reponsum entitled "Family Violence," approved by the Conservative Movement's Committee on Jewish Law and Standards on September 13, 1995.

11. See n. 7 above regarding one such possible role, namely, being called to the Torah.

12. M. *Megillab* 4:3 and *Yad, Hil. Tefilah* 8:4 both mention only a requirement for ten. See, however, *Shulhan Arukh, Orah Hayim* 55:1, 4, that specifies that males are required and that a woman may not count when there are fewer than ten men.

13. Mordecai on B. *Berakhhot*, note 173. Rabbi Philip Sigal seems to put much weight on this text in justifying the counting of women for a prayer quorum, although he states other arguments as well. See Philip Sigal, "Women in a Prayer Quorum," *Judaism* 23:2 (1974); reprinted in Seymour Siegel, *Conservative Judaism and Jewish Law*, 281–292; see especially 287 and n. 20 on 292.

14. For a more thorough discussion of the functioning of custom in Jewish law, see Elliot N. Dorff and Arthur Rosett, *A Living Tree: The Roots and Growth of Jewish Law*, New York, 1988, 421–434.

15. Rabbi Eugene Borowitz specifically takes Rabbi Neil Gillman and me to task for our common commitment to Jewish law, and Rabbi Neil Gillman himself describes "the Dorff / Roth position" as "the classical Conservative ideology and rhetoric" which, he says, "has had minimal impact outside of our own rabbinic circles." Although Rabbi Roth and I do not always agree on specific issues, Rabbis Borowitz and Gillman are right: Rabbi Roth and I share a commitment to a form of contemporary Judaism that preserves Jewish law as a central, organizing feature, however much we may differ on its content in specific matters, and that common commitment differentiates us both sharply from both Kaplan and Borowitz. See Eugene Borowitz, *Renewing the Covenant: A Theology for the Postmodcrn Jew*, Philadelphia, 1991, 282; Neil Gilman, "A Conservative Theology for the Twenty First Century," *Proceedings of the Rabbinical Assembly*, New York 1993, 20f.

16. Uniform Commercial Code, see 1-205; reprinted in Dorff and Rosett, *Op. Cit.*, 434.

17. B. B. M. 74a. I would like to thank Rabbi Ben Zion Bergman for pointing out this parallel to me.
18. Indeed, the few mentions of this in the archives of The Rabbinical Assembly specifically describe mixed seating as a custom and therefore leave it to the rabbi of each congregation to determine; see *Summary Index: The Committee on Jewish Law and Standard*, New York, 1994, 9.14.
19. Pamela S. Nadell, *Conservative Judaism in America: A Biographical Dictionary and Source Book*, New York, 1988.
20. *The Proceedings of the Rabbinical Assembly*, 1955, New York, , 168–190; *Summary Index*, 10.1. The majority decision permitted it at any time The practice in many congregations in the 1980s and 1990s followed the minority decision at that time.
21. *Summary Index*, pp. 10.3 (*minyan*), 10.2 (witness).
22. See Gordon Tucker, "Final Report of the Commission for the Study of the Ordination of Women as Rabbis," in Simon Greenberg, ed., *The Ordination of Women as Rabbis: Studies and Responsa*, New York, 1988, 5–30.
23. *Sifrei Deuteronomy*, Piska 104, Section 190 (Ed. Finkelstein, 230), bases the restriction of testimony to men on a linking (*gezera sheva*) of the word *shenei* (two) in Deuteronomy 19:17 to Deuteronomy 19:15, claiming that the former clearly refers only to men and so the latter is too. The truth is that neither is necessarily referring to men, for *anashim* (men) in v.17 can just as easily be people, as the *Sifrei* itself interprets it! Cf. also the Jewish Publication Society translation, the two parties to the dispute. In *M. Shevuot* 4:1 women are excluded from testifying, and the Talmud (*B. Shevuot* 30a), in trying to justify that ruling, offers a variety of arguments to make *shenei ha-anashim* ("two men") in Deuteronomy 19:17 refer to witnesses rather than litigants, but all those efforts are disputed, and so it ultimately relies on the *Sifrei*'s linking of *shenei* ("two"—two witnesses and two men) in the two verses. Apparently dissatisfied with that proof, or possibly basing himself on J. Shevuot 4:1 (35b), Maimonides in *Yad Hil. Edut* 9:2 instead bases the restriction on "the mouth of two witnesses" (Deuteronomy 17:6), where "witnesses" is the masculine form of the noun. Karo, however, in *Kesef Mishneh*, objects to this justification on the grounds that the masculine form of the noun there also does not necessarily mean men alone, and so, in *Shulhan Arukh Hoshen Mishpat* 35:1, 14, he just asserts the rule that women are barred from serving as witnesses without attributing the rule to the Bible.
24. An important exception was the ability granted to a woman to testify to her divorce or to the death of her husband so that she could remarry; *Yad Hil. Gittin* 12:1, 1–16.
25. Ben Zion Bergman, "A Conservative Approach to Halakhah," *Proceedings of the Rabbinical Assembly*, New York, 1987, 52. In support of his thesis, he points out that Maimonides explains why we do accept the testimony of women when they claim that their husbands divorced them or died because ultimately we can determine whether she lied or not (*Yad Hil. Gittin* 13:29; 13:24 in some editions). This suggests that the reason why women were ineligible to testify in all other cases is not because they were suspected of being incorrigible liars, but rather because, given the circumstances under that they lived, they could not be trusted to give *accurate* testimony.

26. Compare, for example, the opinions of Rabbis Mayer Rabinowitz and Joel Roth on this. Rabbi Roth clearly wants to permit women to be witnesses, and he suggests several ways to justify doing so, but he worries about the effects on the rest of the Jewish community of doing so. Rabbi Rabinowitz, on the other hand, says categorically that "we must reclassify the status of women vis-a-vis *edut* (testimony) based on the realities of our era.." See their respective articles in Greenberg, The *Ordination of Women"*, 117–119 and 149–162.

27. There "'as a minority vote of the Committee to allow women to be witnesses ii, 1974, but it was not rationalized by formal papers. See *Summary Index*, 10.2.

28. For both a reference to that *takkana* of the Chief Rabbinate, and for a more general discussion of the role of *takkanot* in Jewish legal development, see Menachem Elon, *"Takkanah"* and *"Takkanot Ha- Kahal,"* Encyclopedia Judaica 5:71 2–737, especially 727.

29. Making girls and women eligible for the same educational opportunities with the same curriculum as boys and men has been the practice of the Conservative Movement from its very inception, with the notable exception, until recently, of the rabbinical and cantorial schools. Our amendments of the *ketubah*, our pre-nuptial document of condition *(tenai-bekidushin)*, and, if all else fails, our willingness to annul a marriage retroactively, have together freed many women from remaining chained to their former husbands. For a description of these measures, see, Dorff and Rosett, *Op. Cit.*, 523–546. For our elimination of any Jewish legitimacy with regard to a child and spousal abuse, see my responsum, "Family Violence," on these issues, cited in n. 10 above.

30. "'Male and Female, He Created Them:' Equal with Distinction," University Papers, Los Angeles, 1984, 13–23.

31. *Discover*, June 1995, 36; *U.S. News and World Report*, February 27, 1998, 15. Cf. also a summary of earlier research indicating differences between the brain structures and functioning of men and women in "Sizing Up the Sexes," *Time*, January 20, 1992, 42–51.

32. Carol Gilligan, *In A Different Voice*, Cambridge, 1982 . N. Noddings, *Caring:A Feminine Approach to Ethics and Moral Education* , Berkeley, 1984; Deborah Tannen, *You Just Don't Understand* ,New York, 1990.

33. *B. Berakhot* 20b; *B. Shabbat* 31b; *Yad Hil. Avodah Zarah*, 12.3; *Hil. Shabbat* 5.3; *Shulhan Arukh, Orah Hayim* 263.2,3; 271.2.

34. *B. Kiddushin* 30b equals the Talmud's interpretation of *M. Kiddushin* 1:7 to require honor of parents by both sons and daughters.

35. The new book edited by Rabbi Debra Orenstein, *Lifecycles: Jewish Women on Life Passages and Personal Milestones*, Woodstock,1994, presents a rich treasury of new ideas to express women's life passages and personal milestones in meaningful, but distinctly Jewish, ways. A similar book needs to be written for men!

36. *Exodus Rabbab* 5:9; 29:1; *Pesikta DeRab Kahana, "Bahodesh Ha-Shelishi,"* on Exodus 20:2 (Ed. Mandelbaum), vol. 1, 224.

Chapter 5

❖   ❖   ❖

HALAKHAH, MINHAG AND GENDER

Richard Rosenthal

The subject is "gender," a word that comes to scholarship from the grammarians by way of the lawyers. A weapon in the political and legal struggles of our day for women's rights, the term was invented to avoid using the word "sex." Sex was a difficult word to use; its varied meanings damage it. It is a dangerous word threatening discourse, whereas gender is mild, lessening the danger. Who can be afraid of masculine and feminine nouns and verbs? "In grammar, gender is understood to be a way of classifying phenomena, a socially agreed upon system of distinctions rather than an objective description of inherent traits."[1] But the word has not stood still. Gender has left its innocent origins and become political. This should not disqualify it in our discussion, for a word that is political is alive. It reflects issues that are at the heart of our age. "Gender" positions are a real issue. This allows us to use our contemporary experience to look at the past.

A contemporary category becomes a new window to look at the past. Through this window we are allowed to see what was missed by those who came before us. This is not said in criticism. They had their world view that gave them their windows. Our

Notes for this section begin on page 127.

perspective gives us a view and language that allows to do what others have done in every generation, to interpret by restatement.

I have chosen to treat the fate of a mitzvah. It is not at the vital center of *halakhic* debate. Precisely for this reason it is easier to study as successive generations reshape its meaning, guided not only by *halakhah,* but also by *minhag,* the customs of communities shaped by local practices that in turn were influenced by time and place.

The mitzvah is stated Deuteronomy 22:5: *lo yiyeh khli gever al ishah velo yilbash gever simlat ishah ki to-avat adonai eloheikha kol oseh eleh* ("A woman must not put on man's apparel, nor shall a man wear woman's clothing; for whoever does these things is abhorrent to the Lord your God."). It is an interesting statement in its form: two parallel clauses are completed by a third clause explaining the consequence of disobedience. The word translated as "apparel" in the first clause, *kli,* is more commonly translated in the *Tanakh* as "object," "vessel," or "implement." The Targum translates it as "weapon." In rabbinic Hebrew it means "apparel," although "weapon" and "armed" also occur in rabbinic Hebrew.

What is the meaning of the biblical rule? A negative command, it limits. Clearly, men and women are to avoid certain things belonging to the opposite gender. In the case of women we are not sure what "apparel" is. Commentators and translators have speculated. Professor Tigay in the Jewish Publication Society Torah commentary sums up the opinion of both traditional and modern commentators on the verse in three categories: (1) one should not disguise oneself as a member of the opposite sex because this would permit indiscriminate mingling and lead to fornication; (2) transvestism is inherently abhorrent because it obscures the sexual differences God created, "male and female created He them." (3) Transvestism is abhorrent because it was part of pagan rites or magical practices.[4]

Among traditional commentators Rashi explains that men and women exchange garments in order to blend in with members of the opposite sex. Their only purpose must be fornication. Ibn Ezra translating *k'li* as in the Targum, military apparel, remarks that women were not created to fight in war but to perpetuate the seed, clearly defining the social role of men and women. He, too, sees this confusion leading to fornication. A beardless man mixes easily with women to commit adultery. Ibn Ezra adds an interesting observation that this rule is not only the custom of Israel but of most people.[5] All these interpretations are based in the rabbinic extension of the verse.

A key to understanding our verse is the concluding phrase that tells us that such behavior is "abhorrent to the Lord your God." "Abhorrent" (earlier translations say "an abomination"), is used to describe a number of forbidden practices. Louis Epstein speaks for many modern scholars of an earlier generation when he informs us with certitude: "The obvious meaning [of "abomination"] is a prohibition against the practice of homosexuality in any form, with which is generally associated wearing the garment of the opposite sex."[6] Von Rad tells us that the expression "denotes cultic taboos which endanger the religion of Yahweh" and goes on to say that "we learn from a later source (Lucian of Samosata) that in the worship of Astarte such masquerading took place."[7] Eissfeldt comments that the editors of Deuteronomy took an expression that had been in local use and adopted it to emphasize the purity of the Yahweh cult.[8]

Moshe Weinstein makes a thorough investigation of the expression. He tells us that in the task of investigating all the occurrences of the phrase by examining its subject matter, its

> "connection with miscellaneous moral, religious, and cultic interdictions ... can be of little help ascertaining its original cultic significance. We shall learn more by investigating the general nature of the individual malefactions than from their specific subject-matter. Now the general feature common to them all is the two-facedness or hypocritical attitude of the malefactor. ... It is this two facedness or false pretensions assumed when dealing with one's fellow man or in the execution of one's sacrificial dues that is an abomination to God."[9]

To Weinfeld, Deuteronomy is influenced by the Wisdom tradition of the *Tanakh*. He identifies a spirit in the book that he calls "humanism." Part of the humanistic broadening of the law is its inclusion of women in laws concerning both interpersonal and cultic matters. Weinfeld is only partially helpful by changing the direction in our search for the meaning of "abomination unto the Lord." Cross dressing is certainly a form of two-facedness, pretending to be what one is not. But it must mean more, especially when we remember that it is part of a tradition that is characterized by equalizing many of the distinctions between men and women.

If we bring all these interpretations together we can say that we have a commandment that may have a cultic origin but seeks, by focusing on clothing, to regulate the behavior of men and women. It is a demand for morality. Weinfeld, by placing Deuteronomy in the Wisdom tradition, makes it part of a tradition that is distinguished by moralizing about human behavior. It is important for our purposes to add to our investigation information from another direction.

It is useful to listen to feminists critics. Alice Latey writes: "Distinction between the sexes—not only biological distinction but social distinction—is to be express by a strict regulation of what clothing is appropriate for whom."[10] There is always a social dimension to rules. The social meaning is implicit not only in the public spoken law but more importantly in the unspoken assumptions that are hidden from sight and that govern all relationship in a given society.

Some conclusions about our verse. Its *Sitz im Leben* can be guessed at but never clearly determined. The rule stands alone, nowhere in the *Tanakh* are we told of someone cross dressing. What can we make of the rule makers mind? Clothing is social, civilizing. A human takes "the nakedness into which he is born, and which is 'given' to him" and is no longer satisfied. He "makes for himself clothes," the apron serving both as a protection and an indication of genital potency."[11] Men and women are separated by apparel. This seems to be a universal human experience. Unisex is an invention of our time. The clothing we use can be described as modest or provocative, it is designed to hide or to reveal. That is, it plays a sexual role. "It is not sexuality which haunts society, but society which haunts sexuality. Sex-related differences between bodies are continually summoned as testimony to social relations and phenomena that have nothing to do with sexuality."[12]

No wonder that commentators mention aspects of sexuality in relation to the practices of Israel's neighbors. We must qualify that by noting human sexuality was the central metaphor of the fertility cult that so shocked the prophets. If this material is, as

Weinfeld tells us, of Wisdom origin, or as others say, of prophetic or Levitical origin, the conclusion remains the same. A look at all three of these traditions shows the use of sexual metaphors. The language of sage, prophet, and priest insists that basically there are two kinds of women. Mothers, wives, sisters, women of valor, and harlots and temptresses who seek to entice us on the way.

Consider the distinction in our verse between what men and women are forbidden to put on. The *kli* apparel of a man is forbidden for women, *simlah* clothing (perhaps a wrapper), of a women is forbidden men. In sexual matters men's misbehavior is always different from women. For example, Ibn Ezra helps us see the difference: women's sin is "harlotry," men's "adultery." The harlot is the temptress who tries to lead men astray. Adultery is a legal term, limited by definition to a sexual act between certain parties. After adultery has occurred the female partner is called a harlot. There are no such nasty words used for the man. Harlotry is a word for public disgrace, adultery is a private act that is against the law. When it becomes public in the ritual of the *Sotah*, it is the woman who is tried.

Law is a distorted mirror of the world. But the world never stands directly in front of the mirror. Most often its back is turned, hinting at the unstated assumptions of the world it seeks to control. In scripture we must look at non-legal material to understand the assumptions behind the law. If we look at the creation stories that distinguish between men and women, we see tensions between them. We are first told that "male and female" He created them. Humans are equal in creation. The second story, which may have had equalitarian mythic predecessors, has woman emerging from man. The biblical editor reshapes and focuses the meaning of the first story through the prism of the second. An original unity gives way to sexual role distinction.

We are able to understand this focusing well because we are living through a time when gender roles are going through rapid transformation. As I said earlier, we know that gender roles are socially, that is politically, determined. The function and role of men and women is always being renegotiated and remains in flux. Think of it in our terms: many women adopt men's styles to enter the market place, while men do not wear women's clothing to do housework. We notice that women are defined by men.

Sexual undertones remain. There are also homosexual undercurrents in all of this and themes that are hidden; only they revealed in men's fears of their own and others tendencies. But let me repeat that this symbolism is male. Women who dress like men in our society are seen as seeking power and potency; men dressed as women are often called mentally ill. Looking back at the verse from our present situation we can see the male bias in the law. But we can also see that there are great tensions in the law. It is through the cracks in the law opened by these tensions that we can see women waiting to emerge.

Turning to rabbinic literature at this point we can see the development of our law. The rabbis as they restate the law, conclude that there was more to it than cross dressing. There has to be intention to do wrong. *Sifrei* says: "'A woman must not put on man's apparel.' What does Scripture come to teach us? That a woman shall not put on a white garment and a man shall not be clothed in a colored garment. It is taught (that it is) an abomination." A matter that is in the category of "abomination" is generalized by stating the matter that a women shall not dress in the way a man dresses and walk among men, nor shall a man adorn himself with women's ornaments and walk among women. Rabbi Eliezer ben Jacob said: "From where do we know that a women shall not wear armor and engage in warfare? We learn it from 'A woman must not put on man's apparel[13] and a man shall not adorn himself with women's ornaments as our text teaches 'nor shall a man wear woman's clothing.'"[14]

David Hoffman's reconstruction of Midrash *Tannaim*[15] says the same thing in a different order. The talmudic passage dealing with our verse makes the new meaning even clearer. "Rabbi Jochanan said: 'One who removes (the hair of) the armpits or the genital area is to be lashed because (he disobeyed the commandment) 'neither shall a man put on a woman's garment.'"[16] The text continues by telling us "that a man is not to use cosmetics as women do." In the same vein we learn in another place in the Talmud that a man is prohibited from picking "out white hairs from black ones."[17] The Talmud concludes that we do not follow the plain meaning of the verse. But rather it must mean more.

What has happened is that we are no longer dealing with the wearing of clothing but the presentation of the self. Men and women present themselves differently. Men are serious, somber, they dress in white. Women are frivolous at best, enticing at worst. The *Mishnah* list some of the things women do to present themselves: plait their hair, paint their eyelids, rouge their faces.[18] Women are expected to concern themselves with their physical appearance, but men are above such behavior. Women may indulge themselves, behaving in such a way that in a man would be considered vanity. Woman are prized for their beauty. Remember that Hillel in his kindness admonishes us always to praise a bride for her beauty.

In addition all women endanger the world defined by the rabbis by their effect on men. They are a potential source of disorder and pollution. Jacob Neusner[19] tells us that in the thought world of the *Mishnah*, men are normal. They define and order this world and the next. Women are abnormal; they are a continual threat. This attitude became normative in the *halakhic* world view. An extreme example will help make the point. Rabbi Isaac Aboab wrote: "Our pious sages saw men according to their nature desiring women and busying themselves with them continually, for the evil inclination incites and tempts to transgress in forbidden things more than permitted ones. Therefore it is necessary to separate man from this temptation and to deliver him from this temptation ... as it is said in tractate *Shabbat*. ...[20]: 'A woman is a skin bottle full of filth and her mouth is full of blood and all run after her. ...'"[21]

The Talmud in *Nazir* 58b and 59a, defines much of the future discussion. The issues future commentators will raise, which of the extensions of the biblical rule are Torah law, *midoraita*, and which are rabbinic enactments. That is not directly relevant to our issue. But the discussion does list all of the forbidden behaviors that are connected to our verse: shaving of the armpit and genital area by men, cross dressing, and mixing with members of the opposite sex; moreover women should not bear arms, and men should not use cosmetics as women do.

It is with this reshaped meaning that our verse emerges from *tannaitic* literature. Let us see what the codes do to its meaning. Maimonides lists the verse in the *Sefer Hamitzvot*[22] as two mitzvot following the Talmud's explanation of their meaning. But a change occurs when he puts them in the *Mishneh Torah*. He classifies them among the laws of idolatry. They appear in the same chapter as the law forbidding the cutting of the corners of the beard. Maimonides explains this law with a historical note. The corner of the beard are not to be cut because it was the way of idolatrous priests to trim the corners of their beards.[23] By implication our mitzvot also are to avoid idolatry. In his eyes, the avoidance of idolatry is central to Judaism. It is equal to all of the commandments; turning to idols is a denial of the fundamental precepts of Judaism. Maimonides rationalizes the comment by using historical interpretation.

He also limits the rabbinic interpretation of the prohibitions. Men should not shave armpits and genital hair, but "this rule is limited to where women alone remove this hair; a man should not trim himself in a way peculiar to women."[24] A woman may not adorn herself with men's special ornaments ... and a man must not adorn himself in a mode peculiar to women ... in a place where such garments and jewels are only worn by women, it all according to the custom of the country."[25] Custom (*minhag*) is an important element in deciding what has been forbidden. Maimonides adds important limitations to the law. The way men and women actually dress and groom themselves in the society in which Jews live is the test that will shape the law.

By seeing the prohibitions largely connected with idolatry Maimonides seems to move away from the puritanical mindset of his predecessor. *Sefer Hahinukh*, which is normally faithful to Maimonides, attempts to correct this by combining Maimonides' point of view with the rabbis' reading. Explaining the women's prohibition, he says that it is rooted in the desire "to keep our holy faith far from licentiousness ... Our sages use the metaphor for our God hates libidiousness ... for it is an extremely ugly thing that captures the human heart and turns humans from the goodly way and fitting thoughts to the evil way and frivolous thoughts ... It is also the purpose of this *mitzvah* to keep one far from idolatry for it is the way of idolaters to behave thus."[26] He tells us that the source of his explanation is Maimonides. Despite this, it is clear that the main thrust of this argument is away from Maimonides and is turned toward what had become the main understanding of the prohibition. He is following the tradition of the codifiers in the period between Maimonides and himself.

We can see the development more directly if we look at *Sefer Yiraim*. Rabbi Eliezer of Metz was one of the disciples of Rabenu Tam, and he speaks out of the tradition that French and German Jewry will follow. He describes the talmudic sources and list all their prohibitions. But he has an additional note that we should pay attention to because we will hear more about it later. He says: "Dressing [that is, cross dressing] either accidentally or playfully is forbidden. Scripture does not distinguish between normal and accidental [wearing of clothing]. I have seen men dressed in women's clothing playfully and it was distasteful in my eyes."[27] He saw it himself. It must have been customary for Jews at wedding celebrations to have people cross dressing for the amusement of the guests. Who these people were, we can only guess at. It seems too early for the kinds of wedding celebrations that we will discuss later, but obviously Rabbi Eliezer was disturbed at people's behavior at weddings.

Smag[28] follows Rabbi Eliezer as does *Smak*,[29] but neither mentions his concern with his contemporaries who cross dress in fun. Apparently this did not a concern them. If it had been important, they would have mentioned it. Rabbi Moses wrote his code for Spanish Jews, whom he had found very lax in their keeping of mitzvot in his journeys as a traveling preacher. Rabbi Isaac, feeling that he was living in an age when Torah was forgotten, wrote his code to call the Jews of France and the Rhineland back to the mitzvot. At any rate we can see that the talmudic meaning of the mitzvot was transferred through the generations. *Smag* spends a great deal of time on the question of which part of the mitzvah is from the Torah and which is rabbinic.

When we turn to the *Tur*[30] and *Bet Yosef* we can see the longevity of the talmudic argument. The same discussion is continued especially by Joseph Caro. Both continue Maimonides stricture that all is governed by the customary usage of the place. The *Tur* adds an additional extension of the things forbidden to men: they may not look into a mirror unless it is necessary. The Talmud had forbidden holding a mirror on *Shabbat* but permits using a mirror fixed to a wall[31] and it also tells us that we should look in a mirror when we go to a non-Jewish barber.[32] So the prohibition against looking in a mirror is another way of distinguishing between men and women, emphasizing the non-seriousness of women. They are permitted frivolous vanities because that is their nature.

The *Shulhan Arukh*[33] summarizes the law mentioning that men are forbidden from shaving the armpits and genital areas in a place where only women do this. Isserles is stricter and forbids shaving totally because it is a sign of idolatry. It is also forbidden to rub this hair with the hand in order to remove it, but it is permitted if his clothing rubs and removes it. One who has painful scabs in these areas is permitted to remove the hair. A woman may not wear male adornments such as a turban, or dress in armor, or shave her head like a man. A man may not adorn himself like a woman by wearing colored garments or a golden chain. Isserles again is stricter, remarking that even one of these garments is forbidden even though it is clear that the wearer is a man. He adds that hermaphrodites and others of uncertain sex[34] are forbidden to dress as women. A man may not pluck even one white hair out of the dark hair nor may he die his hair. He may not look in a mirror.

We can see clearly how the codes regularize and extend the talmudic texts, explaining them, adding occasional strictures, and in the case of Maimonides revitalizing them. But the language remains essentially the same because the rabbis maintain the continuity of the tradition. It is the explication of the talmudic texts upon which they base their authority and power. To maintain their authority they hold on to the exact language. In the medieval world the four ells of Torah define the place where they stand. But they are not alone. To know only the rabbinic text is not to know the fullness of the lives of Jews. Anthropologists speak of "the Great Tradition," in our case the religion of the rabbis, and the "Little Tradition," the popular religion of every day life.[35] It has been the genius of Jewish tradition that at certain stages *minhag*, the product largely of popular religion, breaks into the world of *halakhah* and sets it aside. As we have seen, Maimonides speaks of custom determining what must be done. Once the extra-halakhic usage of people becomes established it is law. "*Minhag* is Torah" is the rabbinic saying. In matters of everyday law the Talmud already enjoins us "everything is according to the custom of the country."[36] We can see an interesting example here. Shabtai Kohen, commenting on "a woman may not wear male adornments ..." refers us to the laws of Purim. There[37] Isserles comments: "Concerning the wearing of masks on Purim when men wear women's clothing and women wear men's clothing there is no prohibition in the matter because there is no intent. It is joy in general." It is the opposite of the comment of Rabbi Eliezer of Metz quoted above. His authority comes from a responsum of Rabbi Juda Mintz of Padua:

> "Concerning the matter of wearing masks which are customarily worn by young men and women; old and young on Purim ... (I bring) evidence from my observation in this matter of the great and pious of the world among whom I grew up. They saw their sons and daughters, their brides and grooms, dressing in masks and exchanging garments from man's garment to a woman's and the reverse. If, God forbid, there had been head shaking at sin, that they would have laughed and not reproved. How much more so if they had evidence of a prohibition in the matter. They agreed that there was complete permission and that there was not in the matter of this kind of dressing even the hint of sin..[38]

Mintz goes on to show that this interpretation of the law grows out of the history of the interpretation of the various acts the rabbis have forbidden. All of them in one way or another have been limited by the customs of the place, and here he brings empirical evidence from his own experience. Would the pious scholars of his youth have stood idly by when the law was being transgressed? From this we know that at Purim and at weddings it was customary to dress up, and therefore it is permitted.

Padua was a dependency of Venice. Venice had tolerance for Jews. ..." during the long centuries of the history of the Jews in Venice no solitary instance of a popular attack upon them is on record."[39] The Jews of Venice were at home in their society and participated fully in its social and cultural life. Jews danced, attended feasts, gambled and played, banqueted with rich meals, wore the highest fashions. This was true for much of Italy. This situation had existed since the fourteenth century and came into its broadest expression in the time of the Renaissance.[40] They were at one with their environment. Women had greater freedom, which they expressed on the one hand by the luxury of their lives and on the other by their intellectual lives. It was in the Italian communities that the sumptuary laws came into their own. These laws sought to regulate, among other things dress and life cycle celebrations. Jews wasted money and stirred the envy of non-Jews.[41] This can also be seen in the Italian rabbis' attempt to control romantic elopements. Many communities established enactments to forbid them.[42]

Purim has always had a sense of celebration, of turning the world on its head." Raba said: It is the duty of a man to mellow himself (with wine) on Purim until he cannot tell the difference between 'cursed be Haman' and 'blessed be Mordecai.'"[43] On Purim we reverse the normal order. Not only in drinking but we read the *Megillah* at night, encourage the making of noise to wipe out the sound of the name of Haman. A banquet, which serves as a reminder of the banquet Esther made for Ahasuerus, is one of the mitzvot of Purim. Purim bothered the pious. Joy was an essential part of the holiday. But it should be the joy of mitzvah, whose purpose it was to appreciate the miracle of the Purim story. Wrote the Shaloh: "I have seen many persons overtaken by wine go out in terrible sinfulness in these days of Purim increasing in playfulness and frivolity. They are not scrupulous in praying on these days on the contrary shout loudly at the time of prayer."[44] Or consider the comments of Joseph Yuspa Haan Neurlingen: "wise man should keep his eyes in his head and be careful not to get drunk completely nor fill his belly more than is fitting …"[45] Protectors of the established order they felt threatened by the radical possibilities of Purim and wanted everyone to stay off its slippery slope.

Masquerade became part of the celebration. In Italy it all must have been influenced by Carnival, which was an important part of Italian life. Carnival had its origin in the Roman Saturnalia. This was a time when the order of the world was inverted, daily conventions were transgressed, and people indulged in all sorts of excesses. These characteristics were transferred to the Christian Carnival. "Inversion is at the root of Carnival symbolism and explains the presence of such customs as transvestite costumes, or clothes worn inside out, the poor playing the role of the rich, and the weak that of the powerful."[46] The reality of the carnival world was an alternate world that not only served as a kind of safety valve releasing pressure from the brutalities and oppression of every day life but also allowed people to dream of how things might be different. There was even a Jewish King of Fools, cleaned up and made respectable. R. Yuspa Shamos tells us that in Worms the students of the Yeshivah came to the synagogue on the Shabbat after Purim, dressed in all their dignity, led by one of their number who they called head of the students. He was dressed as a fool. They sat on the *bimah* taking the place of the community dignitaries. The rabbi blesses them and then they enter the women's section for the Rebitizin's blessing.[47]

In Italy, the rise of the *commedia dell'arte* consolidated the use of masks and gave them an artistic character.[48] The various characters represented by the masks were universal types. These masked entertainments occurred not only on Purim but also at wedding celebrations. The stage, like the carnival, is an alternate reality. It presents life within three walls, welcoming the observer to become part of its reality; a product of the Renaissance, it spread across Europe. Glickel of Hameln tells of the celebration of the greatest moment in the life of her family, the marriage of her daughter, Zipporah to Kossman Gomperz, the son of Prussia's most important Jew, Elia Gomperz. Part of the glorious celebration, attended by the heir to the Prussian throne and other aristocrats, was a group of "masked performers who bowed prettily and played all manners of entertaining pranks. They concluded their performance with a truly splendid Dance of Death.[49] This was not what it sounds like, but was a stylized dance of familiar types of humans who did a kind of burlesque. All this happened in the presence of Glickel's Rabbi Meir. He did not object but apparently was so engrossed in the proceedings that he forgot to write the *Ketuvah* and had to read one out of a book.

Wedding parties have some of the celebratory aspects of Purim. There is an abandonment of stability, a letting go. Marriages were financial arrangements between parents rather than the romantic joining of lovers. They were celebrations of wealth and power. But still there was drink and entertainment that challenges the normal order of life. The most important thing was not coming under the Huppah but partaking in the banquet. The *hupah* represented order and continuity. The couple stood in the presence of a representative of the community and the families and consented to become husband and wife. But at the banquet, chaos reigned; the new world of bride and groom emerged from it. Dissolution and reconstitution occurs. The bride and groom reenact Adam and Eve, who define the basic human relationship. Amidst masked play that explored potential human relationships the newly married couple took their place in the community of Israel.

These Purim and wedding customs continue in some form or another until the present day. In a 1780 engraving by P. Wagenaar we see stylish, elegant men and women dancing at a Purim ball in Amsterdam. Masking is connected to the Purim *shpiel*, which brought the drama into Jewish life. Yiddish motion pictures continue the tradition. The secular Jews who created them gave their interpretation of Jewish life. In one of the classics, *Yidel Mitem Fidel*, Molly Picon disguises herself as a boy as she travels with her father working as a traveling klesmer.[50]

As happened with Carnival, weddings were regularized and controlled so that in a tamer form they would not challenge the proper order. But since alcohol was involved with both, there was no way that the community could always control events. There is an astonishing comment in *Arukh Hashulhan* on the words of Isserles permitting masquerades in the *Shulhan Arukh*: "Concerning the custom of former days of wearing masks and of men and women exchanging clothes nowadays we do not behave in this way."[51] Rabbi Epstein, writing in the late nineteenth century, must have lived a sheltered life for the riotous celebration of Purim had a rebirth with the rise of Hasidism. *Life is With the People* describes how it was celebrated in the shtetl.

> The favorite historical holiday is Purim ... the gayest of all. ... the child sees his elders in an unfamiliar light ... frivolity is permitted and even prescribed ... Suddenly on Purim things "criticized as un-Jewish" are "becoming." Drinking, even to excess, practical jokes, masquerading in odd costumes, wearing of women's clothes by men ... The license of Purim is exercised more by the Hasidim than by the rabbinists and the very *sheineh layt* unbend only enough to do honor to the tradition, without violating the decorum that is their second nature.[52]

The Hasidim prized Purim. They punned on the name of Yom Kippur, calling it *yom kipurim*, a day like Purim. Both were times when the worshiper came close to God by letting go of the self in repentance. On Yom Kippur we seek to undo the sin of the golden calf, which Israel worshiped through eating and drinking, thus we fast. But on Purim the miracle happened because the Jews fasted. Therefore we make atonement by eating and drinking. Indeed Purim is on a higher rung than Yom Kippur.[53] They reinterpreted the carnival message of Purim as a way to greater holiness. Dov Baer, the Maggid of Meseritch wrote: "A man needs to drink on Purim until he can not distinguish between 'Cursed is Haman' and 'Blessed is Mordecai' because he needs to establish himself on the love of Purim. All will ascend to the Creator, may He be blessed. This is the meaning of 'can not distinguish' for all is equal in His eyes. We serve God even with 'cursed is Haman" because that is our physical self."[54] We must get drunk on Purim despite the fact that scripture often warns us of the evils of drink.[55]

As to masquerades: we are told that Israel sinned in the days of Nebuchanezer by bowing down to idols facing (*lefanim*) the idol. God in return faced them (*lefanim*) with punishment. That is why we hide our faces behind masks at times of joy so that we will not be recognized. Another reason we dress up is that in the Garden of Eden we will be dressed in precious garments. If we dress in a similar garment in this world we will be as spiritual as in the Garden of Eden.[56] In all of these Hasidic teachings disorder is held to be more important than order. The world is blessed by people who take the risk and in ecstasy serve God. Sobriety and seriousness as ideal male behaviors are abandoned. Rabbi Nachman urges his followers to give way to joy by dancing and clapping on Purim, Hanukkah, and weddings for so is God served.[57] The Baal Shem Tov's comment is to the point: If you want a horse to neigh you must slacken the reins. Holiness emerges out of chaos.

If we turn now to some of the important Orthodox decisors of the twentieth century we find something new. Our rule is used as a way to isolate Jews and to help create separate communities distinguished by dress. Answers to questions that grow out of our verse are almost all concerned with women and most of them are answered stringently. They are all aimed at restricting the lives of women by prescribing permissible ways of dress to a very narrow, defined pattern and thus defining them socially.

For men the issue is different. Men are rarely addressed, and when they are, it is with consideration. Thus Rabbi Yechiel Jacob Weinberg in a long responsum answers several questioners who want to dye their beards because they look older than their actual age. This is damaging them because they cannot make proper marriages or they are denied promotions in their professions or businesses. He discusses the long history of the questions. Dyeing of beards has been forbidden for a number of reasons, but the essential question is whether the prohibition is from the Torah or from the rabbis. Then we should also ask whether in the present question men are affecting the style of women by beautifying themselves or are attempting to mislead others about their true age for their personal profit. He permits dyeing, but he also cautions that one must tell one's true age.[58]

Similarly, Rabbi Moshe Feinstein permits the dyeing of beards when it is not an attempt to defraud by deception.[59] Rabbi Eliezer Yehuda Waldenberg permits the plucking of white hairs out of a black beard when the purpose is not beautification but simply to shape the beard properly. He permits this, although plucking is one of the specific acts the Talmud forbids. But he shows that this prohibition is rabbinic, which inclines him to permit.[60]

Both Rabbi Weinberg and Rabbi Feinstein in the above responsa also speak about men using mirrors. They see this as customary usage for men in our society. This is how men groom themselves. Indeed, both add that it is especially important for Torah scholars to appear in public well dressed. Otherwise they would bring dishonor on the Torah. Rabbi Ovadiah Yossef also gives permission for men to use mirrors quoting the Talmud: "Any scholar upon whose garment a [grease] stain is found is worthy of death."[61] His conclusion: "In our time it is also the custom of men to look in the mirror, it has no aspect of 'a man shall not wear a woman's garment,' and it is permitted."[62] Thus it is custom, the way of the world, of Jews and non-Jews, that determines the permitted practice for men.

In two cases regarding women the decisors are lenient. Rabbi Moshe Feinstein is asked whether women who live in Gush Ezion on the West Bank may carry pistols to protect themselves against Arabs. He permits it because "in places that are close to murderous Arabs who have no normal fear of the government, it is permitted for women to bear arms not only to save themselves from actual killing but also from the strikes in skirmishes that necessarily involve both women and men.[63] His language assents to the program of settlements that has placed women in a vulnerable position in the first place. He also mentions that he permits the gun because of the mortal danger,[64] not mentioning that normally if one can avoid putting oneself in danger, one should do so. He also insists that this does not permit a woman to become a soldier. He concludes by saying that women should learn to use the pistol and to carry it in a place where it is easy to draw. Rabbi Ovadiah Yossef addresses a similar question: Are female teachers of kindergartens and schools to train in using arms and to carry them to protect themselves and their children? Emphasizing the danger of terrorists, he permits it to help avert the danger, provided that the women are careful to keep the rules of modesty when they are training.[65]

Rabbi Yossef also concerns himself with a question that has only a tangential relationship to our verse but a direct connection to gender issues and the mood of our time: Are women obligated to come to the synagogue on Shabbat *Zakhor* to hear the reading of *Parshat Zakhor*? He has written two responsa on the subject.[66] He investigates the nature of the mitzvah; is hearing remembering mentally or actively speaking? What are the actual limitations of the fact that women are not obligated to perform positive commandments limited by time, and how does this affect their attendance at the Sabbath morning service and their listening to the Torah reading? What does it mean "to wipe out" the memory of Amalek or to "conquer the land"? If it calls for an obligatory war, what are women's roles in such a war? Rabbi Eliezer's reading of our verse prohibits women from bearing arms. This is seen as forbidding them to serve as soldiers. Rabbi Yossef as always writes very fully on the subject. Nowhere does he mention the Holocaust or Israel's continuing struggle for the land of Israel, but his conclusion must have been deeply influenced by them: "Even though many of the *Aharonim* explain that women are not obligated to go to the synagogue to hear *Parshat Zakhor*, nevertheless it is right and proper for women who are able to go to the women's section of the synagogue on Shabbat *Zakhor* to hear *Parshat Zakhor* to strive to do so to discharge their obligation according to all decisors and the Eternal will bless them."

But the more general attitude toward women can be seen in a responsum of Rabbi Feinstein.[67] He is asked by a Boston rabbi about affluent and important women who are part of the movement for women's liberation. They are observant Jews but are fighting against some Torah laws; they also pray wearing a tallit and similar things. He answers by proclaiming the immutability of Torah and then attacks the women: "ordinary women who are not rich accept the obligation of raising boys and girls for it is a work most important to God and the Torah. God so created both sexes ... that women's nature is better adapted to the raising of children and therefore they are not obligated to study Torah." Women may accept mitzvot they have no obligation to perform and receive their reward. This includes hearing the shofar, *lulav*, and wearing zizit. Only the wearing of Tefilin is forbidden because they require "extra care to have a clean body." It is interesting how the ancient folk belief about the uncleanliness of women never dies. He bases this on *Tosfot*,[68] which he notes does not mention the reading of our verse by Targum *Yonatan*, which reads it forbidding women from wearing tallit and tefilin because they are male ornaments.[69] The women are using the mitzvot to try to change the Torah which is unchangeable. He then defends the Torah: women's roles differ from those of men, but women are equally holy.

The responsa is strangely apologetic and angry. One can find the same tone in many responsa on the subject of women wearing trousers. A good introduction to our subject is a responsum of Rabbi Yossef written in 1973 to a principal of a religious high school.[70] The principal mentions that he is confronted with miniskirts, which break out of the limits of modesty. Wouldn't it be better, especially in winter, if the girls wear trousers?

Rabbi Yossef speaks first of miniskirts quoting Shabbat 62a: "'Because the daughters of Zion are haughty?'[71] That means that they walked with haughty bearing ... and on coming near to the young men of Israel, they kicked their feet and spurted it on them, thus instilling them with passionate desire like with serpent's poison." He uses his erudition to give many references to the effect that women's wanton behavior has on men: "they walk with leg and thigh revealed stimulating the evil inclination in the young men of Israel." He adds a note: "thousands of young men were killed in battle in the late Yom Kippur war. Who knows if it was not for this grave sin ... as it is said: 'For the Lord your God walks in the midst of your camp, to save you, and to give your enemies before you; therefore shall your camp be holy; that he should see no unclean thing in you, and turn away from you.'"[72] Thus miniskirts are forbidden.

Trousers are worse. This is not at first obvious from the sources, for many have permitted trousers. The reasons vary: (1) they are only forbidden when they look like men's trousers; (2) they are allowed when necessary because of heat or cold; (3) the custom of the place is the custom; (4) *Sefer Hassidim* permits women to disguise themselves as men and young men as women in order to save themselves at a time of persecution; (5) women's pants differ from men's in cut parallels; (6) the history of the acceptance of pants parallels that of the use of the mirror by men.

Opposed to this is the tendency of the *Aharonim* to be stringent and also the increasing transformation Maimonides' avoidance idolatry to avoidance of the way of non-Jews. Rabbi Jossef sees himself in this tradition. He forbids both miniskirts and trousers. Women should wear garments that fall below the knees. He closes by saying that trousers may be preferred over miniskirts but only until the daughters of Israel are convinced to wear modest garments.

There are a number of other responsa forbidding the wearing of trousers by women. Trousers are almost always characterized as "arrogant" and "filth." It is hard to miss the rabbis disdain. Rabbi Eliezer Waldenberg quotes a tradition going back to the *Hatam Sofer* that says that our time is different from all other ages because never before have we been challenged by the licentiousness of women. He reports that "one like me who has sat for more than thirty years in the seat of a judge and knows the result of the bitterness of the destruction of many families as a result of the breaking of the yoke and the stripping away of modest clothing."[73] This global statement, as well as the connection of trousers with both sexuality and feces connects the whole process with control. We seek to control others. It begins with toilet training and continues through sexual discipline. If we look back at such classic works as the *Rokeah*, it becomes clear that the control of the body and its fluids creates social control. It is also important to note how an article of clothing can be given an independent existence. It has a life of its own. Perhaps to put it better, it becomes a symbol of modernity and of the non-Jewish world out there. It must be eliminated before we can make our way back to virtue. To quote Rabbi Waldenberg again: "As a matter of fact wearing trousers brings one to abominations, more so than wearing short dresses. As we know the licentious women stand in the middle of the street or on its corner with other licentious women like them and come close and rub themselves against others by way of the trousers, something that would be impossible in skirts." If I am reading this correctly he is referring to prostitutes seeing using trousers to ply their trade.

We have a similar responsum from Rabbi Isaac Jacob Weiss.[74] He adds some information we had not heard before. The prohibition begins at bat mitzvah and not only applies in public but also when a woman is alone at home with no men present or when she hides the offending garment by wearing it under her clothes. With this, trousers have become demonized. Perhaps we can tie this together with a comment of Rabbi Feinstein.[75] Asked how children might be taught to understand the commandment of not cross dressing, he answers that children are not obligated by the prohibition. Their mothers should use care in the way they dress them. When the feeling of shame develops in children, they will learn to dress properly. Wrong, inappropriate clothing is connected with shame. We blush in our shame knowing we have done wrong: toilet training, sexual education, and proper clothing have all become one.

Daniel Sperber has shown us the many faces of *minhag*. It can begin in the world outside the Jewish community or within it. It has its source in misreading of text, adoption of pagan custom, adjusting to the general society. It is alive, changing all the time. Sometimes it looks forward, at other times it tries to preserve the way of the past. It is a way of dealing with the multiple social pressures on Jews. *Halakhah* seems at first the opposite of *minhag*. We hear the repetition of the same text through the generations. But they do not lead to the same conclusions. The law is always shaped by the decisions of the judges. The writers of codes and the answerers of questions shape it. In our time, traditional decisors have tried to shape the world in their own image by the decisions they reach. In the traditional decisions, as in the liberal ones, the world view of the writer is decisive.

Those rabbis who wanted Jews to retreat from the modernity that reshaped women's roles have used dress codes to form their communities. Men and women's clothing symbolizes who they are. To don the proper clothing is the way in, to take them off is the way out. The world and its customary way of dressing had no claim on Jews. Jews were thus encouraged to separate themselves from the mainstream.

In our survey we have seen how a biblical prohibition has traveled through the centuries. Even though we cannot determine the exact cause of its origin, it has been used as a form of social control. The rabbis extended its meaning to include many forms of the presentation of the self. Through most of its history the application of the rule has been modified by *minhag*. In modern times Orthodox decisors have interpreted it in a very different way by using it to enforce separation.

Notes

1. Joan Wallach Scott, *Gender and the Politics of History*, New York, 1976, p. 19.
2. Commentators who use the words "transvestism" bring a modern psychological category to their work and already have interpreted the text radically by using this term.
3. Genesis 1:27.
4. Jeffery H. Tigay, *Deuteronomy, The JPS Torah Commentary*, Philadelphia and New York, 1996, p. 200.
5. This moral universalism is in interesting contrast to the views held by some modern Jewish scholars, as we shall see below, who insist on creating immoral non-Jewish straw men to knock down.
6. Louis M. Epstein, *Sex Laws and Customs in Judaism*, New York, 1976.
7. Gerhard von Rad, *Deuteronomy, A Commentary*, Philadelphia,.1966.
8. Otto Eisfeldt, *Einleitung in das Alte Testament*, Tuebingen 1964.
9. Moshe Weinfeld, *Deuteronomy and the Deuteronomic School*, Oxford, 1972, p. 19.
10. Alice L. Lattey, *An Introduction to the Old Testament*, Philadelphia,.1988, p. 19.
11. G. van der Leeuw, *Religion in Essence and Manifestation*, Princeton, p. 209.
12. Maurice Godelier quoted by Scott, Ibid., p. 45.
13. This follows the Targum's translation of *kli* as military apparel, armor.
14. *Sifre Deuteronomy*, (ed. Finkelstein), chapter 226.

15. *Midrash Tannaim* to Deuteronomy 22:8; Ibid.
16. *Nazir* 59a.
17. Shabbat 94b.
18. Shabbat 94b.
19. Jacob Neusner, *The Way of Torah*, New York, 1987.
20. 152a.
21. Isaac Aboab, *Menorat Hamaor*, Jerusalem, 1961, p. 66.
22. Negative Commandments 40 and 41.
23. *Mishnah Torah, Avodah Zarah* 12:6.
24. Ibid. 12:9.
25. Ibid.12:10.
26. *Sepher Hahinukh* (ed. Shevel) Jerusalem, p. 793.
27. Eliezer of Metz, *Sefer Yiraim*, (Israel Goldblum ed.) Vilna.
28. Rabbi Moses ben Jacob of Cousi, *Sefer Mitzvot Gadol Hashalem*, vol. 1, Jerusalem, 1993, p. 96.
29. Rabbi Isaac of Corbeil, Sefer *Amudai Hagolah*, Jerusalem, mitzvah 33.
30. *Yoreh Deah* 176.
31. Shabbat 149a.
32. *Avodah Zarah* 29a.
33. *Yoreh Deah* 172.
34. *Tumtum ve-androginot.*
35. See the discussion and notes in Steven M. Lowenstein, *Two Sources of Jewish Tradition: Official Religion and Popular Religion*, Los Angeles, 1984.
36. *Minhag* is fully discussed by Israel Schepansky, *Kuntros Haminhag Beyisrael*, appended to volume four of *The Takkanot of Israel*, New York and Jerusalem, 1974.
37. *Orah Hayim* 796.
38. Judah Mintz, *Responsa*, Salonica, 1666, # 15.
39. Cecil Roth, *Venice*, Philadelphia 1930.
40. See the description in M. Guedemann, *Geschichte des Erziehungswesens und der Kultur der Juden in Italien während des Mittelalters*, Wien 1884.
41. On sumptuary laws see Israel Schepansky, *The Takkanot of Israel* (Hebrew), volume IV, New York and Jerusalem, 1984, p. 480 ff.
42. Abraham Freimann, *Seder Kidushin V'nisuin*, Jerusalem, 1964, 322 ff.
43. *Megilah* 7b.
44. Isaiah Horowitz, *Shnei Luhot Habri*t, Jerusalem, 1975, Part one, p. 87.
45. *Yosef Omez*, Frankfurt am Main, 1928.
46. Maria Julia Goldwasser, "Carnival," *The Encyclopedia of Religion*, New York and London, 1963, p. 99.
47. *Minhagim deK.K. Wormeisa LeRabi Yuspa Shamos*, (Benjamin Shelomoh Hamburger (ed.), Jerusalem, 1988. This custom seems to have lasted through the centuries in Yeshivot. Rabbi Ovadiah Yossef is asked about them and forbids them. See *Yabia Omer*, Jerusalem, Part 8:50.
48. Ibid. 100.
49. The Memoirs of Glickel of Hameln, Marvin Lowenthal tr., New York, 1965; See also Solomon Schechter, *Studies in Judaism*, (Second Series), Philadelphia, 1908, p. 136f.

50. Eve Secular, "*A Yingl mit a Yingl Hot Epes a Tam*: The Celluloid Closet Of Yiddish Film," *Jewish Folklore and Ethnology Review*, vol. 6:1.
51. Yechiel Halevy Epstein, *Arukh Hashulhan, Orah Hayim*, Warsaw, 1911, 796.
52. Mark Zborowski and Elizabeth Herzog, *Life Is with People*, New York, 1952.
53. Aaron Wertheim, *Halakha v'Halikhot B'hasidut*, Jerusalem 1960, p. 191.
54. Israel Klapholz (ed.), *Torat HaMagid*, Tel Aviv, 1969, p. 27.
55. For a sense of the Hasidic understanding of the nature of Purim see *Inyanai Megilah* in *Sefer Ta-amai Haminhagim*.
56. Tzvi Elimelech of Dinov, *Sefer B'nai Yissahar*, Israel 1966.
57. Nathan of Nemerov, *Rabbi Nachman's Wisdom*, translated and annotated by Rabbi Aryeh Kaplan, Brooklyn, 1973.
58. Yechiel Jacob Weinberg, *Seridei Esh*, Jerusalem 1977, part 2:1.
59. Moshe Feinstein, *Igrot Mosheh, Yoreh Deah* Bnai Brak, 1981, 2:61.
60. Eliezer Yehuda Waldenberg, *Tzitz Eliezer*, Jerusalem, 1967, part 13:77.
61. Shabbat 114a.
62. Ovadia Yossef, *Yehaveh Daat*, part 6:49.
63. Moshe Feinstein, Ibid., *Orah Hayim* 4:75.
64. *Pikuah nefesh*.
65. Ovadiah Yossef, *Yehaveh Daat*, part 8:58.
66. Ovadiah Yossef, *Yabia Omer*, part 8, *Orah Hayyim* 54 and *Yehaveh Daat*, Part 1:84.
67. Moshe Feinstein, Op. Cit., *Orah Hayyim* 4:49
68. *Eruvin* 96a.
69. This is an interpretation of the reading of *k'li* as arms—tallit and *tefillin* are the arms a Jew wears.
70. Ovadiah Yossef, *Yabia Omer*, part 6 *Yoreh Deah*, 14.
71. Isaiah 3:16.
72. Isaiah 23:15.
73. Eliezer Yehuda Waldenberg, *Tzitz Eliezer*, part 11:62.
74. Weiss, Op. Cit., part 2:`108.
75. Feinstein, Op. Cit., *Hoshen Mishpat* 2:62.

Chapter 6

❖   ❖   ❖

THE WOMAN IN REFORM JUDAISM
Facing or Avoiding the Issues

Walter Jacob

As we define Reform Judaism for ourselves at the beginning of the twenty-first century, egalitarianism is one of its principles. We treat men and women alike; we accord equal opportunities to each gender and see the religious value of their acts in an equal fashion. We usually state that this has been a guiding principle from the beginning of the Reform movement. Is that really so? How important was feminism in early Reform Judaism? How did this express itself in halakhic discussions among the various Reform leaders? These questions need to be answered; in doing so, however, we shall see them as a reflection of the broader gender issues that have faced us and as one example of halakhic renewal and creativity when the traditional interpretations could no longer serve Judaism or the Jewish people.

Our views of gender have changed dramatically in the last two centuries and it was impossible to accommodate these views and their philosophical underpinnings within the framework of Jewish tradition. In this area and in some others we have reached the same impass as did Judaism two thousand years ago when it was successfully reconstructed by the Pharisees. Biblical Judaism

---

Notes for this section begin on page 147.

had to accommodate to the radically new social, philosophical, and economic conditions of the Greco-Roman Empires. Others had conquered ancient Israel and even taken large population groups into exile, but this conquest was more long lasting and different. Alongside political domination there were strong cultural and philosophical challenges. The intellectual world of Judaism had to defend itself as never before. Most Jews, furthermore, no longer lived within the borders of the conquered Jewish land. A variety of groups provided possible future directions for Judaism, and the Pharisees were the most successful among them. They enabled Judaism to accommodate itself to the new conditions. Over a number of centuries, they renewed Scripture through hermeneutic interpretational systems. The Torah took on new meanings. The "oral law" further extended the scope of the Torah and served as a companion to the written Torah. The new system eliminated many economic restrictions by limiting them to the Land of Israel at a time when most Jews lived outside the land and so they could be competitive. Similarly, the *prosbul* made it possible for a society with a different economic basis to flourish. In addition to all of this, religious life was redefined through the creation of the synagogue and of family law that existed only in outline form in the Bible, was expanded. This creativity continued through the period of the Mishnah and the Talmud.

Other groups within the community had other solutions or opposed the Pharisees. Even within the ranks of the new rabbinic Pharisaic Judaism, leaders disagreed about what was legitimate. How should Judaism be reinterpreted? The famous debates between Hillel and Shamai were only the best known of these disagreements. The many centuries of dynamic creativity and internal tensions have been well outlined by modern scholarship.

Judaism in the last two centuries has faced the same kind of cultural and philosophical challenges. It has also needed to adapt. Reform Judaism and, later, Conservative Judaism have followed this path with many internal divergent points of view.

We can trace some of these developments by looking at the changing attitude toward women in the Reform movement. Sometimes this was a reaction to external pressures; at other times internal motivations were at work. We shall begin not with Moses Mendelssohn, but with the abrupt call to modernity issued by Napoleon when he assembled a Sanhedrin in 1806.[1] The very use of this title for the assembly indicated that Napoleon sought to re-establish an old institution and to infuse it with new power. Napoleon wished to propel the Jewish subjects of his vast empire into the modern nation state; it was also an experiment as he was dealing with the smallest religious group and later would face the Protestants with their factions and then the Roman Catholic church. The meeting of the Sanhedrin took place in Paris in 1807; twelve questions were placed before the assembled Jewish dignitaries. The first three dealt with family law and so indirectly with women. Napoleon obviously wished to bring about changes and limit the power of religion; the assembled dignitaries sought to preserve the Tradition and Jewish rights, even while integrating themselves into the broader French community. They avoided the question raised by the title "Sanhedrin;" to do so would have led them into endless debates for which most of the delegates, who were not Jewish scholars, were unqualified. They took the title as honorific and an effort on the part of Napoleon to raise the status of the Jewish community. As Jews in the next generations continued to refer to the assembly as "Sanhedrin," they gave it greater authority than a mere assembly.

The initial question, "Are Jews allowed to marry several wives?" was easily answered by citing the prohibition of Rabenu Gershom against polygamy.[2] The next two dealt with divorce and intermarriage and, of course, were more difficult to answer. The answers were straightforward and did not deal with feminist issues. They show us that the assembled delegates were not concerned with women's rights at all. No women were among the delegates, as was to be expected. The group was eventually dominated by the Orthodox rabbinic representation, especially in matters concerning family law. The document reveals a struggle between modernization and tradition; the issue of women's rights or participation was not on their agenda or, for that matter, on the agenda of Napoleon.

Those who framed the responses were divided into two groups; one was principally interested in equal rights and had no halakhic concerns. On the other hand the rabbis were keenly aware of the halakhic consequences. No halakhic discussions were carried on at the meetings, but the answers, at least in their Hebrew version, were carefully worded to reflect halakhic concerns.

A new type of woman had emerged in the salons of Berlin and elsewhere in the enlightened atmosphere of upper-class Berlin and other cities. These were bright Jewish women, now educated in a western fashion while their husbands were engaged in trading and business ventures with scant attention paid to western culture. The educated wives led salons in which the leading intellectuals of their time met; the salons were gathering places for Jews and non-Jews who assembled to discuss philosophy, literature, science, and art. They represented an initial step into the broader intellectual world.[3] We must remember that these women often became estranged from both their husbands and Judaism and sometimes left Judaism.[4] The numbers of this elite group were very small, and there seemed to be no pressing need for organized Judaism to deal with them. They were, in any case, a group on the periphery of Jewish life, far from the centers of Judaism. Contemporary rabbinic scholars were probably unaware of them or felt that they could be ignored as, after all, they were only women.[5]

The initial steps in the direction of women's equality came from the Reform movement and its founder, Israel Jacobson, who established the first modern Jewish school for both boys and girls in the small Jewish community of Seesen (Westphalia) in 1801 with a new ceremony, Confirmation, which represented graduation and coming of age.[6] The establishment of this school represented a policy decision of Jacobson and his coworkers and was undertaken without any halakhic discussion or any rabbinic participation. The reaction to this effort was mixed, but the opposition also did not base itself on *halakhah*. The effort lapsed with the fall of the Kingdom of Westphalia in 1813; after that no further experiments in religious or Jewish educational reform were possible there. We know nothing more about the education of girls in this period and may presume that none was available.

Somewhat later in Hamburg, we know that the service of the new temple dedicated in 1818 was designed in part to appeal to women, who knew little Hebrew but who could participate in the service, which included some vernacular as well as a German sermon. Forty-three percent of the seats were for women, a much higher percentage than in an Orthodox synagogue.[7] A contemporary scholar, Aaron Chorin, expressed himself strongly that Jewish services should appeal to both sexes.[8] An appeal for the proper education of women was published by Abraham Geiger along with reports on the state of youth education in the various regions of Bavaria, Prussia, Westphalia, and so on,[9] but we are not informed about any positive response. Strangely enough, these educational steps were neither defended on halakhic grounds by the incipient Reform movement nor attacked by the Orthodox. These initiatives got under way slowly.

The first efforts to change the status of women were defended through traditional methods. Enough rabbinic statements permitted the use of the vernacular in prayer and others permitted the education of women. When these matters were attacked, it was more out of fear of what would come next. This was similar to Ezekiel Landau's attack on Mendelssohn's Torah translation. He knew that traditional Judaism could not be opposed in principle but saw it as a dangerous opening to the outside world.[10]

The Pioneers

The first official change, as we have seen, came about through education and Confirmation; the latter eventually raised some mild halakhic objections, as a new ceremony and as an imitation of Christianity, but that was minor compared to the other reforms that were vigorously attacked.

Some of the early Reform prayerbooks omitted the blessing "You have not made me a woman," and this change was discussed by Abraham Geiger who objected vigorously to the traditional explanation that it merely indicated that the male thanked God for the obligations of assuming the commandments.[11] This, however, did not lead specifically to Orthodox opposition, as it was one of many changes in the liturgy that were far more radical: dropping the *musaf* service, eliminating the repetition of the *amidah*, and rejecting virtually all *piyutim*, and others. A thorough review of the fine study by Jakob Petuchowski shows absolutely nothing on this *berakhah*.[12] David Novak, who analyzed this *berakhah* and its meaning subsequently, indicated little interest in this change among the traditionalists when it was made by the early Reform movement.[13] In addition to these liturgical changes, the women's section in various synagogues was expanded to accommodate their regular attendance as happened first in the Hamburg synagogue.

Four rabbinic scholars—Abraham Geiger (1810–1874), Samuel Holdheim 1806–1860), Zacharias Frankel (1801–1875) and Leopold Loew (1811–1875)—concerned themselves with major practical problems and with a theoretical approach to women's issues. Geiger wished to show that the changes in the liturgy that he suggested for marriage and divorce were part of a continuum. He demonstrated that women, despite all short-comings, were treated better in the biblical period than in the surrounding culture and that their condition improved gradually later. The Talmud and subsequent rabbinic literature continued this pattern, albeit with centuries in which there was scant progress. Geiger felt that one could justify changes in the matters of the *agunah*, *halitzah*, and divorce by pointing to major changes that had taken place in the past and that had been prompted by new social conditions in the surrounding society.[14] While Geiger was rabbi of Wiesbaden (1837) he called on his colleagues to make the following changes in the status of women:

1. A declaration of death by the state would be sufficient to free an *agunah*.
2. As soon as the state issued a divorce document, it was to be considered valid even though the husband might refuse to provide the traditional *get* or express willingness to do so only through extortive conditions.
3. *Halitzah* should be removed, abbrogated entirely, and in any case, be deemed unnecessary if the obligated brother could not be found or if his wife objected.

Although Geiger justified a new approach through his progressive reading of the Tradition, he realized that a strict interpretation of the Tradition would not permit any of these changes.[15]

Samuel Holdheim considered all such changes as a radical break with the past and felt that they should be so acknowledged.[16] Holdheim considered Geiger's approach dishonest; revolutionary changes should be proudly proclaimed.[17] Holdheim's book went much further and discussed the entire range of marriage, rabbinic rights versus the civil authority, and the very nature of Jewish marriage. The status of women was to change, as marriage was to consisted of two parts. The civil obligations were enforceable by the state whereas the religious ceremony conducted by the rabbi dealt with the moral and ethical basis of family life. For him *dina demalkhutah dina* governed marriage and divorce, although traditionally this was not so. This was part of Holdheim's struggle to solidly establish the civil rights of Jews and to answer Bruno Bauer and others who asserted that Judaism did not permit a proper allegiance to the state.[18] His lengthy arguments buttressed by numerous rabbinic quotations led to a response by Zacharias Frankel.

Frankel was unwilling to place marriage and divorce into the category of *dina demalkhuta dina* or to consider marriage as primarily an economic act and therefore easily transferable to the state.[19] He considered it unnecessary for Jews to give up their marriage and divorce laws in order to become fully equal citizens of the state. Although also a reformer, he was among the most conservative and wished to preserve as much of the traditional approach to *halakhah* as possible. This was also a judgement of how far it was possible to take the German Jewish communities that were recognized by the government and that consisted of a broad range of opinion. His views became influential, as they were expressed through the rabbinic seminary in Breslau, which he led (1854–1875) and its graduates. Later, Geiger's views were expressed through the *Hochschule für die Wissenschaft des Judentums* in Berlin (1872).

The fourth scholar, Leopold Loew, was rabbi in Szegedin, Hungary. His studies should also remind us of the central role that Hungarian Jews played in the development of Reform Judaism. When the Austro-Hungarian Empire collapsed, this group was forgotten, although it made up a considerable percentage of Hungarian Jews. He approached the status of women in marriage through a series of essays demonstrating how marriage laws and customs had developed through the centuries. He then dealt with modern times and the changes he considered necessary.[20] Loew began with a discussion of Frankel's approach to the various issues and also placed them in the context of the then current Austrian and Prussian laws. He disagreed with Frankel's emphasis on the theological aspects of marriage and the minimization of its contractual obligations. Loew made it quite clear that every Jewish contract contained an ethical element and that this was not limited to marriages. The Jewish formula—*harei at* ... indicated a contract in which Jewish religious obligations were emphasized through the phrase *k'dat moshe veyisrael*; this is in contrast to all other contracts. Loew also used the opportunity to object to the Hassidic practice of placing the burden of economic maintenance on the woman so that her husband could devote himself to studies. He considered this a misguided *pilpul* on the biblical phrase that she was to be his helpmate; of course it also placed the woman in a highly disadvantageous position.[21] Loew opposed Holdheim's radicalism;[22] he also sharply disagreed with the Orthodox rabbinate of Hungary.[23] The essays present a historical overview of marriage, divorce, and associated issues; they show development and so place the role of the woman in a different light, but make no radical suggestions. The last segment of this essay was devoted to responsa; they, however, dealt exclusively with the nature of the rabbinic court, its make-up and its function and so provided an insight into the issues surrounding the modern rabbinate, with state regulations and the taxation of the necessary documents. Loew demonstrated that the *ketubah* (which he translated and annotated) was a fiction as far as the civil authorities were concerned and so neither taxable or enforceable in civil courts; this responsum was intended to eliminate a burdensome tax as was a responsum on *halitzah*. As there was no need to recognize *halitzah* civilly, this document was also not taxable.[24] In a series of essays, Loew sought to raise the status of women through direct statements, responsa, and historic analysis.

These four approaches to women's issues and the subsequent rabbinic meetings were part of the internal debate within Reform/Liberal Judaism. All agreed that changes were necessary, sought different bases for them, but disagreed on now far reaching the changes should be.

Conferences

These discussions involved larger numbers of rabbis and, to some extent, lay leaders. The first rabbinic Conference was held in Brunswick in 1844; both divorce and *halitzah* were on the agenda. Civil divorce was accepted as a precondition for a religious divorce, and both marriage and divorce laws were given to a committee for further study.[25] At the next rabbinic conference, in Frankfurt, in 1845, matters went further, as there was a motion by Samuel Adler that women be considered absolutely equal to men with all religious obligations; this was referred to committee since there was not sufficient time to discuss it thoroughly. They also decided that "modern bathing establishments" could serve as a *miqveh*.[26]

A year later in Breslau (1846) *halitzah* was declared abolished.[27] A six point program was read to the Conference, but owing to lack of time was not passed. It recommended that the rabbinical conference declare women to be entitled to the same religious rights and subject to the same religious duties as men, and in accordance herewith make the following pronouncements:

1. That women are obliged to perform such religious acts as depend on a fixed time, in so far as such acts have significance for our religious consciousness.
2. That women must perform all duties toward children in the same measure as men.
3. That neither the husband nor the father has the right to release from the vow a daughter or a wife who has reached her religious majority.
4. That the benediction *shelo asani ishah* (Praised be Thou, O Lord, our God, who hast not made me a woman), which owed its origin to the belief in the religious inferiority of women be abolished.
5. That the female sex is obligated from youth up to participate in religious instruction and the public religious service and be counted for minyan, and finally,
6. That the religious majority of both sexes begin with the thirteenth year.[28]

In Leipzig in 1869, rabbis met again and moved forward on many issues, recommending that bride and groom exchange rings at weddings; that civil evidence of death be enough to free a woman to remarry; that *halitzah* be changed, if observed at all, so as not to be offensive; that divorce documents be in the vernacular, not Aramaic; that they could be delivered by mail; that a woman might remarry if her husband refused to provide a religious divorce. In other words, civil divorce was to be completely recognized. They also decided that the entire matter of divorce should be reviewed in the interest of equality. In addition, they passed a resolution that dealt with good religious education for both sexes.[29]

Little new was added in Augsburg in 1871, but earlier statements were strengthened, for example, it was suggested that consent be asked of both bride and groom in the wedding ceremony and that rings be exchanged; this had already been the practice for some time in Berlin and Frankfurt.[30] There were further statements on marriage, divorce, *halitzah*, and the *agunah*. The mood of the resolutions was conciliatory. The one on *halitzah* indicated that it did not fit into our time and was no longer necessary, but if someone wished to use it, the rabbis would be willing to oblige.

We do not have detailed minutes of these rabbinic conferences, but only summaries and some echoes in contemporary newspapers and journals. We do not know, therefore, what halakhic considerations may have been raised. The general tenor, however, shows that a revolution had taken place. The assembled rabbis considered themselves legislators and assumed the right to make major changes. If we place these changes in the context of the *takkanot* of previous centuries and the Middle Ages, we must recognize that they were far more radical. Only the decree attributed to R. Gershom eliminating polygamy approaches these changes in the status of women, marriage, and family law.

The assembly Napoleon brought together had been called a Sanhedrin, and it responded as the Emperor wished and did not quibble about the title the assembly had been given.

The rabbinic assemblies did not call themselves a Sanhedrin or raise the endless halakhic issues that such a body would face.

Instead, they simply proceeded as if they were a Sanhedrin, had the power to legislate, and did so in a far broader manner than any rabbinic assembly of the Middle Ages. This pattern has continued in the Reform, Conservative and Reconstructioinist movements. Changes may have been defended halakhically, but they were made within the framework of the right to reinterpret or radically change older Jewish assumptions, both biblical and rabbinic. This has been the pattern of each of these movements for the last two centuries.

North America

This pattern was adopted even more readily in North America. Statements similar to those in Germany were made later at the Rabbinic Conference in Philadelphia in 1869, though it was less conciliatory; they added nothing new and merely clarified matters.[31] The American rabbis were in the fortunate position of serving Reform communities, not congregations in which there were Orthodox minorities as in Central Europe, so they could make decisions much more readily. The last great rabbinic conference before the founding of the Central Conference of American Rabbis was held in 1885 in Pittsburgh. Kaufmann Kohler's (1843–1926) message to the Conference, among other matters, praised women for their charitable and educational efforts and then continued:

> I do not hesitate to claim for myself the priority of the claim for *woman's* full admission *into the membership* of the Jewish Congregation. Reform Judaism has pulled down the screen from the gallery behind which alone the Jewish woman of old was allowed to take part in divine service. Reform Judaism has denounced as an abuse the old Hebrew benediction: 'Blessed be God who has *not made me a woman*,' borrowed from Plato, who, notwithstanding his soul's lofty flights in the highest realm of thought, never realized the high dignity of woman as the co-partner and helpmate of man. Reform Judaism will never reach its higher goal without having first accorded to the congregational council and in the entire religious and moral sphere of life, equal voice to woman with man.[32]

The Conference issued a series of sweeping theological statements that went much farther and were conceived in a much broader manner than those of any earlier conference. Although it dealt with the issues of social justice and mosaic and rabbinic law, it did not in any of these areas mention women or women's rights. Kaufman Kohler did not include any statement on women in his original draft of the "Principles." On several occasions there were references to "man" and in section eight he dealt with the "barriers separating men from men, class from class, and sect from sect. ..." This would have been a perfect place to deal with the issue of women's equality. As we have no detailed record of the discussion, we do not know why it was omitted. Nor were these issues raised in those sessions that treated some very practical questions faced by the American rabbinate.[33]

Each of these last- century rabbinic conferences protected the woman and provided additional rights as well as a status different to the Orthodox tradition; however, without providing either a philosophical or halakhic basis. Traditional authorities were quoted, but no one except Geiger made an effort to build on them.

Many other matters not discussed at all had simply fallen into disuse. *Nidah*, which plays such an important role in the rabbinic literature and also in the responsa, was not mentioned in any of the deliberations. Nor was *miqveh* an item of significance. Some modern synagogues had a *miqveh*, but most did not. In the prayerbooks the offensive *berakhah* was simply omitted or changed in various ways within the *birkhat hashahar*. There was no debate specifically about this *berakhah* for women. The introductions that sought to justify the changes made in the liturgies did not deal with feminist issues at all.

As most women's issues were not contested by the Orthodox, the Reformers did not feel compelled to provide a halakhic defense, in contrast to the issues of praying in the vernacular, using an organ, eliminating prayers or the abbreviating the synagogue service.[34]

The most substantial and visible American change, mixed seating, simply occurred, perhaps first with Isaac Mayer Wise in Albany in 1846, along with a mixed choir used earlier in Europe, without debate.[35] Interestingly, Alexander Kohut, the Conservative rabbi who arrived in New York in 1884 stated that he would not opposed mixed seating if it enhanced the piety of the congregation and if a halakhic basis for it could be found.[36] There was no theoretical discussion of this major change in synagogue worship, nor about the inclusion of women in the minyan. Services were simply held for those present.[37]

Why did these innovations occur in North America and not in Europe? The European reformers had to concern themselves with the attitude of the often conservative governments, which viewed any religious change as a threat to civil stability. Furthermore, they had to work within a communal framework that sought to accommodate everyone. Some changes were possible, radical experiments were not.

North America was different. All the communities were new and not well established, nor was there a huge reservoir of hostile traditionalists in neighboring lands. We might assign some other reasons as well (1) The impatience of the moment. No one wished to move slowly and to debate about minor matters. (2) The feeling that this generation had to make radical changes to accommodate itself to new conditions (3) The American optimism which saw the vision of the ancient prophets close to fulfillment. (4) North America was governed by a bent toward the practical rather than to theories, so a more radical stance could readily be taken. Though we should remember that the first Jewish theology was written by Kaufmann Kohler during his years as rabbi in North America (1917) did not deal with the issue of women and their place in Judaism.

Into the Twentieth Century

The treatment of women in the *halakhah* and in the synagogue were among the major concerns of the early Reform Movement. The changes earlier adopted were accepted and their details worked out in different ways in Europe and North America. This included issues of marriage and divorce, which raised the ire of respondists in Eastern Europe. The attack on these matters was less concerted than on outward changes in the synagogue service. The "organ controversy" stirred more individuals to duel with their pen than the *get*. Orthodoxy seemed to fear the very visible ritual changes more than the changes which affected only a small portion of the population and which would, anyhow always draw some sympathetic reaction even from their own adherents. The tempo of change and the agenda in each of the matters previously discussed were set by the male rabbis with no participation by women.

Surprisingly enough, the Reformers were not among the leaders in the next steps of women's rights. By the turn of the century the major discussion of women's issues dealt with women on the labor market and women's right to vote. The labor movement, especially in New York, had an enormous membership among women in the garment industry. Some of them became radical spokespersons, but they did so outside the synagogue and did not attempt to influence the synagogue. As most came from the new immigrants, they probably did not think along those lines, but neither did the "Uptown" rabbis volunteer to play a major role. They supported "Settlement Houses" and educational ventures, but not feminist issues. Resolutions by the CCAR and the UAHC dealt with these issues in a positive fashion, but they reflect the tenor of the times and were not pioneering efforts.

The Right to Vote

The major battle in the first decades of this century dealt with the right of women to vote. This struggle involved numerous Jewish women, but it did not penetrate synagogue or religious life. Various rabbis spoke in support from the pulpit, but few took an active role in the political struggle. Nor was there a dramatic change in the composition of synagogue boards or the right of women to vote in congregational life. Token women begin to appear on synagogue boards, but the leadership seems to have felt that a Temple Sisterhood was sufficient to represent women.[38] No study of this exists, but looking at the minutes of Rodef Shalom in Pittsburgh and at the statements of the UAHC in the early twentieth century, one finds very little that supported this major effort.

Ordination of Women as Rabbis

An occasional woman led services and preached as did Rachel Frank in California in the 1890s;[39] somewhat earlier Emil G.

Hirsch was the first rabbi to invited women to address the congregation from the pulpit.[40] In 1928 Lily Montagu preached in the Berlin Reform congregation, and subsequently women leaders of the congregations were also invited to share the pulpit.[41]

The first time that women's ordination was debated was following the reading of a responsum on the question in 1922. Its text has been provided in this volume. Its author, Professor Lauterbach of the Hebrew Union College, began apologetically with statements about the high regard that the rabbis had for women, but that they were assigned different roles, and then he provided the usual arguments of tradition. Ultimately, as Moses selected seventy male elders to assist him in judgements, so this pattern continued with no discussion and only occasional references. He then argued that if a change were made, the ordination of the Hebrew Union College would no longer continue the "long chain of authoritative teachers," but would be different from the ordination of all other rabbis. ... It would "create a distinction between the title rabbi, as held by the Reform-rabbi and of the title of rabbi in general."[42] He did not wish to jeopardize the "authoritative character of ordination." Furthermore, he felt that women would not exercise "as wholesome an influence upon the congregation" as men. He concluded that this kind of decision would not be unjust, as numerous other avenues are open to women in the field of education, and so on. This responsum was followed by a lively debate, rare for a responsum, in which many indicated that they favored the ordination of women whereas others, as so often on different issues, argued for caution with due attention to the rest of the Jewish community. Rabbi Neumark, also of the Hebrew Union College faculty, whose daughter had applied to the College for rabbinic training, dealt with some of the Talmudic arguments in detail and demonstrated that they could be seen in a different light.[43] It was some time before the courtesy of the floor was extended to the women who were present. Despite this debate, the responsum stood, and eventually the Board of Governors of the Hebrew Union College found it needed to make no decision, as the single woman candidate who had presented herself no longer wished to pursue this path. In contrast to other issues, the rabbinic assembly did not take action independently.

Just two years later, in 1924 Regina Jonas (1902-1944) registered as a student at the *Hochschule für die Wissenschaft des Judentums* in Berlin. Other women also studied there and in 1932, 27 of the 155 students were female, but only Jonas aspired to the rabbinate. In 1930 she completed her studies along with a halakhic thesis on the topic "Can a Woman Become a Rabbi?" She did not receive ordination as the ordaining professor of Talmud, Eduard Baneth, had just died and his successor, Chanoch Albeck, opposed her ordination. She was, finally ordained by Max Dienemann at the end of 1935. She was readily accepted by her liberal colleagues and through her earnest service, partially by others. The Orthodox opposed the ordination, but did not engage in a halakhic discussion. Jonas had opportunities to emigrate, but refused and was killed in Auschwitz in 1944.[44]

When the Hebrew Union College ordained its first woman student, Sally Priesand, in 1973, it was without halakhic debate. She and hundreds of others began to serve the Jewish community. No halakhic justification was sought and, as with some other North American changes, there was no official resolution, either. When the Conservative movement took the same step some years later, it engaged in a lengthy halakhic discussion that sought to justify the ordination on traditional grounds.[45]

Women's Movement in the Late Twentieth Century

During the last forty years Reform Judaism has willingly joined the feminist movement, but it cannot claim to have led it. Complete equality in congregational leadership had existed in some places but now came more quickly everywhere. The ordination of Sally Priesand and several hundred other women subsequently opened the rabbinate and the cantorate fully to women. The synagogue liturgy has slowly changed to avoid all references to sex. Feminist liturgies have been created as have midrashim that emphasize the role of women. Although Reform Judaism has not been a leader in the broader field of feminism, it has led within Judaism and been a catalyst that has moved even the Orthodox community to some radical changes. So, for example, women *halakhists* are now trained in Israel; they will not function on a *bet din*, but will have a major and influential role in the development of traditional *halahkah* in the future.

Reform Halakhah and Women's Issues

In all of this a halakhic approach to issues became significant again only in the middle of the twentieth century. There was a hiatus between the European proceedings in the nineteenth century and the renewed American interest. The spirit of America and the revolutionary fervor of the rapidly growing Reform movement led away from halakhic considerations. At the end of World War II matters changed. In the volumes *Reform Jewish Practice and Its Rabbinic Background* by Solomon B. Freehof (1891–1990), we find discussions of women and their rights, particularly when connected with Jewish rituals and liturgy. So the status of women, conducting services, reading from the Torah, and other matters were discussed with citations from both the traditional literature and Reform Jewish writings that indicated equality. The same kind of treatment was provided in the vast area of marriage and divorce that covers fifty pages of a slim volume of less than two hundred pages. In other words, the issues formally avoided or discussed only in a vague fashion now came to the fore and were provided with a halakhic basis. For the first time we find women in services as well as women officiating discussed in a thorough fashion in the second volume printed some years later. Although congregational practice may have gone in these directions earlier, these matters were neither officially debated nor provided with any rationale.

As responsa reflect questions asked and not an agenda set by individuals or a group, they accurately reflect the rising interest in women and women's rights within the Reform movement, and also at an earlier time show that neither men nor women raised these issues. Responsa need not be limited to internal Jewish questions but could very well have dealt with some of the issues of the day that involved women: the right of women to vote, the employment of women in various professions, the relationships of men and women within the family, and various other matters. None of these issues, however, were ever raised before the Responsa Committee.

In the 500 responsa written by Solomon B. Freehof and another 500 by me,[46] only a few major women's issues have arisen, such as the ordination of women and nonlineal descent. Some took new directions; others followed the path set by earlier responsa or practices and clarified them. When they dealt with ritual questions like may women recite *kaddish*, read from the Torah, or be counted as part of a minyan, along with other issues, equality was taken for granted and did not need justification.

As we review almost two centuries of the Reform movement, we see that traditional *halakhah* connected with women has sometimes been successfully reinterpreted; resolutions, and popular decisions have been given equal significance and have reshaped the role of women within Judaism. Here as in other movements in Judaism, Reform, Conservative, and Reconstructionist leaders have made dramatic changes through resolutions, *minhag*, and *halakhah*. For our time these have brought major changes to rabbinic Judaism while continuing the path set at its beginning through the creative adjustment to new cultural and intellectual forces by the ancient Pharisees and their successors through two millenia.

Notes

1. D. Tama (F.D. Kirwan (trans.), *The Napoleonic Sanhedrin*, London, 1807
2. Louis Finkelstein, *Jewish Self-Government in the Middle Ages*, New York, 1964, pp. 111 ff.
3. Two generations later figures like Bertha Pappenheim emerged as well as a few forerunners both in Germany and in Eastern Europe, but they remained on the rim of society.
4. F. W. Riemer, *Mittheilungen über Goethe aus mündlichen und schriftlichen und ungedruckten Quellen*, Berlin 1841, pp. 428 f. Michael Meyer, *The Origins of the Modern Jew*, Detroit, 1967, pp. 85 ff.
5. I have not been able to find any reference in the responsa literature of the time to the salons or to the women involved in them. The rabbis were well aware of Moses Mendelssohn and his translation of the Torah into German as he corresponded with some of them. They saw the translation as dangerous, but did not deal with Berlin Jewish life. (Alexander Altman, *Moses Mendelssohn*, Philadelphia, 1973, pp. 376 ff, 382)

6. The records indicate that the school enrolled girls. Michael A. Meyer in his *Response to Modernity*, Oxford, New York, 1988, p. 39f., indicated that although the documents stated that in 1810 girls should were to participate in the Confirmation/graduation exercises, there is no indication that this occurred. Mordecai Eliav, *Jewish Education in Germany in the Period of Enlightenment and Emancipation*, (Hebrew), Jerusalam 1960.
7. Samuel Echt *Die Geschichte der Juden in Danzig*, 1972, in Michael Meyer Op. Cit. p. 408.
8. Aaron Chorin, *Ein Wort zu seiner Zeit*, Vienna, 1820, p. 55.
9. A. Geiger, *Wissenschaftliche Zeitschrift für jüdische Theologie*, Vol. 3, 1837, p. 7.
10. Alexander Altman, *Moses Mendelssohn*, Philadelphia, 1973, p. 382.
11. A. Geiger, *Wissenschaftliche Zeitschrift..*, 1837, Vol. 3, p. 7.
12. Jakob Petuchowski, *Prayerbok Reform in Europe*, New York, 1968.
13. David Novak, *Law and Theology in Judaism*, New York, 1974, vol. 1, 2.
14. A. Geiger, "Die Stellung des weiblichen Geschlechtes in dem Judentume unserer Zeit," *Wissenschaftliche Zeitschrift für jüdische Theologie*, Vol. 3, 1837, pp. 10 ff.
15. Ibid., p. 18ff.
16. Abraham Geiger, *Wissenschaftliche Zeitschrift für jüdische Theologie*, Vol. 3, 1837. Samuel Holdheim, *Die religiose Stellung des weiblichen Geschlechts im talmudischen Judenthum*, Schwerin, 1846, *Ueber die Autonomie der Rabbinen und das Princip der jüdischen Ehe*, Schwerin, 1843.
17. Samuel Holdheim, *Ueber die Autonomie der Rabbinen und das Princip der jüdischen Ehe*, Schwerin, 1843.
18. Bruno Bauer, *Judenfrage*, 1843; also in *Deutsche Jahrbuecher*, 1842.
19. Zacharias Frankel, "Grundlinien des mosaisch-talmudischen Eherecht," *Jahresbericht des juedisch-thehologischen Seminar*, Breslau, 1860, pp. 1–17.
20. Leopold Loew, "*Eherechtliche Studien*", *Gesammelte Schriften*, Szegedin, 1893, Vol. 3. These studies were published from 1860 to 1866 in his periodical *Ben Chananja*.
21. Ibid., p. 28.
22. Ibid., pp. 192 ff. He demonstrated, for example, that Holdheim had omitted a key word in his quote from Moses of Coucy that seemed to permit intermarriage, but did not.
23. Ibid., p. 217, where he dealt with the Orthodox objection to holding wedding ceremonies within the synagogue.
24. Ibid., p. 324.
25. *Yearbook, Central Conference of American Rabbis*, Vol. 1, Cincinnati, 1891, pp. 81 ff.
26. *Yearbook of the Central Conference of American Rabbis*, vol. 1, pp. 92-94.
27. David Philippson, *The Reform Movement in Judaism*, Cincinnati, 1930, p. 219.
28. *Protokolle der dritten Rabbinerversammlung*, Breslau, 1846, p. 265,
29. *Yearbook*, vol. 1, pp. 107–110. David Philipson, *The Reform Movement in Judaism*, p. 298.
30. *Yearbook*, vol. 1, p. 112. Philipson, Op. Cit., 310.
31. *Yearbook*, p. 119.
32. W. Jacob (ed.), "Authentic Report of the Proceedings," *The Changing World of Reform Judaism, the Pittsburgh Platform in Retrospect*, Pittsburgh, 1985, p. 96.

33. Ibid., 111 ff.
34. *Eleh Divreh Haberit, Nogah Hatzedek, Or Nogah, Tzeror Hahayyim, Lev Haivri*, Responsa of Moses Sofer, Judah Aszod, Moses Schick, Hillel Lichtenstein, David Hoffmann, and others.
35. David Philipson, Op. Cit., 335. Mixed seating did arouse some debate in the Conservative movement and the congregations remain split on this issue with the decision left to each congregation. *Summary Index: The Committee on Jewish Law and Standards*, New York, 1994, 9.14.
36. Alexander Kohut, *Ethics of the Fathers*, New York, 1920, pp. 100 as cited in Naomi W. Cohen, *Encouter with Emancipation,* Philadelphia, 1984, p. 181.
37. Only in the latter part of the twentieth century was the matter of a minyan even brought up. Solomon B. Freehof wrote about it, but it was already so much of a set practice that this was not a real issue.
38. National Temple Sisterhood established in 1913.
39. Michael A. Meyer, *Response to Modernity, A History of the Reform Movement in Judaism*, New York, 1988, p. 287;
40. Naomi W. Cohen, *Encounter with Emancipation*, Philadelphia, 1984, p. 198.
41. Wolfgang Hamburger, "Die Stellung des Reformjudentums zur Frau," *Emuna*, Vol. 10 (1975) Supplementheft 1, p. 19.
42. "Shall Women be Ordained Rabbis," *Central Conference of American Rabbis Yearbook*, Richmond, 1922, p. 160.
43. Ibid., p. 175 ff. The resolution which recommended the ordination of women was adopted by the Conference with a vote of 56 to 11. It reads

    "The ordination of woman as rabbi is a modern issue; due to the evolution in her status in our day. The Central Conference of American Rabbis has repeatedly made pronouncement urging the fullest measure of self expression for woman as well as the fullest utilization of her gifts in the service of the Most High and gratefully acknowledges the enrichment and enlargement of congregational life which has resulted there from.

    Whatever may have been the specific legal status of the Jewish woman regarding certain religious functions, her general position in Jewish religious life has ever been an exalted one. She has been the priestess in the home, and our sages have always recognized her as the preserver of Israel. In view of these Jewish teachings and in keeping with the spirit of our age, and the traditions of our Conference, we declare that woman cannot justly be denied the privilege of ordination."

    The resolution, therefore opposed the responsum and both are part of the record, but ultimately the Conference left the matter in the hands of the Hebrew Union College and did not pursue the matter further.
44. A full biography as well as Jonas' rabbinic thesis with annotations and comments has been prepared by Elisa Klapheck, *Fräulein Rabbiner Jonas—Kann die Frau das rabbinische Amt bekleiden,"* Teetz, 2000, pp 24 ff.
45. Simon Greenberg, ed., *The Ordination of Women as Rabbi: Studies and Responsa*, New York, 1988.
46. Solomon B. Freehof, *Reform Responsa*, Cincinnati, 1960; *Recent Reform Responsa*, Cincinnati, 1963; *Current Reform Responsa*, Cincinnati, 1969; *Modern Reform Responsa*, Cincinnati, 1971; *Contemporary Reform Responsa*, Cincinnati, 1974; *Reform Responsa for Our Time,* Cincinnati, 1977; *New Reform Responsa*, Cinnnati,

1980; *Today's Reform Responsa,*, Cincinnati, 1990. Walter Jacob, *American Reform Responsa*, New York, 1983; *Contemporary American Reform Responsa*, New York, 1987; *Questions and Reform Jewish Answersm, New Amnerican Reform Responsa*, New York, 1992; *Halalkhah*, Pittsburgh, (1993- 2000)Vols. 1-7.

Chapter 7

❖ ❖ ❖

PROGRESSIVE HALAKHAH AND HOMOSEXUAL MARRIAGE

Moshe Zemer

In 1997 the Responsa Committee of the Central Conference of American Rabbis decided by a majority of 80 percent that same-sex unions do not qualify as kiddushin, which is the only form of Jewish marriage. In a long and learned responsum published in full in the *CCAR Journal*, the committee decided that a Reform rabbi should not officiate at a ceremony of marriage or commitment between two persons of the same gender.[1] As a member of the committee, I voted with the majority, agreeing with its conclusions and almost all its *halakhic* reasoning. Nevertheless, I decided to write a concurring decision to bring forth certain factors that were not considered in the committee's deliberations. This is neither a critique nor commentary of the responsum, but rather a form of *tosafot* and *hashlamot*.[2]

K'vod Habriot-Human Dignity

We are considering very sensitive matters. They relate to persons who have suffered from discrimination and persecution. They

---

Notes for this section begin on page 168.

are human beings created in the image of God and dedicated Jews. We must, therefore, deal with these subjects in a sensitive way. It might be helpful to recall Maimonides' ruling in a different context. "The Great Eagle" exhorts the *dayan* before making judgment: "Let all of his deeds be for the sake of Heaven, but let not the dignity of human beings be light in his eyes."[3]

Respect for human dignity is one of the foremost qualities required of a judge, a rabbi, and every Jew. Yet, respect for human dignity does not negate ruling according to one's principles, conscience, and understanding of Jewish tradition, which may be contrary to another person's opinions and needs.

Most studies of homosexuality in Jewish tradition emphasize its negative aspects and the prohibition of this practice in the Torah and rabbinic literature.[4] The Torah castigates such behavior in males as one of the forbidden sex relationships (Lev. 18:23, 20:23) and condemns it as an abomination or abhorrence. The rabbinic sages took steps to prevent such forbidden intercourse. They also condemn lesbianism as *peritzut* (licentiousness), even though it was not considered a form of sexual intercourse. These prohibitions have been a consistent aspect of the tradition. This study will not accentuate these negative views of homosexuality in the tradition. Rather, it will attempt to study other aspects of the tradition that would determine the possibility of Jewish religious marriage for same-sex couples.

The Criteria of Progressive Halakhah[5]

There are those who believe that if Progressive and Reform Jews explore the ramifications of halakhah and tradition on current problems, they are succumbing to Orthodoxy. This belief reveals a lack of insight into the chasm between the approaches of these two streams of Judaism to revelation and halakhah. Evolving, modernist halakhah must be founded on reinterpretation of scholarly study of the classic texts of Judaism, which discovers variety, flexibility, and creativity in halakhah and draws on new information derived from archaeological excavations and documents unknown to our ancestors. Rabbi Louis Jacobs explicated: "The ultimate authority for determining which observances are binding upon the faithful Jew is the historical experience of the people of Israel, since, historically perceived, this is ultimately the sanction of the *halakhah* itself."[6]

Serious modernist Jews accept or reject the content of Jewish tradition not because of convenience or caprice, but as a matter of principle, based on their liberal theological understanding of revelation, history, and halakhah. Modernist Jews have a different basic conception of the divine authority of halakhah. The progressive view initiates and supports inquiry aimed at uncovering the latent principles of halakhah and Jewish tradition and then applies them to reach *halakhic* decisions.

This theological position on the divine authority of halakhah, together with a sensitivity to ethical concerns, inner spirituality, and social justice, is the crucial factor in the opinions issued by modernist halakhists. Some of the foremost thinkers of the twentieth century have set forth criteria for *halakhic* decision making and observance of the commandments by modern, non-fundamentalist Jews. Most Orthodox decisors reject these criteria because the very process of choosing and selecting which traditional precepts should be observed is incompatible with the traditional view of the absolute authority of the divinely authored and sanctioned halakhah.[7]

It is incumbent upon us to determine which of these criteria of Progressive halakhah apply to *pesikah* in the case of same-sex marriage. Does Progressive Judaism sanction homosexual marriage?

To resolve this issue we must determine what are the criteria and principles for *pesikah* (decision making) in progressive halakhah that may be applied to such a question. A number of such progressive criteria may help us ascertain the moral and liberal Jewish religious approach to this problem. My contention is that decisions in such important matters should be decided on the basis of these criteria and principles.

Major Thrust of the Tradition

The rules and principles mentioned here may serve as a guide for liberal tradition and halakhah. As with any collection of precepts, these principles will be useful only if we make the effort to delve deeply into our tradition and go beyond a superficial glance and incomplete understanding. Professor Jakob Petuchowski of Hebrew Union College stated:

> In the process of examining the traditional material, one must not remain satisfied with first impressions. Rather should one pursue the meaning of a given observance in the Jewish past. Moreover, since, within a span of four thousand years, the meaning was not always uniformly understood and interpreted, it becomes particularly important to discover the main thrust within this tradition.[8]

If we examine closely the flux of Jewish tradition over the ages, we find that there was always a balanced orientation that emphasized enlightened spirituality and generally stayed clear of extremism. We must find this mainstream in the tradition. It is not enough just to decide what is appropriate for our own community and generation. Tradition is what is passed on from generation to generation and spreads throughout the entire Jewish world.

The first of the criteria, "the major thrust of the tradition," according to Professor Petuchowski, should lead one to pursue the meaning of a given observance in the Jewish past and its main thrust within this tradition. What then, has been the main thrust of heterosexuality or homosexuality within the millennial tradition? Instead of analyzing the many prohibitions and castigation of homosexuality, let us look at the obverse side of this question. What is the approach of the tradition to heterosexuality?

Zugiut

The rabbis accentuated the significance of heterosexual relationships more than they denounced same-sex relations. This may be expressed in the concept of *zugiut*, "coupleness," the quality of being a couple, a sexual or erotic partnership. The term, per se, postdates rabbinic literature, but the concept is prevalent throughout the rabbinic period. We find the view of *normative zugiut* throughout the written Torah and the Oral Law. The story of creation illustrates this phenomenon: "God created the human in his image, in the image of God he created him, male and female he created them" (Genesis 1:27). This specification of the two sexes is not incidental, as we see in the next verse, which presents God's first commandment of procreation to those created in the Divine image: "And God blessed them and said to them: 'Be fruitful and multiply and fill the earth and conquer it'" (Gen. 1:28) This commandment applies only to heterosexual couples.

Almost all descriptions of the family unit in the Bible include a reference to parents of both sexes. Thus we find in the Decalogue, "Honor your father and your mother"[9] and in the Holiness Code: "One must revere one's mother and father."[10]

The normative family in Jewish tradition consists of a heterosexual couple with children, from Adam and Eve through matriarchs and patriarchs, Abraham, Isaac, and Jacob with Sarah, and Rebecca, Rachel, and Leah. This is also the recorded tradition in the talmudic, gaonic, medieval and modern literature. Heterosexuality is the rule in the entire Jewish tradition.

Procreation

The first commandment of God, the Creator, to his human creatures is to imitate him by engaging in creation or, more specifically in procreation. This form of *imitateo Dei* is obviously meant exclusively as a mitzvah for a heterosexual couple. The fulfillment of this first commandment serves as a precedent for other mitzvot of the Torah. The rabbis claim that those who fulfill these commandments "are crowned by Scripture as partners with God in the work of creation."[11]

Furthermore, the Torah spells out the passage of the couple from the nuclear family to their new family: "Hence a man leaves his father and mother and clings to his wife, so that they become one flesh" (Gen. 2:24). Rashi interprets "one flesh" to refer to "the child created by both of them in whom their flesh becomes one."[12]

Procreation by these human creatures is an essential aspect of creation. A couple becomes united in the conception of their offspring in which both share. Man and wife cling together emotionally and physically and spiritually. This is not merely a sexual act, but the continuity from one generation to another by bringing into life their offspring. The couple leaves the parental home and establishes its own family.

The Tradition emphasizes again and again the utmost significance of sexual reproduction. According to the Midrash, "God said I created the world only for the sake of procreation, as it is written (Isaiah 45:18) 'God who formed the earth and made it, he did not create it as a waste, he formed it to be inhabited.'"[13]

A number of heterosexual couples, of course, are unable to bring children into the world. Their number is relatively small when compared to fertile couples. The Torah and the halakhah go according to the majority. Today, these infertile couples may seek medical assistance through artificial insemination, In-vitro-fertilization (IVF), or adoption.

Gays and lesbians claim that they also fulfill the mitzvah of procreation in a similar fashion by means of medical science or adoption. The vast majority of heterosexual couples are able to reproduce naturally, and this was the intention of the Torah commandment to be fruitful and multiply to bring children into the world. Medical aid to reproduction was developed as an alternative to the natural process. In most of these techniques the ova of the wife and sperm of the husband are used. Even though the process is artificial, in most cases the genetic makeup of the children is that of their father and mother. It is a genetic family. Lesbians might rely on the donation of sperm by a stranger or friend outside the family circle. Same sex families can never be fully genetic.

Scientists indicate that the rate of success in conception and childbirth by artificial means is much less than in natural sexual intercourse. According to this finding, same sex-couples, on the average, will have fewer children than heterosexual parents.

In order to have children, of course, these techniques can be used only by lesbians, whereas homosexual men are limited to adoption. The resulting childbearing may be relatively small. More than two decades ago there was a widespread debate about the world population explosion and the threat of world wide famine. Political leaders concerned about the dangers of wide spread starvation encouraged society to adopt the policy of zero population growth.

When this proposition was discussed in Jewish communities, the conclusion of the majority was that after the Shoah, the Jewish people could not afford to limit its numbers. On the contrary, it was considered a mitzvah to bring into the world a large Jewish family.

Kelal Yisrael—Responsibility to the Covenant Community

Most of the fundamental principles for evaluating the mitzvot and deciding which should be observed, like internalizing the commandments and heeding the voice of individual conscience, relate to the individual's struggle between soul and heritage. There comes a moment, nevertheless, in the observance of the commandments when Jews are called upon to express their sense of responsibility to their people, to the Covenant Community, or *kelal yisrael*. A Jew cannot live a full Jewish life alone. Many precepts can be performed only in public as part of a community, in a prayer quorum or *minyan*, in the synagogue, and at home. For citizens of Israel there is also the community of the Jewish state, which adds the responsibility of observing special precepts, such as defending our homeland and serving our people, as well as other civic obligations, which in Israel assume the character of mitzvot.

Beyond the individual, then, there is *kelal yisrael*, which includes all Jews wherever they live. Each of us bears responsibility for the entire nation; we are all responsible for one another. We must observe certain precepts for the good of the collective even when we have personal reservations about them. This is another criterion for the observance of mitzvot.

Accordingly, we must all ask ourselves not only whether a particular precept is compatible with our individual world view, but also whether observing it would harm or strengthen the Jewish people as a whole.

Rabbi Petuchowski has written that "everything ... which contributes to the survival and to the unity of the Covenant Community of Israel must be regarded as a religious commandment. Everything, on the other hand, which hurts the Covenant must be avoided. Bearing this perspective in mind, the Reform Jew will observe many a *mitzvah* toward which he might feel no personal obligation, because it is not a matter of the individual only [but] also of the community as a whole."[14]

Following this principle, our *halakhic* decisions must take account of more than just ourselves and our synagogue, community, and movement. We must be aware of their ramifications for *kelal yisrael*. When dealing with issues relating to marriage and personal status, to the physical and spiritual welfare of Jews that do not share our views, and to the relations between Jews of the Diaspora and Israel, we must be mindful that we are one people. In spite of diversity and severe conflict, we are all of us bound by that contractual covenant that our ancestors, and we ourselves, made with the God of Israel.

When the North American Reform movement makes a radical decision to abandon a basic tenet of the Jewish heritage relating to marriage, it does not affect its own constituents alone. The Reform, Liberal, and Progressive congregations and movements in Europe, Israel, South Africa, Latin America, and Australia are affected.

Most of them are in the midst of large Orthodox communities, who take advantage of such activities in North America to denigrate the local Liberal Jews. The example of the Progressive rabbis and congregants in Israel is especially difficult. Not only are they fighting for the recognition of Reform conversions, including those from North America, but they have been appealing for the right to officiate at marriages. The fact that their colleagues will officially marry gays and lesbians will weaken their case not only with the intransigent Chief Rabbinate, but also with a large portion of secular Israelis and very possibly with the courts. If same-sex marriages are performed by American Reform rabbis, it will harm the struggle of their Israeli colleagues to attain the right to officiate at weddings and conversions.

We must, therefore, consider the needs of *kelal yisrael,* not only the Orthodox and Conservatives, who are in religious opposition to this step, but the secular and especially our own Progressive, Liberal, and Reform rabbis and lay people, who suffer because of these unacceptable marriages. *MARAM,* the Israel Council of Progressive Rabbis, has researched and studied this issue Its rabbis have decided not to officiate at same-sex marriages or ceremonies.[15]

The Scope of Same-Sex Marriages

When we deal with questions relating to homosexuality and lesbianism, one puzzle that appears to remain unsolved is the dimensions and extent of this phenomenon. How many gays and lesbians are there in a particular society? Is this a widespread social issue? Furthermore, what is the proportion of Jewish homosexuals in relation to the entire Jewish population? It would appear that no such census has been taken. How many of these constitute permanent couples?

The Kinsey Report, published in 1948, had been the basis of the statistical assumption that about 8 percent of the adult population is homosexual. Kinsey actually concluded that 8 percent of men were exclusively homosexual. A half century later in 1994 *The New England Journal of Medicine* analyzed a number of scientific studies published independently, that concluded that 2 percent of men were currently exclusively homosexual.[16] There are no statistical data on lesbians. We have no data on the sexual orientation of Jewish males. The most reasonable conjecture is that the percentage of Jewish homosexuals is about the same as that of the general population, namely, 2 percent. The question remains: How many of these homosexuals are involved in a committed, coupled relationship? The answer would undoubtedly be a small proportion of the Jewish population, perhaps 1 percent or less. Coupled gays or lesbians therefore appear to constitute an extremely small portion of the Jewish population. How would Jewish law and tradition react to such a situation?

In several instances the halakhah was not clear to the sages. In one such case we learn: "Rabbah bar Hanin asked Abaye: 'What is the legal ruling?' Abaye said to him: 'Go and see what is the accepted practice of the people.'"[17] What is the accepted practice of the vast majority of the Jewish people today? There is no doubt that the accepted practice is heterosexuality.

A Matter of Choice?

One of the controversies surrounding the phenomenon of homosexuality is whether it is based on a free choice or a compulsory orientation. Are they the way they are because of nature or of nurture? The report of the CCAR Ad Hoc Committee on Homosexuality and the Rabbinate indicates that members of the committee held two major opposing views on the origin and nature of sexual identity: 1) Sexual orientation is not a matter of conscious choice but is constitutional and therefore not subject to change; and 2) Sexual orientation is a matter of conscious choice.[18] Learned studies have produced contradictory conclusions that are similar to these above.

A member of the Responsa Committee claimed that "we tend to regard homosexuality as an orientation, as the product of a complex of causational factors which render it, like heterosexuality, a part of one's psychological makeup rather than the result of a conscious choice on the part of the individual."[19] Yet the same person that made this statement quotes the conclusions of the ad hoc committee "that the scientific community lacks unanimity on this question and that the very definition of sexual orientation depends largely upon the interpretations and constructions which various disciplines and groups place upon that group." He notes that there is vast scientific literature on the nature and causes of human sexual orientation, but we are not qualified to judge the scientific character of this material.[20]

Other researchers have completely different conclusions. Widespread psychiatric research has shown that homosexuality is reversible as a matter of personal choice. He bases his conclusions such research.[21] These studies may raise questions for those who claim that concessions should be made to homosexuals and lesbians in officiating at religious marriage ceremonies, because they have no choice.

Not a few gays and lesbians claim that homosexuality is their preferred, legitimate lifestyle along with or, perhaps, instead of heterosexuality. This seems to be a matter of free choice. They have chosen a gay or lesbian lifestyle. This seems to fit in with the Rambam's view: "Every human being may become ... wise or foolish, merciful or cruel; penurious or generous; and so with all other qualities. There is no one that coerces him/her or decrees what he/she is to do, or draws him/her to either of the two ways; but everybody turns to the way which one desires, spontaneously and of one's own volition."[22]

The Struggle Against Discrimination

As we discuss the possibility of a gay rite of marriage, it will be helpful to study the development of gay rights, both in society at large and within the Jewish community. We note with satisfaction that there has been a considerable improvement in the status of gay men and lesbian women in this last century. Not long ago homosexual relations between consenting adults were considered a criminal offense. In 1895, Oscar Wilde was put on trial in the Old Bailey of London and was convicted of "acts of gross indecency" with other men. Mr. Justice Wills immediately sentenced Wilde to two years imprisonment with hard labor.[23] Today, such a criminal trial and sentence would be unthinkable. In most countries homosexual acts have been decriminalized, but in others they remain on the legislative books, including in certain states of this Union.

Homosexuality was once considered a mental illness. In 1973, the American Psychiatric Association decided by a majority vote to remove the definition of homosexuality as a sexual perversion from the association's *Diagnostic Statistical Manual*.[24] Discrimination against gays and lesbians has been rampant in matters of employment, housing, rights of insurance, inheritance, and survivors' benefits, to mention but a few areas. Court decisions, legislation, and executive orders have, at times, helped homosexuals in their struggle for full and equal civil rights.

In other instances, judges, legislators, and even the President of the United States have ruled against them. For the most part, successes in their struggle were due to the initiative, leadership, and determination of gays and lesbians, many of whom were assisted by heterosexuals that identified with their cause. In spite of the obstacles and homophobia, an impressive list of accomplishments has been achieved by gays and lesbians to improve their lot. No matter what one's views may be, the progress through self-help, political pressure, legal action, and public relations aimed at convincing the "straight" community, has been very impressive.

In spite of the obstacles and homophobia, an impressive list of accomplishments was achieved by gay and lesbians to improve their lot. The UAHC and CCAR have fought for gay rights over the years. Following is a partial list of their accomplishments:

1. In 1977, they called for the decriminalization of homosexuality.

2. In 1987, they supported the inclusion of gay and lesbian rights;
3. In 1990, they supported the ordination of gay and lesbian rabbis.
4. In 1993, they called for legislation that would grant spousal benefits to lesbian and gay partners in a committed relationship.
5. In 1996, the CCAR passed a resolution supporting the right of lesbian and gay couples to share fully and equally in the rights to civil marriage, to oppose governmental efforts to ban gay and lesbian marriage. The CCAR decided that this is a matter of civil law and is separate from the question of rabbinic officiation at such marriages.

Five gay synagogues have been founded from coast to coast in the United States: is this a variation of "separate, but equal?" or a form of "landsmannschaft" in our movement? Jews used to separate themselves by the country of their origin or their vocation; my grandfather would *daven* only in the *Litvisische Schul* (Lithuanian synagogue); a relative was married in the Furrier's Synagogue in New York.

Gays and lesbians are welcome to all services and functions of our synagogues, as well as to regional and national activity. They are welcome to join our congregations and to participate in all their activities, both religious and social. If they prefer, they have the opportunity of joining any of the five gay/lesbian synagogues from coast to coast affiliated with the UAHC, which has welcomed them to its midst and membership. The Reform movement has done as much or more than any other Jewish religious body to further the civil and religious rights of gays and lesbians.

Commitment Ceremonies

Many gays and lesbians have expressed a desire to have their unions sanctified with a commitment ceremony. What is the origin of this custom? It certainly is not a Jewish ceremony. We know that the Christian clergy has introduced these ceremonies for the commitment of gay or lesbian couples in churches.

The Responsa Committee has received many requests to affirm the use of creative, private religious ceremonies. Some of these have no roots in Jewish tradition or theology. A *mohel* was asked to officiate at the *berit milah* of the child of a mixed marriage. The mother is Jewish, the father a believing Catholic. They have requested that the child have a *berit* and then be baptized. The child is to be educated in both religious traditions.

The responsum, given by Walter Jacob, stated that the circumcision and synagogue education would only lead to the confusion of the child. The *mohel* is not to proceed with the *berit*.[25]

In another situation, a rabbi, who serves a New England community, has received a request to participate in the annual ceremony of "blessing the fleet" with the Christian clergy of the area. After a thorough analysis, this interfaith ceremony, was revealed to be a sort of Christian ritual, and finding that there is no precedent for blessing things in Jewish tradition, the Responsa Committee responded in the negative.[26] We can understand from this that not every creative ritual and ceremony may be accepted as properly Jewish.

Nevertheless, if a same-sex couple and the rabbi must choose between a same-sex marriage or a commitment ceremony and cannot avoid either alternative, they should choose the latter. The marriage ceremony can be considered a violation of Jewish Law; the commitment ceremony might be prohibited because it gives the appearance of a wedding ceremony. Neither has any justification in Jewish law and tradition. Of the two, the wedding ceremony is a more serious violation of Jewish law.

The Rabbi, the State and the Marriage

A Reform rabbi and a professor posted the following on the Hebrew Union College alumni internet forum: "However, the fact remains that in New York State, among others, it is against the law. to perform a gay/lesbian marriage. If I perform one, I am breaking the law. If I perform some other sort of ceremony which appears to be a wedding but in fact is not a wedding, I am giving the appearance of breaking the law. These are not, in my thinking, trifling matters."[27]

Rabbis should check the ramifications of such marriages in the state or country in which they serve. The license to marry is received from the state. Does this fact carry any responsibility to the law of the state that forbids or does not recognize the marriage? As of this writing, no state of the Union has enacted legislation permitting the marriage of a same-sex couple. A number of acts and ordinances have been passed to grant certain rights and measures of equality, but no nuptials. Thirty states have passed or are in the process of enacting legislation to prevent same-sex marriages from being performed either in their jurisdiction or elsewhere.[28]

Perhaps the greatest stumbling block to gay marriage was the passage of a bill in the United States Congress entitled the Defense of Marriage Act, which was signed into law in 1996. Among its provisions of this Federal Bill is Section 7: "In determining the meaning of any Act of Congress, or of any ruling, regulation, or interpretation of the various administrative bureaus and agencies of the United States, the word "marriage" means only a legal union between one man and one woman as husband and wife, and the word "spouse" refers only to a person of the opposite sex who is a husband or a wife." The House passed the Defense of Marriage Act on July 12, 1996 by an overwhelming 342–67. The Senate followed suit on September 10, by a vote of 85–14. President Clinton signed it into law.[29]

Some European countries have passed legislation to establish the status of same-sex couples. In 1989, Denmark became the first country to legalize same-sex unions. Although the legal ceremony creates a legal bond, it is not the same as marriage between men and women; gay and lesbian couples were not granted access to adoption, artificial insemination, in-vitro fertilization, or church weddings. The other Nordic states more or less followed the Danish precedent. No European country has fully recognized gay marriage, even those countries that arrange for an official domestic union for the couple.

What about the above question of the New York rabbi who asked whether he may marry such a couple in a state where it is prohibited. Solomon B. Freehof dealt with a question about a different matter, which nonetheless reveals a similar principle. An elderly couple who were living together asked a rabbi to officiate at their wedding without registering it with the civil authorities.

If they were formally married, their joint Social Security would be reduced.

Freehof raises the question:

> Is the Rabbi violating the state law by officiating for a couple who do not have a marriage licence? I have received various legal opinions on this matter. The majority opinion seems to be that it is a violation of the law so to officiate. ... Since this marriage ceremony is being conducted without a license for the purpose of evading or contravening the just and legal regulations governing Social Security, such an arrangement must be deemed illegal, even from the Jewish point of views. ... The marriage in question may, however, be an illegal action by the Rabbi who officiates, if the law of the state requires recording the information of every marriage conducted.[30]

What is a Valid Jewish Marriage?

A valid marriage is one of an unmarried couple of a Jewish man and woman for whose union there is no prohibition in Jewish law. Gays and lesbians are not the only ones unable to contract a valid Jewish marriage. A mixed couple of a Jew and Gentile may not have a Jewish wedding. An adulterous Jewish couple, where one member is still married to another person, may not be joined in matrimony. Furthermore, incestuous couples may not be married. In all these cases the explanation is *ein ha-kiddushin tofsin* (There is no marriage—it does not take hold). The wedding ceremony has no significance and the marriage is null and void. When there is a valid marriage, there exists *havaya* between the couple. This refers to a legal and spiritual binding between the pair. This is the legal status of marriage, which is broken only by divorce or death.[31]

Many lesbians and gays prefer not to have *kiddushin* because of the heterosexual character of the ceremony. A few scholars tend to denigrate this ancient rite. Eugene Mihaly sharply criticized a statement of a group of rabbis who equated *kiddushin* with sacred matrimony. In his view, "*kiddushin* is clearly a rabbinic metaphor and refers to a man's acquisition of a woman through an act of appropriation ... We must not translate *kiddushin* as 'sacred Jewish marriage.'"[32] He goes on to elucidate: "Since the *kiddushin* basically consists of the man giving the woman a *perutah* (the smallest copper coin) in the presence of two qualified witnesses, while he recites the appropriate formula. In this way the woman is acquired."[33]

From this analysis Professor Mihaly draws the following conclusions: traditional halakhah, however, sees marriage primarily as an act of acquisition by the man, as a *kinyan*, a commercial transaction, with the woman as a passive object in the process."[34] This view of *kiddushin* as primarily a business deal has been repeated in recent years with the claim that this betrothal no longer exists in our day. There was indeed an aspect of acquisition in *kiddushin* at an early stage of Jewish law. Bet Hillel determined that a woman may be betrothed with a *perutah*, the smallest coin of the realm, whereas Bet Shammai insisted on a silver *denar* worth 200 times as much.

Nonetheless, it is my claim that Bet Hillel, by allowing kiddushin to be effected with the smallest possible coin, in reality eliminated any financial or acquisitional aspect of the ceremony and converted into a symbolic act.[35] There has not been a commercial feature in *kiddushin* for millennia, nor is there in our day. *kiddushin* remains the holy bonding of a Jewish man and woman.

Mark Washofsky, the chair of the Responsa Committee summed up the majority decision, which defines "Jewish marriage" as kiddushin: That concept, whether understood according to its traditional terms or its Reform interpretation, is a legal institution whose parameters are defined by the sexual boundaries that Jewish Law calls the *arayot*. Homosexual relationships, however exclusive and committed they may be, do not fit within this legal category; they cannot be called *kiddushin*. We do not understand Jewish marriage apart from the concept of kiddushin, and our interpretation of rabbinic authority does not embrace the power to "sanctify" any relationship that cannot be *kiddushin* as its functional equivalent. For this reason, although a minority disagree, our majority believe that Reform rabbis should not officiate at ceremonies of marriage or "commitment" for same-sex couples.[36]

That is the position of this paper, which follows the criteria and principles of Progressive *Halakhah*, as well as the major thrust of our tradition, which does not sanction homosexual marriage.

We have seen that normative *zugiut* from biblical to modern times has been heterosexual. We indicated that the mitzvah of procreation is almost exclusively fulfilled by heterosexual couples, whereas gays or lesbians may have offsprings only with difficulty. *Kelal yisrael*, the Covenant Community, means being concerned for Jews abroad, especially Progressive rabbis in Israel, whose struggle to officiate at marriages and conversions will undoubtedly be harmed by their colleagues in North America marrying two men or two women. We demonstrated the uncertainty of a compulsive orientation that might justify such action. For these and many other *nimmukim*, I concur with the decision of the CCAR Responsa Committee, that Reform rabbis should not officiate at ceremonies of marriage or "commitment" for same-sex couples.

Notes

1. "On Homosexual Marriage," *CCAR Journal*, winter, 1998, pp. 5–35, (written by the Chair of the Responsa Committee, Mark Washofsky).
2. Addenda and complementa.
3. *Hilkhot Sanhedrin* 24:10.
4. The Responsa Committee (decision *supra*, note 1) mentions some of these negative aspects (pp. 8–11), while showing more positive sides (pp. 12 f.).
5. For the sources of this section, see Moshe Zemer, *Evolving Halakhah,*, Vermont, 1999, p. 37 ff.
6. Ibid., p. 44.
7. Ibid. p. 45.
8. See Jakob J. Petuchowski, *Heirs of the Pharisees*, New York, 1961, p. 174.
9. Exodus 20:12 and Deuteronomy 5:16.
10. Leviticus 19:3.
11. See *Shabbat* 119b, Ibid. 10a; *Mahzor Vitry* 328; *Responsa Jacob Weil* 191 and *Responsa Divrei Rivot* 361, among the many sources of this saying for different *mitzvot*.
12. Ibid., Rashi commentary.
13. S. Buber, ed., *Midrash Tanhuma*, Warsaw, 1878, *Parashat B'reishit* 26.
14. Ibid., pp. 177–179.
15. See Zemer, *supra*, note 5, 53–55.
16. R.C. Friedman and J.I. Downey, "Homosexuality," *New England Journal of Medicine*, October 6, 1994, vol., 131, no. 14, pp. 921–931.
17. *Eruvin* 14b; See Rashi to *Berakhot* 45b.

18. *CCAR Yearbook*, vol. 100, 1990, 109–110. 57 51.3, pp 159 f.
19. Supra note 1, p. 12.
20. Ibid.
21. Nathaniel S. Lehrman, "The Reversibility of Homosexuality," *Midstream*, April, 1998, pp. 30 f.
22. *Hilkhot Teshuvah* 5:2 .
23. H. Montgomery Hyde, *Famous Trials, Oscar Wilde*, Middlesex, 1962, pp. 222–273.
24. *American Journal of Psychotherapy*, 1978, 32:414.
25. Walter Jacob, *Questions and Reform Jewish Answers*, New York, 1992, #109, p. 173
26. W. Gunther Plaut and Mark Washofsky, *Teshuvot for the Nineties*, New York, 1997,
27. HUCALUM, Digest 239, 29 November, 1999 (copied in another digest).
28. In December, 1999, the Supreme Court of the State of Vermont made a precedent- making decision in favor of three same-sex couples who had appealed in 1977 for the right to a recognized marriage. The judges did not give a verdict recognizing homosexual and lesbian marriages, but they made it clear to the Vermont legislature that it has the following choice: either to give full recognition to such states of matrimony or to establish a comprehensive arrangement of "domestic partnership" that would give them the same rights as married couples.
29. Internet, Thomas Legislation.
30. Solomon B. Freehof, *Contemporary Reform Responsa*, Cicinnati, 1974, pp. 100–103.
31. *Kiddushin* 5a; *Yevamot* 13b.
32. *Teshuvot on Jewish Marriage*, Cincinnati, 1985, p. 40.
33. Ibid. pp. 29–30.
34. Ibid. pp. 40–41.
35. Moshe Zemer, *Journal of Reform Judaism*, Spring 1988, p. 32.
36. *CCAR Journal*, Winter 1998, p. 29.

Chapter 8

❖ ❖ ❖

REFORM JUDAISM AND SAME-SEX MARRIAGE
A Halakhic Inquiry

Peter S. Knobel

This paper seeks to explore the question of whether same sex marriage would be permitted under a liberal understanding of *halakhah*.[1] Since the CCAR Responsa Committee has published a long and complex responsum on the topic and has concluded that rabbis should not perform ceremonies of commitment either under the rubric *kiddushin* or even under an alternative designation, this paper is in part a response to this conclusion. The analysis here, however, depends on the lengthy analysis of Reform Judaism and marriage.[2] To clarify the issues I wish to begin with some methodological considerations.

The current debate about same-gender marriages or commitment ceremonies is part of a broader discussion of the methodology of Reform Jewish decision making and its relation to or its lack of relation to *halakhic* process. Is there a difference between how we respond individually and how we respond collectively? Is there a place for sustained intellectual debate about crucial issues, that will have an influence on our personal deci-

---
Notes for this section begin on page 180.

sions? The Responsa Committee of the CCAR—under Rabbis Walter Jacob, W.Gunther Plaut and now Mark Washofsky and the Freehof Institute of Progressive *Halakhah* has been one of the most significant venues for these discussions. In my view, the seriousness of this enterprise requires that those who differ with their conclusions offer a sustained rebuttal. Judaism is essentially about reading sacred texts, seeking God's will in these texts, and applying these insights to Jewish living.

In an important paper entitled "Culture Wars," Prof. Mark Washofsky, chair of CCAR Responsa Committee, analyzes the current debate in Reform Judaism about proper methods of decision making. He identifies himself as "a text-and-tradition type." He assumes that "text-and-tradition types" will inevitably conclude that same-sex marriages or same-sex commitment ceremonies are not permitted in Reform Judaism. He writes:[3]

1. *The acknowledgment of particularity.* We text-and-tradition types discuss questions of Jewish practice from the assumption that there is something identifiable that can be called Jewish practice. This something is a particular phenomenon, one which has emanated from the historical experience of a particular religious community which we call Israel. While it is imaginable that the Jews might have developed different religious institutions, different concrete means by which to respond to the call of the divine, they in fact came up with *these,* the particular observances which make up what we know as the tradition. Thus, in the case before us, we must begin our thinking with the fact that while marriage is a universal social institution, the particular form of marriage which has historically prevailed among the Jews is called *kiddushin* and that there is no such thing as Jewish marriage other than *kiddushin*.[4] While it is theoretically possible that an alternative form of Jewish marriage might be created today, such theoretical possibilities do not provide the point of departure for our discussions for we begin our religious conversation from within the parameters of that which is and has always been *Jewish* practice, the religious way of life of a particular people.[5]

2. *The valuation of our particular tradition.* This particular people, moreover, is our people, and its particular religious tradition is an integral element of our own Reform Jewish religious life. Unlike some of those folks who speak the other languages I have described today, text-and-tradition speakers do not assume a stance of objective neutrality (let alone skeptical distance or scornful hostility) toward the particular traditions that have

come down to us. While we are liberals and while we stand ready to criticize those aspects of the tradition which can no longer function in our religious universe, we do not start our thinking by identifying the "good" with the "contemporary," as though the latter were a litmus test of Jewish legitimacy. We do not understand ourselves as essentially modern (or postmodern) people who are ready to accept a traditional practice only to the extent that it fits into a system of religious value that is already hewn from the stone of contemporary thought. *Lehefekh:* we see ourselves as essentially *Jewish* people who are willing to introduce changes into traditional practice when this becomes necessary.[6] This difference in stance is a significant one: while some others begin their discussions with no great sense of commitment toward preserving tradition, we seek to validate and to incorporate traditional practice into our lives whenever we can. We assert the primacy of the particular over some abstract, universalizable notion of religious value. To use someone else's theological language, we might call this a preferential option for the traditional[7]. What makes a practice Jewish, in this view, is the very fact that we have inherited it from the Jewish past, that it has been Jewish for longer than a few days, and that this practice has a venerable record of service within the concrete life of a people that has regarded that life as an exercise in holiness. True, the tradition arose in times and within cultural contexts much different than our own, but this does not make it our enemy, something other and alien to us. When the traditional practice seems to endorse immorality or oppression, we believe that it is better to make adjustments or to find new interpretations (which more often than not already exist in the sources) than to junk the whole system. For example, if the classical conception of *kiddushin* involves the legal and economic subjugation of women, we would prefer to look upon our own marriage institution as a an egalitarian *perush* on the traditional one, in which the woman sanctifies the man in the same way as the man traditionally sanctifies the woman, rather than to declare that the time has come to invent a new institution of Jewish marriage.[8] For such a new institution, whatever its advantages over the old, is unavoidably and entirely a creation of our own, and not something we have inherited from the Jewish past.[9]

3. A *language of text and sources.* Once we acknowledge that Jewish practice is a *particular* phenomenon, and once we value the tradition as a positive thing and the appropriate starting point for our thinking, it follows that the language we use to express our religious consciousness ought to be the language that has traditionally been used to express it. These are the texts and sources of our sacred literature, including the halakhic literature, which has always occupied a central position in Jewish

religious talk. I repeat that I do not want to engage here the theological debate over the question of *halakhah's* authority, or any authority, for that matter, over the individual Reform Jew. I want simply to emphasize that the very way we vocalize our approach to marriage and to all other religious issues is not through the use of grand but essentially empty slogans as *betzelem elohim* or *ve'ahavta lere'ekha kamokha*,[10] and not through a stance of critique whose terminology is borrowed wholesale from Kant, Hegel, Nietzsche, Marx, Freud, or Foucault.[11] Rather, our language is a traditional one; its grammar, syntax, and vocabulary are the texts of those books that have served as our sources of value and argument for many centuries. We read these texts, to be sure, as Reform Jews, a community that has fully experienced and endorsed modernity. The perspectives we can bring to *halakhah*, we immodestly assert, constitute a vital contribution to the history of its interpretation. With all that, however, the language we use to verbalize our understanding of religious practice is the language of text and tradition. And the primary difference between us and others is that we want to speak this language and have trouble defining our work as Jewish unless we manage to speak.

When you take this approach and speak this language, you tend to construct your world differently than do others. Let us take as an example the issue of *kiddushin*. Some Reform Jews argue for the abandonment of *kiddushin* as the proper designation for marriage in our communities, on the grounds that we in fact abandoned that Rabbinic institution long ago. As proof for this assertion, they will cite the fact that we Reform Jews, at least in the United States, will accept a civil divorce as sufficient for remarriage. If we no longer demand a religious divorce, the argument goes, then we have already rejected the Rabbinic understanding of marriage, *kiddushin* as a legal-halakhic institution, replete with its civil and financial connotations.[12] We have transformed marriage into a spiritual and emotional union. Yet this argument by no means describes the theoretical basis on which our forbears actually decided to dispense with the requirement for *gitin*. As they reasoned it, divorce in Jewish tradition has always been a matter of civil rather than religious law; as such, since Jewish law can accept the validity of the civil actions of a non-Jewish court, a decree of divorce under the secular law is valid for us according to Jewish law as well. In other words, although our predecessors initiated a far-reaching change in Jewish religious practice by recognizing the validity of civil divorce, they justified this change by using halakhic language. They explained their action, however revolutionary it seemed, not as a revolution at all but as a move fully consistent with the theory and rhetorical style of the Rabbinic legal tradition.

In the passage above, Professor Washofsky has described clearly what is at stake. It is the nature and method of Reform decision making. Decisors using the same method may, however, come to different conclusions. It is the responsibility of those who wish to introduce new understandings or new practices to do so from within rather than outside the vocabulary and style of halakhic decision making.[13] The CCAR Responsa Committee has produced a masterful document "On Homosexual Marriage 5756.8," which says: "A Reform Rabbi should not officiate at a ceremony of marriage between two persons of the same gender, whether or not this ceremony is called by the name *kiddushin*." A minority of the committee disagreed and said "A Reform rabbi may officiate at a wedding or commitment ceremony for two homosexuals, although for important historical and theological reasons that ceremony should perhaps not be called *kiddushin*."[14] The responsum makes clear that same sex marriage is a complex and difficult issue. It tells the reader at the outset: "We discovered we were no longer talking *to* or even arguing *with* each other, rather we were conducting a series of parallel monologues in place of the dialogue that has served us so well in the past one."[15]

Before proceeding to the substance of my argument, it seems important to delineate the principle within halakhah itself that grants the *posek* authority to make changes and the warrants for those changes.

Menachem Elon, in his comprehensive work on Jewish law, writes about the authority of contemporary decisors to determine the law in a different manner from the past.

Thus was established and accepted the fundamental principle of decision making in Jewish law: The law is in accordance with the view of the later authorities. It should not be thought that this principle diminished in any way the respect later generations accorded to earlier generations. It was precisely this respect that induced the later authority responsible for declaring the law to ponder his own decision earnestly, fearfully, and humbly, because he was aware that he was dealing with a question already considered by the earlier authorities. Nevertheless, when he finally reached his conclusion his view, and not the view of the earlier authorities, became law. [16]

The contemporary decisor, or in our case, the Responsa Committee, must carefully weigh the decisions of prior generations and "ponder earnestly, fearfully and humbly," but ultimately the decision lies in the hands of the contemporary sage either to uphold the past or to rule differently.

The task of determining and fashioning the halakhah was entrusted to the halakhic authorities of every generation, to perform according to the tradition they possessed and according to their human reason and intelligence. The halakhic authorities that constituted an integral part of the general community and whose own lives were affected by the problems of their generation, were authorized to examine the previously existing halakhah in the light of their own later circumstance; and their decisions established the law. In this way, the halakhah continued and developed. Linked to and interwoven with current life and problems, it guided at the same time was shaped by contemporary life.[17]

Our contemporary intellectual, social, ethical, scientific, and economic environment is part of the equation. Our decisions are in response to the problems engendered by the context in which we live. In the case of our attitudes toward homosexuality, there has been a dramatic change over the last two decades. Homosexuality has been uprooted from the categories of sin and illness and been replanted as sexuality identity.[18]

Dorff and Rossett offer the following observation: significant changes in Jewish law sometimes come through outright revision, but more often they were produced by shifting the weight according to varying constructions of precedents.[19] Reform Judaism has for more than a century been revising its marital halakhah. For the last two decades we have been reevaluating our position on homosexuals and homosexuality. The discussion about same-sex marriage or commitment ceremonies should be understood as the latest step in a long and complex process. The issues have been considered not only by the rabbinate, but by the Union of American Hebrew Congregations.

Joel Roth, in his book *The Halakhic Process A Systemic Analysis,* describes in detail the authority of the *posek* and various factors that inform a decision. In the Orthodox community the *posek* is an individual, and in the Reform and Conservative movements a committee of experts plays the same role. The book clarifies systemic principles of legitimate change within the halakhic system.

The authority of the decisor is extensive: In the most extreme instance this principle applies, *peiamim she bittulah shel Torah zehu yesodah* (sometimes the abrogation of Torah which is its foundation). As Roth writes, "when the ultimate goals of the Torah would be better served by its abrogation, even in its entirety, it is within the purview of the sages to take that step." The circumstances that might warrant such action are never defined. In the final analysis, the determination of the need for such action lies with the sages themselves. As Moses rendered the decision on his own, so too must the sages make the decision on their own.[20]

Another important systemic principle for making a change is *et laasot la-donai heferu toratekha.* Roth notes sages amended or abrogated norms in order to strengthen the Jew's commitment to the will of God.[21] He cites Rashi on *Berakhot* 54a s.v.*ve-omer*. There are times when we abrogate (*she-mevattelin*) the words of the Torah in order to act for the Lord. ... It is permissible to violate the Torah and to do what seems to be forbidden."[22]

The sages used medical and scientific sources to change the law. What counts is the specialist's expertise. It is a matter of record that the number of matters of law in the first sense stipulated in the talmudic sources and contradicted either by the expert scientific opinion of later ages or by the personal observation of later sages has produced many problems. How could it be that the talmudic sages had been mistaken? Surely it was not reasonable to suppose that the talmudic sages had misperceived their own reality. It was more reasonable to surmise that the reality had changed, and once it became acceptable to make such a claim, medical and scientific sources that might result in the abrogation of previously held legal norms could be introduced without impugning the reliability or integrity of the talmudic sages. A new systemic principle referred to as *shinnui ha- ittim* ("a changed reality") became the vehicle that enabled later sages to make use of new medical and scientific knowledge without vitiating the smooth functioning of the halakhic system.[23]

Roth further writes: If new medical/scientific evidence indicates that a norm no longer applies to a majority of cases, and the norm itself was ground in earlier medical and scientific evidence that it did apply to a majority of cases, the extralegal sources allow the reopening of the question of the factual basis upon which the norm was predicated. In such a case, the extralegal sources allow the norm to be overturned by the claim of *shinnui ha-ittim* if the evidence is strong enough.[24]

New information can also alter the meaning of a text. Archaeological, historical, and philological research is used to analyze a text. Such an analysis can potentially reveal that the text has been misunderstood. The goal of the critical study of rabbinic texts is to discover the *peshat* of each statement, comment, and question in a passage, and then to establish the *peshat* of the entire passage. If the end product of such an analysis results in an interpretation different from the interpretation of the passage offered by the classical commentators or from that codified by the codifiers, its legal status is the same as that of another interpretation or a variant reading, and carries with all the options that we have seen new interpretations and variant readings to provide a *posek*. And, obviously, the greater the degree of certainty the new interpretation is in fact the *peshat,* the less will bet he hesitancy of the *posek* to employ his systemic rights.[25]

In claiming that he understands the *peshat* of a statement better than any of his predecessors, a modern scholar would be doing no more than those sages who have claimed that, had some earlier sage had access to knowledge to which the later sage has access, the earlier sage would have retracted his view.[26]

The prohibition of same sex intercourse is mentioned twice. "Do not lie with a male as one lies with a woman; it is an abhorrence."[27] If a man lies with a male as one lies with a woman, the two of them have done an abhorrent thing; they shall be put to death;[28] their blood guilt is upon them.[29]

The CCAR responsum analyzes these passages as follows: In both cases the prohibition appears as part of a list of forbidden sexual acts, (incest, adultery, relations with a menstruating woman, and sex with animals) associated with the customs of the Canaanite peoples whose land is assigned by God to Israel.[30] Indeed, the Canaanites have defiled the land by committing these abhorrent acts (*to-eivot*; 18:26, 30) and the land, as it were, cooperates with God's plan by "spewing" out its offending inhabitants to make way for the Israelites (18:24ff, 20:22ff). The Torah admonishes Israel to keep far from these practices and instead to observe God's statutes, which are a source of life (18:5) and holiness (20:7–8, 26).[31]

Rabbinic literature adds relatively little to this legal material. The Talmud contains few mentions of overt homosexual acts and no reports of executions carried out as punishment. We cannot determine how prevalent homosexual behavior may have been in the society of the time. At any rate the rabbinic sources, which we use as the building blocks of our own textual conversation, imply that the phenomenon was either not widespread, or successfully hidden or suppressed. Thus, although Rabbi Yehudah forbids a lone unmarried male from pasturing a beast and two unmarried males from sleeping together under a common blanket, the *hakhamim* permit these practices, because "Jews are not suspected of homosexual relations and of buggery." On the other hand, one who avoids even *yihud* (being alone together) with another man or a beast is deserving of praise.[32]

It is clear that sages had no concept of sexual identity. The Torah and the rabbis prohibited a particular sex act. This act performed between a male and female was emblematic of marriage and therefore prohibited to those who are not proper marriage partners. In addition, the identification of homosexuality with Canaanite and Egyptian practices suggests that the rabbis connected homosexuality with idolatrous practices.

Sexual orientation is a new category.[33] Rabbinic literature does not have a concept of sexual orientation. It deals with permitted and prohibited sexual behavior. The Torah prohibits male-male intercourse and makes no mention of female-female sexual contact. Joan Friedman, points to a passage in *Yevamot* 76a. Since R. Huna said: Women who practice lewdness with one another are disqualified from marrying a priest. And even according to R. Eleazar, who stated that an unmarried man who cohabited with an unmarried woman with no matrimonial intention renders her thereby a harlot, this disqualification ensues only in the case of a man; but when it is that of a woman the action is regarded as mere obscenity.

And the following passage from Maimonides *Yad Issurei Bi'ah* 21:8 says: It is forbidden for women to commit lewdness with one another. This is one of the "practices of Egypt" concerning which we were warned, as it is said. "You shall not copy the practices of the Egyptians. Said our sages, What did they do? A man would marry a man and a woman, or a woman would marry two men." (*Sifra* to Lev. 18:3) Even though this practice is forbidden, they do not impose flogging as a penalty since it does not have an explicit prohibition of its own and no intercourse is involved. Therefore they are not disqualified from a marriage to a *kohen* on the grounds of being considered a whore, nor is a woman prohibited to her husband if she has done this, for this is not a matter of *zenut*. But it is appropriate to flog them for rebelliousness for violating this prohibition. And a man should take care that his wife does not do this and should prevent women that are known to engage in such practice from coming to visit her or her, going to visit them.

Friedman writes: "Throughout the rabbinic discussion there is no evidence of any awareness of such a phenomenon as *sexual orientation* among either men or women. A married woman engaging in lesbian relations is seen simply as a woman engaged in illicit sexual acts—not as someone whose entire sexual and emotional being draws her to seek intimacy with women rather than men.

In fact it would be no exaggeration to say that the conceptual framework within which we understand sexuality and sexual relations is irrevocably different from that of our tradition. The chasm between them is as wide as the Enlightenment. ... We cannot simply start quoting *halakhic* sources without stopping to ask ourselves about the context of these sources and its implications for their relevance.

The responsum continues: "To the extent that the sources offer a rationale for the Toraitic and rabbinic condemnation of homosexual behavior, we find that the concern over the breakdown of marriage, the bearing of children, and "normal sexuality," the proper and accepted relations between the genders, figures prominently. The Talmud explains that the prescription that the male shall "cleave unto his wife" (Gen. 2:24) comes explicitly to prohibit homosexual intercourse; that is to say, homosexual behavior threatens marriage and childbirth."[34] Bar Kaparah offers an agadic etymology for *to- evah*, the biblical term for "abhorrence": *toeh atta bah*, "you go astray after it.[35] The fourteenth-century Spanish commentator R. Nissim b. Reuven Gerondi explains: "One abandons heterosexual intercourse *(mishkevei isha)* and seeks sex with males."[36] That is to say, since sexual union is traditionally expressed within the context of marriage, the indulgence in homosexual intercourse is destructive of this most basic unit of society and community.[37] This theme continues in the medieval *Sefer Hachinukh, mitzvah* 209:

God desires that human beings populate the world He created.[38] Therefore, He has commanded that they not destroy their seed through acts of unnatural intercourse which do not bear fruit (that is, children). These acts violate not only the commandment of marital intercourse *(mitzvat onah)* but also every standard of sexual propriety, since by its nature homosexual intercourse is despised by every person of reason. Thus, the human being, who was created to serve his God, should not bring shame upon himself through such disgusting behavior. And for these reasons the rabbis prohibited a man from marrying a barren woman or one who is past childbearing years.[39]

From the sources cited by the Responsa Committee, the major concern of the rabbis seems to be that homosexual activity will be nonprocreative, and will prevent men from marrying and women from marrying and producing children. Some of the most tragic family circumstances created by forcing gays or lesbians to live straight lives and marry has been the pain caused to spouses and children when gays and lesbians can no longer pretend to be heterosexual. In a society that accepts gays and lesbians, they will not feel compelled to be what they are not. The *mitzvah* of *peru urevu* (procreation) is limited to males.[40] In Reform Judaism the *mitzvah* would equally apply to males and females. We have also come to recognize that some people genuinely ought not be parents, and therefore we have limited the *mitzvah* to those who are physically and psychologically capable of performing parental duties. The issue of procreation is complex. New reproductive techniques, however, are being used with increasing success to overcome the problems of infertility. Artificial insemination has become a relatively common technique. Males are faced with a more difficult ethical dilemma, but surrogate motherhood[41] and adoption are possibilities. There are issues of gestational, genetic, patrilineal, and matrilineal parenthood. They are complex but not insurmountable issues.

Rabbinic teaching considers celibacy unnatural. It is not he who marries who sins; the sinner is the unmarried man who "spends all his days in sinful thoughts." (*Kid*. 29b).

Notes

1. "The term halakhah, is also used to signify the process which legal conclusions are reached. To this end the term refers to all the factors that use or that might be considered by a *posek* before rendering his *pesak* (decision). When these factors are expounded together with the resultant norm, it rarely appears clear or definitive. It is rather complex, ambiguous, and replete with ground for disagreement." Joel Roth *The Halakhic Process a Systemic Analysis*, New York, 1987, p.1.
2. Peter Knobel, "Love and Marriage Reform Judaism and *Kiddushin*," W. Jacob and M. Zemer, *Marriage and Its Obstacles in Jewish Law*, Pittsburgh, 1999, pp. 57 ff.
3. I have chosen to quote an extended section of Prof. Washofsky's statement because of the profound esteem in which I hold him. His knowledge of texts and clarity of thought make him one of the most important voices for those of us who believe that Reform halakhah is not an oxymoron. The text is taken from an unpublished paper and I am grateful to the author for permission to quote it.
4. Prof. Washofsky assumes that Reform Jews use the term *kiddushin* in the same way that traditional Jews use the term. I have argued in "Love and Marriage Reform Judaism and *Kiddushin*" that although we still use the term *kiddushin* for marriage we have altered its meaning. We have changed the halakhic paradigm; we reject its origins in property law, and we reject its patriarchal nature. Although on a superficial level Reform marriage and traditional marriage appear to be the same, they are really different. I find myself convinced by the halakhic case made by Rachel Adler in her groundbreaking book *Engendering Judaism*. Marriage as we understand It is *Brit Ahuvim* an egalitarian covenant of lovers.
5. We cannot begin this discussion de novo as if Reform Judaism had not previously modified Jewish marriage law. Reform Jews have in very decisive

ways changed the meaning of *kiddushin,* and the real question is, given the changes, does it still constitute *kiddushin* in any meaningful sense of the term as used by tradition? Or to put it another way do Reform Jews and the "tradition" use the terms differently and therefore, following a Reform definition of *kiddushin,* same sex marriage would be legitimately included.

6. This is a very important point. The question is whether such a time has arrived. *Halakhic* change often takes place gradually. In the body of the paper, I will argue that the halakhic process provides for significant change when there is a social, moral economic or scientific breakthrough that makes it appropriate. Reform decisors are more self-conscious than Orthodox decisors in their use of extra-halakhic considerations to change the halakhah. We have often ignore the halakhah when we make changes than offer a halakhic justification for the change. Prof. Warshofsky's paper "Reinforcing our Jewish Identity: Issues of Personal Status," *Central Conference Of American Rabbis Yearbook,* 1994, describes the competing narratives that dominate Reform decision making.

7. Simeon Maslin, in the introduction to *Gates of Mitzvah* argues that the burden of proof is not on the one who wishes to preserve prior practice, but upon the one who wishes to make the change.

8. From a halakhic perspective mutual *kinyan* is no *kinyan.* "*Processes in which both parties are active participants are explicitly rejected.* The man must take and the woman must be *taken.*" Rachel Adler p. 176: Egalitarian marriage is a new institution or at least a very significant modification of an older institution. Judith Hauptman in her book *Rereading the Rabbis: A Woman's Voice* makes it clear that there are trends within rabbinic Judaism to mitigate the partriarchal character of marriage but at best they make of women second class citizens. She points to precedents, that, if they had been adopted, would have made even more profound changes in favor of equal rights for women. "The changes they (the rabbis of the Talmud) made and, in particular *the direction in which they were headed* makes them fitting precursors for us. As we face our own problems with the practice of Judaism today, we can turn to the rabbis of the Talmud for solutions. They laid the groundwork and pointed the way. ... In the Talmud , women seemed content with gaining a measure of control within a patriarchal system. Today armed with the knowledge that Jewish law is open to change, women are likely to seek to become full-fledged members of the Jewish community." pp. 247–249.

9. If we move from property law to partnership law we may be creating something new but we are doing it within the framework of "tradition."

10. Here I disagree. These phrases need not be empty slogans. They have halakhic implications, and they have a history of usage with Reform Judaism that also constitutes a portion of the "tradition." Modern philosophers are part of the cultural backdrop that affects the reading of texts. We cannot pretend they do not exist. Their authority for us may be limited and we may choose consciously to reject their language but Reform Judaism is itself a product of modernity and inhabits a postmodern reality. These intellectual trends are part of the apperceptive mass of our constituency. We seek what might be described as a "Maimonedean synthesis."

11. These thinkers and others provide a cultural backdrop which has halakhic significance. The works of Rachel Adler, Judith Plaskow, Daniel Boyarin, and Howard Eilberg-Schwartz probe the rabbinic mind and culture that reveal to us rabbinic conceptions and biases.
12. We have modified but not rejected *kiddushin*. The question of *gitin* is complex, but the essential point is that the rejection was based on halakhic language. The challenge of those who reject *kiddushin* as a proper paradigm for Reform Jewish marriage or who would included gay and lesbian marriage within the *kiddushin* paradigm is to use "halakhic language" and to make it consistent "with the theory and rhetorical style of the Rabbinic legal tradition."
13. Such arguments are important only to those understand Reform Judaism within the general rubric "rabbinic Judaism."
14. CCAR Responsa Committee "On Homosexual Marriage" 5756.8, p. 1 I have indicated in my paper cited in footnote 1. Whether Reform marriage halakhically should be considered *kiddushin,* is questionable. And if, in fact, it is not would we not be better to use a new name and a new ceremony. There are immense difficulties with this suggestion. One of the most important is the acceptance of such a change by ordinary Jews and whether it will be a *pithon pe* for the Orthodox.
15. Ibid., p. 1
16. Menachem Elon, *Principles of Jewish Law,* Philadelphia, 1994 p. 272.
17. Ibid, p. 273.
18. The majority of psychiatrists and psychologists have accepted the APA decision to remove homosexuality from its official list of pathologies. See citations provided by Bradley Artson in his "Enfranchising the Monogamous Homosexual: A Legal Possibility A More Imperative," *S'vara* Vol .3 #1, 1993 p. 19. Some health professionals still do not agree with the decision. Reform and Reconstructionist Judaism and liberal Protestants have been explicit in the acceptance of gays and lesbians. More conservative Christians and Orthodox Jews still maintain that homosexual behavior is a sin.
19. Elliot N. Dorff and Arthur Rosett, *A Living Tree the Roots and Growth of Jewish Law,* New York, 1988. p .224.
20. Roth p. 180.
21. Ibid. p. 171.
22. Ibid. p. 172
23. Ibid. p. 237.
24. Ibid. p .244.
25. Ibid. p. 373.
26. Ibid. p.3 74 The historian Shaye J.D. Cohen writes, "The sort of homosexual relationships which we are encountering more and more frequently in our society and about which you are speaking, that is stable monogamous loving relationships between adults of equal status—relationships of this kind were unknown in antiquity ... Consequently we may assume that the rabbis of antiquity did not know and therefore were not addressing, this type of homosexual relationship." Artson, " Enfranchising," p. 22.
27. Lev. 18: 22

28. See M , *Sanhedrin* 7:4, *BT Sanhedrin* 54a-b, and *Yad, Isurei Bi'ah* 14, the penalty is *sekilah,* or "stoning" according to its particular halakhic form (M. *Sanhedrin* 6:4).
29. Lev. 20:13.
30. Footnotes 30, 31, 32 are quoted from the CCAR Responsum. Male homosexual intercourse features as one of the wicked deeds of the Sodomites (hence, "sodomy"; Gen. 19:5) and of the Benjaminites in Gibeah (Jud. 19:22). In addition, the *kadesh* or male prostitute (I Kings 14:24, 15:12; 11 Kings 23:7) proscribed in Deut. 23:18 may have provided male homosexual intercourse; this, at any rate, is how the Talmud *(Sanhedrin* 54b) interprets the verse, although Targum *Onkelos* reads it differently.
31. Rabbinic tradition, however, affirms that male homosexual intercourse *(mishkav zakhur),* like the other *arayot,* is forbidden to Gentiles as well; *Sanhedrin* 58a-b; *Yad, Melakhim* 9:5.
32. The concept of holiness is here identified with that of *distinctness,* of separateness from other peoples and their way of life (20:24, 26), a theme to which we shall return below.
33. " It is only in our generation that homosexual behavior has been found to involve not merely a single overt act or series of such acts, but often to reflect a profound inner condition and basic psychic orientation, involving the deepest levels of personality." Hershel Matt as cited by Bradley Artson, "Gay and Lesbian Jews: An Innovative Jewish Legal Position," *Jewish Spectator*, Winter 1990–91 Vol. 55, #3, p. 6.
34. Footnotes 34–39 are cited from CCAR Responsum; *Sanhedrin* 58a. Note Rashi's comment to the next part of the Genesis verse, "And they shall become one flesh." " a child is created by both male and female and it is in the child that her flesh. becomes one."
35. *Nedarim* 51a.
36. Ran, 5a, s.v. *to'eh atta bah*.
37. See also *Gen. Rabah* 26:5 and *Lev. Rabah* 23:9: the generation of the Flood was destroyed because they wrote wedding contracts for males and animals.
38. See *Gitin* 4 1 b and *Arakhin* 2b: the world was created only for the sake of the commandment "be fruitful and multiply", as it is said (Is 45:18), "He did not create it for waste, but formed it for habitation."
39. *Yevamot* 6lb-62b; *Yad, Ishut* 15:7. A dispute exists in the literature as to whether a man ought to continue to try to beget children even after he has fulfilled the Toraitic *mitzvah* of procreation. Rambam holds, at least as a matter of Torah law, that one who has fulfilled this commandment may then marry a woman who is not capable of bearing children.
40. *Yevamot* 65b *Kiddushin* 34b-35a.
41. I have certain reservations about how women are recruited as surrogate mothers which may lead to the exploitation of poor women.

Part Two

❖   ❖   ❖

SELECTED REFORM RESPONSA

These responsa on gender are a representative selection from more than one thousand American Reform responsa published in the twentieth century. We are grateful to the Central Conference of American Rabbis and the Hebrew Union College Press for permission to reproduce them.

Reform Judaism and Divorce

American Reform Responsa, New York, 1983, # 162

Walter Jacob

QUESTION: What is the traditional Jewish attitude toward divorce? What is the Reform attitude toward divorce? Is a *get* necessary before remarriage can occur?

ANSWER: Judaism looks upon divorce with sadness (*Git.* 90b; San. 22a), but recognizes that it might occur. It makes divorce easy and simple when the parties are no longer compatible, in keeping with the Biblical statement (Deut 24:1–2). According to the Talmud, divorce could be given by a man for virtually any reason, even the most minor one (*Git.* 90a). This was subsequently restricted according to the decree of Rabbenu Gershom (Finkelstein, *Jewish Self-Government in the Middle Ages*, pp. 29ff; *Shulhan Arukh, Even Ha-ezer* 119.6). A divorce always originated with the husband, and the wife accepted the document. A court could force the husband to give a divorce, and a man might be punished and imprisoned for his refusal to give a divorce; this remains true in in modern Israel. If he remains unwilling after punishment, nothing further can be done (*B.B.* 48a; *Yad, Hil. Erusin* 2:20; Amram, *Jewish Law of Divorce*, pp. 57ff; Schereschewsky, *Dinei Mishpahah* 285ff). There are also certain circumstances under which a court may demand a divorce, although neither one of the parties involved has requested it. The detailed reasons for a divorce have been codified in the various early codes and in the *Shulhan Arukh, Even Ha-ezer* (1.3; 11.1; 39.4; 70.3; 76.11; 115.5; 134; 154.1–7, etc.). The actual procedure and the document of divorce have been surrounded by many restrictions in order to ensure their complete validity. The procedures have been prescribed in greatest detail (*Shulhan Arukh, Even Ha-ezer* 119ff). The various problem areas have been treated extensively by Rabbinic law; for example, the mental incapacity of the husband or wife, the disappearance of the husband, or his presumed death. In these instances and in ordinary divorce, Orthodox law has found itself in a difficult position, for only the man can actually grant a divorce, and if he is unwilling or unavailable there is little that can be done.

As divorce proceedings frequently involve a great deal of bitterness, the husband may be unwilling to provide a religious divorce (*get*) along with the civil divorce unless a large payment or some other concessions are made. Sometimes a religious divorce is stipulated as part of the arrangement in a secular divorce. The Conservative movement has sought to remove itself from this predicament by including a special statement in its marriage document. It provides for authority of a rabbinic court to grant a divorce in cases where the husband is unwilling to do so or if he becomes unavailable (Isaac Klein, *A Guide to Jewish Religious Practice*, pp. 98f). This kind of ante-nuptial agreement, as well as other possible solutions, have been suggested by various traditional scholars (Freiman, *Seder Kiddushin Venisuin*; Berkovits, *Tenai Benisu-in Uveget*), but they have met strong opposition among other Orthodox authorities.

The limitations of the Orthodox procedure for granting a divorce are, therefore, quite clear. In theory, divorce should be easy to obtain; in practice, the stipulation that only a male may initiate the proceedings, the lack of enforcing power of the Jewish court and the many details necessary for the procedure make the *get* virtually unobtainable for many women.

The Reform Movement, since its inception, has concerned itself with the problems of both marriage and divorce. The matter was raised at the Paris Sanhedrin in 1806, when it was asked whether divorce was allowed and whether civil divorce would be recognized. It was clearly stated that a religious divorce would only be given if a valid civil divorce had preceded it (M.D. Tama [Kirwan tr.], *Transactions of the Parisian Sanhedrin*, 807, pp. 152ff). This statement weakened the status of religious divorce, although that was not the intent of the respondents.

The Brunswick Conference of 1844 appointed a committee to look into all the questions connected with marriage and divorce. They reaffirmed the Paris statement that marriage and divorce were subject not only to Jewish law, but to the laws of the land in which Jews reside. Although various reports and motions were presented to the rabbinic conference in Breslau in 1846, as well as to that of Leipzig in 1869, none of these resulted in any definite action. In 1871, in Augsburg, another commission was appointed to study the matter and to bring definite recommendations to a further meeting (*CCAR Yearbook*, Vols. 1, 2, 3). Holdheim had earlier suggested that divorce be eliminated entirely from the set of Jewish proceedings and that civil divorce simply be accepted (Holdheim, *Über die Autonomie der Rabbinen*, pp. 159ff). This was the point of view the Philadelphia Conference of 1869 accepted, with only Sonnenschein and Mielziner expressing the sentiment that the *get* should not be entirely abolished, but should be modified in some form (Mielziner, *The Jewish Law of Marriage and Divorce*, p. 135), a view Geiger also held (S.D. Temkin, *The New World of Reform,* p. 61). The resolution of the Philadelphia Conference remained somewhat unclear, as it permitted the rabbinic court to look into the decree of the civil court and reject some grounds for divorce.

The discussion of divorce continued at later rabbinic conferences, but without any formal action being taken. Generally, the civil decree was simply accepted (*CCAR Yearbook*, Vol. 23, p. 154; Freehof, *Reform Jewish Practice*, vol. 1, p. 106). One might say that this is in keeping with at least one talmudic decision, as quoted by Ezekiel Landau when he stated that the *get* is really a matter of civil law (*Dinei Mamonot* in *Noda Biyehuda, Even Ha-ezer* 114, based on Yev. 122b). Kaufmann Kohler, in his discussion of the problems of marriage and divorce and their relation to civil laws, recommended that civil divorce be recognized as long as the grounds for such divorce were consonant with those provided by previous rabbinic tradition (*CCAR Yearbook*, Vol. 25, pp. 376ff). His recommendations were heard by the Conference, but not accepted in any formal manner. Technically, of course, the child of a woman (and possibly a man) that has remarried without prior religious divorce would be considered illegitimate (*mamzer*). Such a child would, according to Orthodox law, be considered unlawful and akin to one born of an incestuous or adulterous relationship (*Mishnah, Kid.* 111.12; *Kid.* 49a; *Shulhan Arukh, Even Ha-ezer* 4.2). This was the attitude taken toward Karaites until recently. In fact however, nothing the Reform or Conservative Jews do can avoid this possible predicament. It does not matter to the Orthodox authorities whether we simply recognize civil divorce or proceed to initiate our own form of *get*. The latter would also not be recognized by them.

The entire matter of divorce has come up a number of times again more recently. Several Canadian congregations have decided that they would provide a *get* in a somewhat modified form, as have the Reform (not the Liberal) congregations of Great Britain. Petuchowski has suggested that an appropriate *get* be instituted by the Reform Movement in keeping with the spirit of Jewish tradition, i .e., both the consecration of marriage and its dissolution should have religious forms. Others have stressed the psychological value of a religious divorce.

At the present time, the Central Conference of American Rabbis makes no provision for a religious divorce and civil divorce is recognized as dissolving a marriage by most Reform rabbis.

A Reform *Get*

Walter Jacob, Questions and Reform Jewish Answers, New York, 1992 # 233

Walter Jacob

QUESTION: Should Reform Rabbis issue a formal document of divorce *(get)*? Should we consider the document in the new *Rabbis Manual* to be a *get*? (Morton Cohen, Los Angeles, CA; Karen Silverman, New York, NY; Michael Smith, Pittsburgh, PA)

ANSWER: An earlier responsum entitled; "Reform Judaism and Divorce" (W. Jacob (ed) *American Reform Judaism* # 162), provided the historical background of the divorce proceedings. It did not, however, deal with the technical problems of a *get*. This decision should supplement the previous responsum.

The *get* became important traditionally because of the question of *mamzerut*. In other words, the child of a union with a "married" woman or one otherwise forbidden would be placed in jeopardy and it is important for such an offspring to assume the status of its parent's marriage.

As we look at the entire area of divorce in the North American Jewish Community, we must ask ourselves what alternative paths are open to us. We can simply follow the procedure of the past, acknowledge civil divorce. This will continue to be appropriate for a large number of individuals, however, some individuals now desire a religious act to finalize the separation. It is religiously and psychologically satisfying to both parties

We might seek a uniform solution for all groups, Reform, Conservative, and Orthodox so that the document would be universally recognized. That is a praiseworthy goal, but with the current mood of the Orthodox community may be unattainable. Perhaps some liberal Orthodox would be willing to work out a compromise, but it would not satisfy the rest and so it hardly seems worth the enormous effort.

It might be easier to establish a common basis for divorce with the Conservative movement or a mutual recognition of each others documents. This process would best be initiated in specific communities. That would provide working models and might lead to a greater understanding of the actual needs rather than satisfying the theoretical claims of each movement.

As we return to summarize the history of divorce within the Reform movement, we see that various rabbinical conferences and synods of the last century in Germany and in the United States tried to deal with the question of divorce alongside other problems. In the Paris Sanhedrin of 1806, the decision of those assembled was that no religious divorce would be granted unless a valid civil divorce had preceded it (N. D. Tama (ed.) Kirwan (tr.) *Transactions of the Parisian Sanhedrin* 1807, pp. 152 ff.). This decision has been adopted by all groups within Judaism in every modern country. The Liberal synod, which gathered in Leipzig (1869), passed a number of other resolutions on this issue. They were favored by most of those present including Abraham Geiger. It was agreed that the religious divorce needed to be simplified and that (a) it should be given as soon as a civil divorce had been settled; (b) rabbis should make an effort at reconciliation before a civil divorce is filed; the document of the divorce should be brief, in the vernacular, and presented to both parties; (d) the religious divorce should be granted even if one of the parties objected; (e) the woman may remarry even if she has no divorce; (f) a divorcee may marry a *kohen* as may a proselyte. *(Yearbook Central Conference of American Rabbis* vol. 1, pp. 106 ff.) The question of the equality of the sexes in matters of divorce was to be discussed at a later synod (Ibid. 108).

The synod held in Augsburg in 1871 established a committee to deal with divorce. It was to report at a future meeting, and one of the concerns expressed was the equal treatment of both sexes. No later meeting was held.

In the United States, divorce was discussed at the Philadelphia Conference of 1869 which declared that divorce was a purely civil matter and needed no religious steps whatsoever. Therefore, a *get* was not necessary. A rabbinic body should, however, investigate the conditions under which a divorce had been given to ensure that they also meet the criteria for a Jewish divorce. At that meeting in Philadelphia two rabbis, Sonnenschein and Mielziner, felt that the *get* should be modified rather than completely abolished, a point of view expressed somewhat earlier by Geiger.

It has been the general position of the Central Conference of American Rabbis to follow the stand taken by Kaufmann Kohler who recommended that civil divorces be recognized as long as the grounds for such a divorce were in keeping with the rabbinic tradition *(Central Conference of American Rabbis Yearbook,* vol. 25 pp. 376 ff.). The matter, however, never came to an official vote within the Conference.

The Orthodox rabbinate of France in 1907 suggested that a civil divorce decree annulled the marriage and the woman would be released and free to marry according to Jewish ritual subsequently. This suggestion, which was attacked by Orthodox authorities throughout the world, is much akin to Reform Jewish practice (A. H. Freiman, *Seder Kidushin Venisuin*, p. 390).

In 1924 the Orthodox rabbis of Turkey proposed a "conditional marriage" to solve the problems of divorce and a husband's unwillingness to procure a *get*. This was subsequently rejected by Ben Zion Uziel of Israel (A M. Freiman, *Seder Kidushin Venisuin*, pp. 391 ff.).

The mood among both rabbis and members of our congregations has changed, especially as the number of divorces have increased. Some individuals now seek a religious resolution to the end of their marriage. This has led to the creation of the Document of Separation *(Seder Peredah).* in the new *Rabbis Manual.* Others have been willing to obtain an Orthodox or Conservative *get* despite the hardships involved and the secondary status given to the woman in those proceedings.

As we look at the problems connected with a Reform *get,* let us look at the traditional *get*. The original requirements connected with it were rather simple, and a divorce was easily obtained. The husband prepared for the divorce by asking a *sofer* (scribe) to write the document for him and indicated that he wished to divorce his wife. The specific name of the husband and the wife were given in the document; the city in which it was prepared was also indicated. No reason for the divorce was mentioned in the document itself.

This document was then signed by two adult male Jewish witnesses who were unrelated to either party or to each other. It was then given to two other witnesses or perhaps to the same individuals who delivered it to the woman. Upon her acceptance the divorce became effective. The witnesses to the signature and to the delivery of the document could subsequently attest to the fact that everything had been accomplished by the law.

This document, therefore, depended entirely on the husband and its acceptance by the wife. A rabbinical court *(bet din)* had no real standing in this matter unless a further dispute arose. It may or may not have supervised the various stages of the document, i.e., the proper composition, witnessing and delivery, but that was not essential. The court did not initiate the procedure nor did it provide any kind of hearings in the matter.

These proceedings were straightforward and uncomplicated until questions of custody and financial control were raised. As such issues are nowadays settled by the civil courts, we need not be troubled by them.

Throughout the centuries, questions have been raised about the names of the individuals in the documents, the fitness of the individuals who were witnesses, the state of mind of the author of the document and the state of mind of the recipient, the qualifications of the scribe, etc. Eventually this simple document became rather complex. Its Hebrew or Aramaic text was fitted into precisely thirteen lines. The names of each of the individuals involved had to be spelled absolutely correctly, and there were frequent discussions about the precise name of the individuals, nicknames, etc. Furthermore, even the city involved had to be spelled properly, often in order to locate it precisely; a river or stream flowing through the city was also mentioned. If it was the first *get* written in a location, then each subsequent *get* had to be written in the same manner. The delivery of the *get* had to be properly attested, and since the decree of Rabbenu Gershom (1000 C.E.) a *get* could not be given to a woman against her will. Delivery had to be established through the woman's actual acceptance of the document; it could not be deposited with her. A vast literature deals with each of these questions in every century.

Most of the issues involved that troubled previous generations are of no concern to us as the civil court has already dealt with them in its own way and in a manner acceptable to us. At this time, therefore, we have accepted civil divorce.

Agunot
Questions and Reform Jewish Answers, New York, 1992, # 234

Walter Jacob

QUESTION: Should we marry women considered *agunot* by Orthodox rabbis? (Martin Cohen, Los Angeles, CA)

ANSWER: In the long span of Jewish history, aside from the normal problems and aggravated circumstances surrounding divorce, the chief issue has been that of the *agunah,* a status caused by the disappearance of the husband or by his refusal to provide a religious divorce *(get)* for his wife. The second problem has often been solved through communal pressure, which stopped short of actually forcing a *get,* as that would not be legally valid (Solomon ben Aderet *Responsa W* #40; Simon ben Zemah Duran *Responsa* II #68; *Tur* and *Shulhan Arukh Even Haezer* 134 and 154; *Responsa Reanana* #43; *Responsa Mabit* II #138; *Piskei Din shel Batei Hadin Harabanim,* vol. 2, pp 300 ff).

Much more difficult is the problem of a husband who disappeared. Usually in the past this condition occurred when the husband had disappeared in time of war or during a long journey to distant lands. Despite a presumption of death, as it could not be proven, the wife continued to be considered as married. During the period of heavy eastern European emigration to the United States and other western lands, some men were lost at sea or in the wild West, whereas others slipped away and thus relieved themselves of family responsibilities. In modern times, in addition to these cases *of a agunah,* we have thousands of Orthodox women whose husbands simply refuse to provide a *get* and leave their wives with no solution. After civil courts have dissolved the marriage, only moral persuasion can be exercised on the husband, and that is frequently difficult because of the hostility which exists between the individuals. Although some states, for example New York, now recognize the obligations of a *ketubah* and would enforce its provision until a *get* had been given, this is only minimally helpful, as it is easy to escape its jurisdictions.

The problem of the *agunah* in modern times has been solved in a number of different ways. Our Reform method simply acknowledges civil divorce. For the Orthodox an annulment is possible, but very difficult. Some traditional Jews solve the problem when the original marriage was Reform or Conservative by not accepting the witnesses who signed the *ketubah* and so denying its validity. As no marriage has taken place in their eyes, no *get* is necessary (Moses Feinstein, *Igrot Moshe Even Haezer* #74, #75; David Hoffmann, *Melamed Lehoil Even Haezer* #20)

Although this path may be technically correct from an Orthodox point of view, it is insulting to all Reform and Conservative Jews; it also does not satisfy psychologically. One of the problems with this approach is the Jewish doctrine that Jews who engage in intercourse do so with serious intent; furthermore, individuals, who have lived together for a period of time and are recognized as husband and wife by the community in which they live, are so accepted (*Git* 81b). The Orthodox authorities who suggested the above mentioned solution claim that this ruling does not apply to sinners (Moses Feinstein, *Op Cit.*, #75; Jehiel Weinberg *Seridei Esh Even Haezer* #28).

A variety of modern proposals have incorporated some statement about divorce, or at least about the jurisdiction of the rabbinic court in the *ketubah* in order to solve the problem. The modern Orthodox scholar, Eliezer Berkovits, made such a proposal and urged the use of a conditional marriage; he subsequently defended it in his book *Tenai Benisuin Vehaget*. The rabbis of Turkey in 1924 made a similar proposal which was later rejected by Ben Zion Uziel of Israel (A. H. Freiman, *Seder Kiddushin Venisuin*, pp. 391 ff).

A most determined effort in this direction was made by Louis Epstein for the Conservative Rabbinical Assembly in 1930; he suggested that a conditional divorce be given at the time of marriage. This approach which is *halakhically* sound was rejected by the Orthodox rabbinate and Epstein's efforts to defend it failed.(I. Epstein *Hatzaah Lemaan Takanot Agunot; Lisheelah Haagunot)*. Many considered it inappropriate to deal with divorce in the wedding document. The Conservative Rabbinical Assembly has added a clause to its *ketubah* which simply states that the couple places itself under the authority of the Conservative *bet din*. This removes one of the objections to the document of Epstein (*Rabbinic Manual* pp 37 f) The effort of the Conservative Rabbinical Assembly was made under the guidance of Joshua Liebermann and has been incorporated in the *ketubot* used by the Conservative movement.

A more radical suggestion was made by the French Orthodox rabbinate in 1907, which urged that all *ketubot* include a clause that indicated that a civil divorce decree would annul the marriage and the woman would be released and subsequently free to marry according to Jewish ritual. This suggestion was attacked by Orthodox authorities in other lands (A. H. Freiman, *Seder Kiddushin Venisuin*, p. 390).

These efforts have tried to deal with the problem of *agunot* but largely to no avail, as the complications have usually led women who sought a second marriage to use a Reform rabbi who recognized a civil divorce or a "Document of Separation" (W. Jacob (ed.) *American Reform Responsa* #162) or to turn to the civil authorities. We should continue to perform such marriages of *agunot* as a way of helping the Jewish community with a difficult problem. We recognize civil divorce as sufficient. Our solution is within the range of those proposed by some Orthodox authorities and so is part of our effort to unite the Jewish community.

Ordination of Women

Yearbook, Central Conference of American Rabbis, Cincinnati, 1922, Vol. 32, pp. 156 ff.

Jacob Z. Lauterbach

The very raising of this question is due, no doubt, to the great changes in the general position of women, brought about during the last half century or so. Women have been admitted to other professions, formerly practiced by men only, and have proven themselves successful as regards personal achievement as well as raising the standards or furthering the interests of the professions. Hence the question suggested itself, why not admit women also to the rabbinical profession?

The question resolves itself into the following two parts: first, the attitude of traditional Judaism on this point, and second, whether Reform Judaism should follow tradition in this regard. At the outset it should be stated that from the point of view of traditional Judaism there is an important distinction between the rabbinate and the other professions in regard to the admission of women. In the case of the other professions there is nothing inherent in their teachings or principles which might limit their practice to men exclusively. In the case of the rabbinate, on the other hand, there are, as will soon be shown, definite teachings and principles in traditional Judaism, of which the rabbinate in the exponent, which demand that its official representatives and functionaries be men only. To admit women to the rabbinate is, therefore, not merely a question of liberalism; it is contrary to the very spirit of traditional Judaism which the rabbinate seeks to uphold and preserve.

It should be stated further, that these traditional principles debarring women from the rabbinate were not formulated in an illiberal spirit by the Rabbis of old or out of a lack of appreciation of women's talents and endowments. Indeed the Rabbis of old entertained a high opinion of womanhood and frequently expressed their admiration for woman's ability and appreciated her great usefulness in religious work. Thus, e.g., they say, "God has endowed woman with a finer appreciation and a better understanding than man" (*Nidah* 45b); "Sarah was superior to Abraham in prophecy" (*Tanhuma*, Exodus, beginning); "It was due to the pious women of that generation that the Israelites were redeemed from Egypt" (*Sota*); and "The women were the first ones to receive and accept the Torah" (*Tanhuma*, (ed. Buber), *Metzora*, 18, p. 27a); and "They refused to participate in the making of the golden calf." These and many other sayings could be cited from Rabbinic literature in praise of woman, her equality to man and, in some respects, superiority to him. So we may safely conclude that their excluding of women from the rabbinate does not at all imply deprecation on their part of woman's worth.

But with all their appreciation of woman's fine talents and noble qualities, the Rabbis of old have also recognized that man and woman have each been assigned by the Torah certain spheres of activity, involving special duties. The main sphere of woman I activity and her duties centered in the house. Since she has her own duties to perform, and since especially in her position as wife and mother she would often be prevented from carrying on many of the regular activities imposed upon man, the law frees her from many religious obligations incumbent upon men, and especially exempts her from such positive duties the performance of which must take place at certain fixed times, like reciting the "*shema*" or at prescribed seasons, like Sukkot (*M. Kiddushin* 1.7): "*Vekhol mitzvot aseh shehazeman geramah, anashim chayavim venashim peturot.*"

This fact, that she was exempt from certain obligations and religious duties, necessarily excluded her from the privilege of acting as the religious leader or representative of the congregation (*sheliah tzibur*). She could not represent the congregation in the performing of certain religious functions, since, according to the rabbinic principle, one who is not personally obliged to perform a certain duty, cannot perform that duty on behalf of others and certainly cannot represent the congregation in the performance of such duties: "*kol she-eino mechuyav badavar eino motzi et harabim yedei hovatan.*" (*R.H.* 111.8; *Berakhot* 20b)

On the same principle, she was expressly disqualified from writing Torah scrolls. Since she could not perform for the congregation the duty of reading from the Torah, the text prepared by her was also not qualified for use in connection with the performance of that duty (*Gitin*, 45b; *Mas. Soferim* 1.14). Women were also considered exempt from the obligation to study the Torah (*Eruvin* 27a; *Kiddushin* 29b-30a). Some Rabbis even went so far as to object to women studying the Torah (*M. Sota* 111.4). This opinion, of course, did not prevail. Women were taught the Bible and given a religious education, and there were some women learned in the law even in talmudic times. But to use the phrase of the Talmud (*M.K.* 18a), "*isha bei midrasha lashehiha,*" women were not to be found in the *bet hamidrash*, in the academies and colleges where the rabbis assembled and where the students prepared themselves to be rabbis. Evidently, the reason that they could not aspire to be rabbis, was that the law excluded them from this religious office.

This law, that women cannot be rabbis, was always taken for granted in the Talmud. It was considered to be so generally known and unanimously agreed upon that it was not even deemed necessary to make it a special subject of discussion. The very idea of a woman becoming a rabbi never even entered the mind of the Rabbis of old. It is for this reason that we find only few direct and definite statements to the effect that women cannot be rabbis. Only occasionally, when the discussion of other questions involved the mentioning of it, reference—direct or indirect—is made to the established law that women cannot act as judges or be rabbis. Thus, in a *baraita* (*Pal. Talmud Shevu-ot* 4.1, 35b, and *Sanhedrin* 4.10, 21c) it is stated "*harei lamedan sheha-isha einah dana,*" "We have learned that a woman cannot act as judge," i.e., cannot render decisions of law. The same principle is also indirectly expressed in the *Mishnah* (comp. *Nidah* 6.4 and *Shevu-ot* 4.1). The Talmud (*Gittin* 5b) also indirectly states that a woman cannot be a member of a *bet din*, i.e., a rabbi or judge. For there it is taken for granted that she could not be one of three who form a tribunal or *bet din* to pass upon the correctness of a bill of divorce or of any other document (see Rashi, ad loc.).

The *Midrash* (*Numbers Rabbah* 10.5) also quotes as a well-known and established principle that women may not have the authority to render decisions in religious or ritual matters: "*Shehanashim einam benot hora-a.*"

These Talmudic principles have been accepted by all medieval Jewish authorities. Maimonides (*Yad, Hil. Sanhedrin* II.7) declares that the members of every tribunal or *beit din* in Israel, which means every rabbi, *dayan*, or *moreh hora-a* in Israel must possess the same qualities which characterized the men whom Moses selected to be his associates and whom he appointed judges and leaders in Israel. These qualities, Maimonides continues, are expressly stated in the Torah, as it is said: "Get you from each one of your tribes men, wise and understanding and full of knowledge, and I will make them heads over you" (Deut. 1:13). Maimonides here has in mind the idea, entertained by the rabbis of all generations, that the rabbis of each generation continue the activity and are the recipients of the spirit of those first religious leaders of the Jewish people. For, as is well known, Mosheh Rabbenu and the Seventy Elders who formed his Council were considered the prototypes and the models of the rabbis of all subsequent generations (comp. *Mishnah, R.H.* 11.9). Likewise, R. Aaron Halevi of Barcelona (about 1300 C.E.) in his *Sefer Hahinukh* (nos. 74, 75, 77, 79, 81, 83), Jacob Asher in *Tur, Hoshen Mishpat* VII, and Joseph Caro in *Shulhan Arukh, Hoshen Mishpat* VII.3—all expressly state the principle that a woman cannot officiate as judge or rabbi. It hardly need be stated that when some of the sources use in this connection the term "judge" (*dayan*) they, of course, mean rabbi, for which *dayan* is but another name. In rabbinic terminology the functions of a rabbi are spoken of as being "*ladin ulehorot*," to judge and decide religious and ritual questions. And even in our modern rabbinical diploma we use the formula "*yoreh yoreh, yadin yadin*," giving the candidate whom we ordain the authority to judge and decide religious questions and to give authoritative ruling in all religious matters.

To be sure, the rabbis do permit the women to be religious teachers, like Miriam, who, according to the rabbis, taught the women while Moses and Aaron taught the men (*Sifrei Zuta*, quoted in *Yalkut Shemoni, Behaalotekha*, 741 end), and Deborah, whom the rabbis believed to have been merely teaching the law (*Seder Eliyahu Rabbah* IX-X, Friedman, p. 50; compare also *Tosafot*, B.K. 15a, s.v. "*asher tasim*" and parallels). Some authorities would put certain restrictions upon woman even in regard to her position as teacher (see *Kiddushin* 82a, and Maimonides, *Yad, Talmud Torah* 11.4), but in general, the opinion of the rabbis was that women may be teachers of religion (see *Hinukh*, 152, and compare Azulai in *Birkei Yosef* to *Hoshen Mishpat* VII.12); and as a matter of fact, there have always been learned women in Israel. These women scholars were respected for their learning in the same manner as learned men were respected (see *Sefer Hasidim*, 978, and compare also *Sedei Hemed* I, letter Kaf, no. 99), and some of these women scholars would occasionally even give lectures in rabbinics; but they have never been admitted to the rabbinate, since all the rabbinic authorities agree, at least implicitly, that women cannot hold the office of a rabbi or of a *sheliah tzibur* and cannot perform any of the official functions requiring the authority of a rabbi.

This is the attitude of traditional Judaism toward the question of women rabbis, a view strictly adhered to by all Jewry all over the world throughout all generations, even unto this day.

Now we come to the second part of our question; that is, shall we adhere to this tradition, or shall we separate ourselves from catholic Israel and introduce a radical innovation which would necessarily create a distinction between the title rabbi as held by a Reform rabbi and the title rabbi in general? I believe that hitherto no distinction could rightly be drawn between he ordination of our modern rabbis and the ordination of all the rabbis of preceding generations. We are still carrying on the activity of the rabbis of old who traced their authority through a chain of tradition to Moses and the elders associated with him, even though in many points we interpret our Judaism in a manner quite different from theirs. We are justified in considering ourselves the latest link in that long chain of authoritative teachers who carry on their activity of teaching, preserving, and developing Judaism. For our time we have the same standing as they had (comp. *R.H.* 25a). The ordination which we give to our disciples carries with it, for our time and generation, the same authority which marked the ordination given by Judah Hanasi to Abba Areka or the ordination given by any teacher in Israel to his disciples throughout all the history of Judaism.

We should therefore not jeopardize the hitherto indisputable authoritative character of our ordination. We should not make our ordination entirely different in character from the traditional ordination, and hereby give the larger group of Jewry that follows traditional Judaism a good reason to question our authority and to doubt whether we are rabbis in the sense in which his honored title was always understood.

Nor is there, to my mind, any actual need for making such a radical departure from this established Jewish law and time-honored practice. The supposed lack of a sufficient number of rabbis will not be made up by this radical innovation. There are other and better means of meeting this emergency. This could be accomplished if our rabbis would follow the advice of the men of the Great Synagogue to raise many disciples and thus encourage more men to enter the ministry. And the standard of the rabbinate in America, although no doubt it could be improved in many directions, is certainly not so low as to need a new and refining influence such as the influence brought by women to any profession they enter. Neither could women, with all due respect to their talents and abilities, raise the standard of the rabbinate. Nay, all things being equal, women could not even raise it to the high standard reached by men, in this particular calling. If there is any calling which requires a wholehearted devotion to the exclusion of all other things and the determination to make it one's whole life work, it is the rabbinate. It is not to be considered merely as a profession by which one earns a livelihood. Nor is it to be entered upon as a temporary occupation. One must choose it for his life work and be prepared to give to it all his energies and to devote to it all the years of his life, constantly learning and improving and thus growing in it. It has been rightly said that he woman who enters a profession must make her choice between following her chosen profession or the calling of mother and homemaker., She cannot do both well at the same time. Thus certainly would hold true in the case of the rabbinical profession. The woman who naturally and rightly looks forward to the opportunity of meeting the right kind of man, of marrying him, and of having children and a home of her own, cannot give to the rabbinate that wholehearted devotion which comes from the determination to make it one's life work. In all likelihood she could not continue it as a married woman. For, one holding the rabbinical office must teach by precept and example and must give an example of Jewish family and home life where all the traditional Jewish virtues are cultivated. The rabbi can do so all the better when he is married and has a home and family of his own. The wife whom God has made as helpmate to him can be, and in most cases is, of great assistance to him in making his home a Jewish home, a model for the congregation to follow.

In this important activity of the rabbi—exercising a wholesome influence upon the congregation—the woman rabbi would be deficient. The woman in the rabbinical office could not expect the man to whom she was married to be merely a helpmate to her, assisting her in her rabbinical activities. And even if she could find such a man, willing to take a subordinate position in the family, the influence upon the families in the congregation of such an arrangement in the home and in the family life of the rabbi would not be very wholesome. (Not to mention the fact that if she is to be a mother she could not go on with her regular activities in the congregation.)

And there is, to my mind, no injustice done to woman by excluding her from this office. There are many avenues open to her if she chooses to do religious or educational work. I can see no reason why we should make this radical departure from traditional practice except the specious argument that we are modern men and, as such, we recognize the full equality of women to men, hence we should be thoroughly consistent. But I would not class the rabbis with those people whose main characteristic is consistency.

Discussion

Rabbi Levinger: I feel very strongly on this question. When we look at the various denominations in this country who are opposed to ordaining women as ministers we find that they are those who, like the Episcopalians and the Catholics, look upon their ministers as priests. To us the rabbi is merely a teacher and preacher. The question is not whether there are a great many women who want to become rabbis. Perhaps there are none at all. But we are called upon to act on a matter of principle, and if in the next thirty or forty years we produce but one Anna Howard Shaw, we want her in the rabbinate.

Rabbi Witt: I was present at the meeting of the Board of Governors when the matter came up, and it was decided to refer it to the Conference. After reading the responsa that were prepared by Rabbi Lauterbach, I feared that there would be much opposition. I trust that our action in this matter will be unanimous. It is not a matter of tradition at all. I must confess I was not in the least interested in Rabbi Lauterbach's presentation. It seemed reactionary to me. I did not feel that it was the proper presentation of the subject. I need not say that I honor Dr. Lauterbach for the learning contained therein, but the point he presents is not the point at issue. We have witnessed the revolution in the status of women. Five years ago I had to argue in favor of women's rights when that question came up in the Arkansas legislature, but I did not feel that there would be need to argue that way in a liberal body of men like this. There is a principle involved, and I hope that the stand we take will be one in line with all the progressive tendencies of our day; that we will have the vision to see what is before us. From the standpoint of today, shall we say to women that they shall not have the right to function as we are functioning?

The question is: Have they the qualifications to function as spiritual leaders?

What does it require to be a spiritual guide? It requires a great spirit and the quality of leadership. Some women have it and some women have not. Some men have it and some men have not. If we had a great leadership we would not have the questions which were so ably presented yesterday among the practical questions of the ministry. The one thing that was stressed was that if we had devoted leaders who could inspire following, all the problems would vanish.

I believe that this body of men should do nothing that would stand in the way of any forward movement in behalf of the womanhood of America. I cannot believe that a religion that is so splendidly spiritual and forward-looking as our religion will stand in the way of such a movement. I feel that this Conference can only act in one way, and that is to fall in line with what is the destiny of the women of the future.

Rabbi Weiss: In a large measure I agree with the previous speakers. I agree with all that has been said in favor of ordaining women as rabbis. I believe I am second to none in the rabbinate in the matter of idealism. But a vast measure of compromise must enter into all situations of life. I do not believe that we can have life exactly as we would like to have it. There is a vast debt due to cold austere justice, but there are fourteen million Jews in the world, and they must be considered. In the city of New York alone there are a million and a half who look upon you with a degree of respect but who have their own mode of procedure and who would look upon any radical action on your part as a line of cleavage in the House of Israel. I merely mean that we should proceed slowly. I believe that some compromise can be effected, such as allowing women to be teachers or superintendents; but I believe that it would be unwise at the present time to have them ordained as rabbis. Let me give one concrete illustration. Suppose a woman were to sign a marriage document. To many in New York today such a ceremony would hardly be recognized as binding.

Rabbi Brickner: here is much merit in what Dr. Lauterbach has said. He has not stressed the question of opinion, but the question of practicability. Modern psychologists agree that women do not differ from men so much in intellect. In fact, experiments prove that women are the peers of most men. There are women occupying positions in modern industry in which they could not be equaled by many men. It is not a question of equality. All that Dr. Lauterbach says has already been said against women entering other professions. The question with us is one of practicability. The tendency in modern Judaism is to conserve Jewish values. We wish to be in touch with the masses of Jewish people. When I came away from Toronto the other day I clipped from the newspaper the vote of the Methodist Church in Canada. It represents the liberal traditions in Canada. And yet it voted by a small majority against permitting women into the ministry. It is not a question of principle or equality—on that we are all agreed. It is purely a question of practicability.

Rabbi Charles S. Levi: The matter before you is not a matter of the hour, but a matter of all times. It is a matter that touches upon the acknowledged leadership of our people, and reaches the lives of uncounted thousands of our American coreligionists. We are the links in the chain of time. We are the spokesmen who give expression to the great truths which bind the past to the future, and it is for us to keep alive the chain of tradition.

Rabbi Rauch: I listened with great interest to Dr. Lauterbach's presentation and was at first inclined to agree with him, but as he proceeded it struck me that there was a great omission. He gave a fine presentation of the traditional point of view and even hinted at certain modern needs, but I regret to say that he failed to touch on what Reform Judaism has to say on the subject. And yet our whole interpretation of religious life is supposedly based on the principles of Reform Judaism. Now what has the philosophy of Reform Judaism to say in regard to woman? I know from experience because I was born in an Orthodox environment. There was a very clear line of distinction between the boy and the girl, and the education given to the boy and girl. The boy had to learn Scriptures, while the girl was not expected to learn them. Many duties were imposed upon the boy, few upon the girl. This went on for centuries. What happened when Reform came in? One by one the barriers separating the boy from the girl educationally began to be broken down. We admitted the girls into the same schools, and we tried to teach them the same things. Even in the important ceremony of *bar mitzvah* we brushed aside the traditional point of view and we said that the girl should be educated and confirmed the same as the boy. And in our congregations, which is the practical side of our religious life, we have given to women exactly the same status as to men. In my own congregation women conduct the summer services, and they conduct them just as well as—if not better than—they used to be when we got someone temporarily for the summer. In every line of endeavor in our temples we have proceeded on the theory that woman is the equal of man. What do they ask us to do? They want us to make it possible for women to work along the same lines as we men are working. We do not ask privileges for them. Let there be the same demands, the same rigorous training, and let the congregation decide whether the woman is doing the work well or not. I do not think that our course will be hurt by a liberal attitude.

Rabbi Englander: Personally, I was surprised to learn that the Board of Governors submitted this question to the Conference. I thought that after the faculty—a body composed of the teachers—had taken action, that would be sufficient guidance for action on the part of the Board of Governors. However, I wish to touch on one argument which has been raised to the effect that if we admit women as rabbis we would tend to create a schism in Israel. During all the conferences in recent years there have been many actions that we would not have taken had we feared this. We would not have set ourselves on record against Zionism. Had fear been taken into consideration, we would not have taken a stand on many subjects. Twenty years ago, this Conference put itself on record favoring absolute religious equality of women with men. Are we going back on our own action? In spite of all the arguments advanced by Dr. Lauterbach, the faculty set itself on record as favoring the ordination of women, although it stated that at the present time it believed it was impractical for women to enter the rabbinate. But I do not believe that the question of practicability is for us to decide. The only question before us is: shall we, in the light of Reform Judaism, put ourselves in favor of admitting women to the rabbinate?

A motion is made that further discussion be discontinued.

Rabbi Morgenstern: I do not care to express any opinion upon this subject, because—you can readily understand—inasmuch as this question has been submitted by the College authorities to the Conference to get an expression of opinion, I am here rather to listen than to offer any opinion I myself may have. I realize that the time of the Conference is very precious and that you cannot afford to give more time than is necessary to the discussion of this question, but I believe that the question is of such importance that it ought to justify the expenditure of as much time as may be necessary for a thorough discussion of the question. Several of the men lay emphasis upon the significance of the principle of not breaking with catholic Israel. We have heard the arguments, but there are several valuable thoughts which have not yet been presented. And there is one phase of the question which has not been adequately discussed. We can all accept the opinion of Dr. Lauterbach as authoritative, namely, that from the point of view of traditional Judaism the ordination of women would not be permitted. We need not discuss that. But the practical aspect of the question has not been discussed. Namely, is it expedient, and is it worthwhile?

Rabbi Abrams: It seems to me that the question resolves itself into three parts. First, what is the principle? Second, is it consistent? Third, is it practical?

As a matter of principle, women ought to be ordained, as we now recognize that they are entitled to the same privileges and rights as men. Our ancestors never asked, is it practical? They asked, is it the will of God? And thus they settled the question for themselves. But we must ask the question, is it in keeping with the tradition of the past? In the whole paper of Rabbi Lauterbach, we do not find the statement that women could not be ordained as rabbis. Indirectly, we inferred that they may not be ordained because we do not find any women who were ordained. At the most, sentiment was against it; but sentiment has been against women going into many of the professions even today. But that does not mean that they should not be ordained or could not be according to traditional laws.

What is our ordination today? In spite of our claim that we are the descendants of the ancient Rabbis, we must admit that the function of the modern rabbi is entirely different from the function of the Rabbi of old. In olden times, he was the judge. That was his chief function. Preaching and teaching were secondary. If we were to lay claim to be lineal descendants of the ancient teachers, we must go to the prophets of the Bible. We are the followers of the prophets more than of the Rabbis. And if we would follow the example of the women of the Bible, we would find that many women served as prophets and that during talmudic times many of them taught. So we are not inconsistent with the past if we put ourselves on record as favoring the ordination of women.

Rabbi Joseph L. Baron: I enjoyed thoroughly the scholarly paper of my teacher on the negative view of the question, and I shall not deny that the admission of women into the rabbinate will, like any innovation, shock some people and call forth opposition and ridicule. But I wish to point out several flaws in the negative argument. Professor Lauterbach intimates that the matter has hitherto never arisen as a practical issue because it has been taken for granted that a woman cannot, in the capacity of a rabbi, carry out, or represent the people in, a function in which she is not personally obliged to participate. How, then, can we infer from this that with the full entry of woman in all the religious functions of home and synagogue, she must still be denied the privilege of ordination? We broke with tradition long ago when we granted women an equal standing with men in all our religious functions.

I disagree entirely with the remark that by taking the proposed step, we shall create a schism. The Russian Jews, to whom reference has been made, do recognize and follow women leaders, as in the radical factions. And if women are not recognized as leaders in the Orthodox synagogue, let us not forget that neither are we recognized as such. There is a distinct difference made, even in the Yiddish terminology, between a *rav* and a rabbi. Again, we broke with tradition long ago when we declared that a rabbi need not be an authority on questions of *kashrut*; and I need not mention which, from the point of view of Orthodoxy, is the greater offense.

When I received the responsum of Dr. Lauterbach a week or two ago, I inquired as to the attitude of the members of a Unitarian Church in Moline, where a woman has been officiating for about half a year, and the reply was very favorable. That minister is not falling behind her male predecessors in her zeal and ability in handling all the problems of the church. So, as to the practicality of the matter, I believe that should be left entirely with the individual congregation.

Rabbi James G. Heller: I do not believe that the Conference has the right to appeal to its duty to "Catholic Israel" in order to settle this question. In the past, many decisions have been taken which evidenced no regard for mere keeping of the peace. The one question at issue, the one question that should be discussed by this Conference, is whether in principle the admission of women into the rabbinate is desirable, and whether it is in accordance with the historic teachings of Reform Judaism. The entire content of Dr. Lauterbach's responsum, to my mind, be summed up in that very logical inconsistency to which he refers toward the end of his paper in so laudatory a manner. He must complete the syllogism contained in his remarks. Since traditional Judaism, Orthodoxy, did not require women to perform certain duties or functions, did not permit them to share in certain duties or functions, did not permit them to share in certain religious acts, it could not allow them to become teachers of these same duties. And, per contra, since Reform Judaism requires and asks of women the performance of every religious duty in the catalogue, it cannot deny them the right to become teachers and preachers.

Rabbi Samuel S. Cohon: I wish to call your attention to the fact that in other professions there is a great deal of prejudice against women even where they administer with considerable success. You would imagine that women would welcome the services of women physicians; but in actual practice it is stated that women are more bitterly opposed to female practitioners than are men.

In the legal profession we also know that in many instances women are debarred from practice. But I believe that many of us who realize how much our wives have helped us, how they have cooperated with us, how they have borne many of the responsibilities, also realize that they should be given the opportunity to assume this work on their own accord, if they so desire. Of course, there will be prejudice against women in the rabbinate, but if one congregation is found that will welcome a woman, the opportunity should be granted.

Rabbi Frisch: We have made greater departures from tradition in Reform Judaism than the one which is before us, so we can afford to dismiss this question without further discussion. But I regard the ordination of women as the last step in the removal of restrictions in the Jewish faith. She is fitted by temperament and by all of her qualifications to the position of teacher, and she has been granted the right to participate in all our congregational activities as the equal of man. Civilization has had cause to regret every restriction it has placed in the way of those who wanted to be free.

I have been wondering whether we are not denying ourselves a new source of strength, a new source of inspiration, by our reluctance to admit women to the rabbinate. I recognize the handicaps, but I believe that the women who surmount the obstacles will be greater spirits than the men who are in the rabbinate today. Will it be any greater reproach for a woman to give up the ministry for the sake of maternity than it is for a man to give it up to seek a livelihood in other work? I think it will be for a nobler reason. If we get women into our midst as rabbis, I believe that we will be enjoying some of the inspiration and strength we feel we need. So I plead that we place ourselves on record as in full sympathy with a further emancipation of women by their ordination as rabbis in Israel.

Rabbi Stern: Emotionally I am conservative and I do not like to break with the past, but I cannot agree with Rabbi Lauterbach in this instance. Is it not essential for us first to decide what is the principle? I believe the practical will take care of itself. It is very interesting to note that in the city of New York a professor in the Seminary, the rabbi of an Orthodox congregation, had a *bat mitzvah* of girls. This is very interesting and shows that the other wing of Judaism is also making progress.

A motion that the opinions of members which have been sent in should be read was introduced. The motion lost.

Rabbi Morgenstern: I think there is one possible source of information that we have not heard from and whose opinion would be very helpful to us. I mean the wives of the rabbis present. It would help us to get an expression of opinion from the women, if some of the wives would be willing to give us their ideas based on many years of experience in this work. I would ask that this opportunity be given to the ladies to express their opinions.

It was moved that the courtesy of the floor be extended to any of the ladies present who cared to take part in the discussion.

Mrs. Frisch: When I entered the hall this morning, I was opposed to the ordination of women as rabbis. I am now in favor of it. I have been much impressed with what I have heard.

The reason I was opposed to the ordination of women was what you would call the practical reason. I now feel that whatever practical reasons I may have had cannot be compared in value with the matter of principle which has been mentioned here this morning.

The practical reason that I had in mind was that I, as a wife and mother, did not understand how a woman could attend to the duties which devolve upon a rabbi and at the same time be a true homemaker. Candidly, I do not see at this moment how it can be accomplished. I cannot solve this question, but there may be some women who would prefer a life of celibacy in order to minister to a congregation.

Personally, I am selfish enough not to be willing to give up the happiness of wifehood and motherhood for this privilege, great though it may be. But I love the work of the rabbinate so much that could I have prevailed upon myself to forget the joys that come with homemaking, I should have become a rabbi. I do not believe that privilege should be denied women, and it behooves us to go on record as being in favor of this development.

Miss Baron: I am connected with Jewish work in New York City and I know that since the Jewish woman have entered this work it has intensified the value of Jewish education. I believe that should the Jewish woman enter the rabbinate, she will be able to intensify the religious feeling of our people.

Mrs. Berkowitz: I am more than satisfied to be the silent member of our partnership, but I believe that it is the function of women to give spiritual value to the world, and especially the Jewish woman—imbued with the Jewish spirit—will naturally bring a certain quality to the ministry which some of our men lack. I think that might be enlarged and strengthened, and therefore I should like to see our women become rabbis, if they wish to do so.

A motion that action on this resolution be postponed until next year lost.
A motion that a referendum vote of the members of the Conference be taken lost.
A motion that this resolution be referred to the Committee on Resolutions lost.

Rabbi Joseph Leiser: The objections of Professor Lauterbach concerning the admission of Jewish women to the rabbinate are inadequate. His thesis, that the rabbinical profession is a career and involves the totality of life to the preclusion of even the function and offices of motherhood, is not valid and is no more applicable to the Jewish woman as rabbi than it is to the Jewish woman as lawyer, doctor, dentist, newspaper writer, musician, businesswoman or teacher. In all these trades and professions, Jewish women are actively engaged beyond the consideration or limitations of sex, and in spite of previous sex taboos. As a profession, the rabbinate ought to be open to women on a parity with that of men, provided women receive a degree for academic training carried on according to approved standards.

But my objection to the position maintained by Professor Lauterbach rests on more fundamental contentions than of sex discrimination in the rabbinate., The professor fails to analyze the rabbinate in the light of its function and activity in the world today. He carries over into America, a modern America the methodology and outlook of an Orthodox rabbi whose function is that of a lawyer, one who renders decisions in an ecclesiastical court from codes drawn up by established standards of behavior. Orthodox Judaism rests upon laws of conformity: one discharges his duties; one learns them and fulfills them, whereas Reform Judaism releases the individual, and enables him to realize his own nature, and therefore allows him to contribute whatever there is implanted within his soul, and mind in humanity.

This difference in motivation is translated to the profession of the rabbi, as it is interpreted in Reform Judaism.

The mere repudiation of the authority of the Talmud and *Shulhan Arukh* is not sufficient to constitute one as a Reform rabbi; nor does the acceptance of these make one an Orthodox rabbi. To be sure, the Orthodox rabbi is learned in the law, since the very nature and constitution require it. But the Reform rabbi is not primarily a legal expert. The modern rabbinate has become an institution, just as the synagogue has developed functions other than those pertaining to worship and the discharging of ceremonial observances. In these days, it serves more than one purpose, and therefore requires more than one type of professional labor.

The variety of activities that are now released in the ordinary synagogue calls for a number of workers, all of whom must be filled with the knowledge of God. The new work recently developed in the synagogue appeals particularly to the woman, who by nature and training is singularly fitted to undertake it.

It will be said in rebuttal that while the need and ability of these modern activities within the synagogue may require the professional assistance of women, these functions do not require the training and professional equipment of a rabbi. This is a mistake. Mere inclination provides access to those qualities of emotionalism and undisciplined enthusiasm which endanger the assistance of a woman. Professional training is required for the expert in the religious institution of the synagogue. In the departments of education, as our synagogues are elaborating them; a Jewish woman is particularly well qualified, provided her training in rabbinics is grounded in a thorough knowledge of the literature.

A Jewish woman is the logical adjunct to young people's societies and organizations, and no synagogue is complete without these new features.

The social activities of a congregation are dependent on the social instincts of a woman. Her rabbinical training enables her to link up these activities with tradition and provides the background of Jewish consciousness to this work.

The pulpit, and whatever pertains to it, is—and remains—a plane wherein man is by nature and temperament best qualified, although not exclusively so. But woman, by reason of self-limitation, is not disqualified. Viewing the rabbi in the light of a prophet and the man of vision, he—more than woman—responds to this unusual endowment. Men are prone to be idealists. They are quick to see visions. They are the dreamers. To men is given the gift of prophecy, but not exclusively (as the careers of Hulda and Deborah testify). Men are called upon by God to be pathfinders, liberators, protagonists of right, brandishing the shining sword of justice before the hosts of evildoers. In the defense of right, men will face the outrages of the world alone.

On the other hand, women are conservative, and seldom are impelled to stand forth and proclaim these eternal convictions. They are pacifists, importunists, moderators, trimming their sails to whatever winds blow on the seven seas of thought. Remember that while it was due to the merit of women that the children of Israel were redeemed from Egypt, it was only merit, not the fierce rebellion of a Moses, saying, "Let my people go free!" that wrought the miracle.

Were the woman as rabbi merely confined to pulpit discourses and the formal aspects of ceremonials, her admission to the profession would be inept and otiose. The synagogue, however, has enlarged its tent cords of service. It is an institution of which the pulpit is part, not the totality. Being only a feature of the institutional labor, there are spheres of activity in the synagogue that not only can be filled by woman, but are primarily her province.

Rabbi Neumark: I. "This fact that she was exempt from certain obligations, she could not represent the congregation in the performance of such duties": (*R. H.* III.8; *Berakhot* 20b). Against this argument the following can be said:

First, the traditional functions of the rabbi have nothing to do with representation of the congregation in the performance of certain religious duties from which women are freed. There are certain categories of men, such as are deformed and afflicted with certain bodily defects, who could not act as readers, but could be rabbis for decisions in ritual matters and questions of law. The same holds true of people with a "foreign accent" in Hebrew.

Second, women are not free from the duties of prayer, grace after meal, and *kiddush*, and they can read for others (cf. *Mishnah* and *B.Berakhot*, 20a,b). Thus, even in our modern conception of the function of the rabbi, which includes reading, woman can act as representative according to traditional law. Of course *tefilah* here is used in its technical meaning—"Eighteen Prayers"—while prayer in is general meaning of divine service had the *shema* in its center, and woman was freed from its obligatory reading. But no Orthodox Jew ever waited with the obligatory reading of the *shema* for the public service; it has, at least in post-talmudic times, always been done right in the morning, privately.

Third, the practice within Reform Judaism has decided in favor of admitting women as readers of the divine service. And since we are interested in the traditional law on the subject only in order to take from it a clue for Reform practice, this argument would be of no consequence even if it were valid, as it is not. If a woman is to be debarred from the rabbinate in Orthodox Judaism because she cannot serve as a reader, then the only logical consequence would be that Reform Judaism, which has decided in favor of the woman reader, should disregard the Orthodox attitude, and admit women to the rabbinate.

II. The reason why a Torah scroll written by a woman was considered unfit is not, as Dr. Lauterbach claims, because she could not be reader of the Torah, but quite a formal one: whosoever has not the obligation of binding (*tefilin*), has not the fitness of writing (a Torah scroll) (*Git.* 45b; *Men.* 42b). The above reason is given in *Soferim* I.13, but there, woman is not debarred from writing a Torah scroll.

III. In *Moed Katan* 18a, it is not said that "women were not to be found in the academies and colleges where the rabbis assembled and where the students prepared themselves to be rabbis![1] It is only said *ishah bei midrasha lo shehiha*, "A woman is not often to be found in *bet hamidrash*. The academies and colleges of those days were not institutions for training rabbis, but institutions of learning, most of whose students were pursuing other vocations. A woman in those days was supposed to keep away from all public places, such as courts and the like, and even, as much as possible, from the streets: *kol kevodah bat melekh penimah*.

IV. As to the direct question of the legal situation, I have discussed that matter in the opinion I have submitted to the faculty of the Hebrew Union College. I want to add the following remarks: 1. The statement of *Yerushalmi San.* 21c and *Shev.* 35b that a woman cannot serve (occasionally) as judge, is not from a *baraita*, as Dr. Lauerbach claims, but occurs in a discussion between two Amorain. 2. *Lamadnu* does not mean "we have learned," but is a technical term for an inference on the virtue of a hermeneutical rule; in this case, *gezera sheva*. 3. Nowhere in talmudic but always by *tanya* literature is a *baraita* introduced by *tanei, lamadnu*, and the like. 4. The emphasis on "men" in the quotation from Maimonides is not justified.

V. As to the practical question of the advisability to ordain women at the Hebrew Union College, I do not believe that the Orthodox will have any additional reason to object. They themselves employ women in their schools as teachers and readers, and our women rabbis will not do more than this. In fact, the entire question reduces itself to this: women are already doing most of the work that the ordained woman rabbi is expected to do, but they do it without preparation and without authority. I consider it rather a duty of the authorities to put an end to the prevailing anarchy by giving women a chance to acquire adequate education and an authoritative standing in all branches of religious work. The practical difficulties cannot be denied. But they will be worked out the same way as in other professions, especially in the teaching profession, from the kindergarten to postgraduate schools. Lydia Rabbinowitz raised a family of three children and kept up a full measure of family life while being a professor of bacteriology. The woman rabbi who will remain single will not be more, in fact less, of a problem than the bachelor rabbi. If she marries and chooses to remain a rabbi—God blesses her—she will retire for a few months and provide a substitute, just as rabbis generally do when they are sick or are involved in an automobile accident. When she comes back, she will be a better rabbi for the experience. The rabbinate may help the women, and the women rabbis may help the rabbinate. You cannot treat the Reform rabbinate from the Orthodox point of view. Orthodoxy is Orthodoxy and Reform is Reform. Our good relations with our Orthodox brethren may still be improved upon a clear and decided stand on this question. They want us either to be Reform or to return to the fold of real, genuine Orthodox Judaism whence we came.

Women Wearing a Talit
*Yearbook, Central Conference of American Rabbis,
New York, 1970, Vol. 80*

Solomon B. Freehof

QUESTION: In some of our congregations it is the custom that whoever comes up to the pulpit to participate in the service puts on a *talit*. In young people's services for our high schools, boys and girls participate and often the girl put on the *talit* at that occasion. According to Jewish law and tradition, is it proper for a girl to wear a *talit* at service?

ANSWER: The commandment to wear a *talit* with fringes is based upon Num 15:37–4. On the basis of this commandment, the anonymous *baraita in Menahot* 43a says that women, too, are in duty bound to wear the garment with fringes. However, Rabbi Simon says there that they are free from that obligation. He bases his opinion upon the fact that Scripture in the passage in Numbers uses the phrase: "Ye shall see them and remember, …" Since Scripture says, "Ye shall see them," that proves that the proper time for *talit* and *tzitzit* is the daytime, not the nighttime. This conclusion puts the commandment to wear fringes into the special class of positive commandments "limited by time" (*shehazman gerama*), and it is a general rule that women are free from the obligation to fulfill positive commandments that are dependent upon time. Of course, being free from the obligation to fulfill the commandment of fringes does not mean that they are forbidden to wear them. It means only that they are not in duty bound to wear them.

When the law is discussed in the *Shulhan Arukh, Orah Hayim* 17.2, Joseph Caro says, following Rabbi Simon in the Talmud (quoted above), that women and slaves are free from putting on the fringes, since it is a commandment based upon time; but Isserles adds: "At all events, if they wish to put on the fringed garment and even recite the blessing over it, they are free to do so, as is the case with all time-limited positive commandments" (that is, they are not compelled to obey, but they are permitted to do so if they wish). However, he adds, if they do put it on, it would appear to be a show of extra pride of piety (*yohara*). But if they are not to put it on because it would look like a show of extra pride of piety on their part, then it becomes necessary to explain the fact that women observe the commandment of the *lulav* and recite blessings over it. Is not the *lulav* also a positive commandment limited by time? The explanation of this difference is given by the *Magen David*: that the *lulav* is a stricter commandment than the one concerning fringes, because if a person does not have a square garment (the fringes must be on the corners of a four-cornered garment) he need not put fringes on at all. It is true that it is now our custom always to wear a *talit katan* with four corners and fringes. Nevertheless, according to law, it is only if a man has a four-cornered garment that he must put fringes on. In other words, the obligation depends on the garment. But with regard to the *lulav*, a man must get a *lulav* and say the blessings. In this case the obligation is incumbent upon the man himself *(hovat gavra)*, not on whether he has the object or not; he must get it if he lacks it.

One of the later deciders, Yechiel Epstein, in his *Arukh Hashulhan, Orah Hayim* 17, says that we should not allow women to put on the fringed *talit*. But then Epstein has the problem of explaining why women bless the *lulav* and formally eat the *matzah* at the seder, which are positive commandments limited by time. He explains by saying that these positive time-limited commandments come only once a year) but the *talit* should be worn every day.

However, all the great (and earlier) authorities permit it. The only question that seems to divide the earlier authorities (none of whom doubts the right of women to put on the *talit*) is the question as to whether, when a woman puts on the *talit* she may make the regular blessing or not. There is a full discussion of this problem in the *Tosafot* to *Rosh Hashana* 33a, s.v.*ha*. This *tosefet* is mainly the opinion of Rabbenu Tam. The discussion is on the general principle of whether anyone (such as women and the blind) who is free from the obligation to fulfill "positive commandments limited by time" should (when he fulfills such commandments voluntarily) pronounce the blessing over them or not. The *tosefet* is based mainly on the discussion in *Baba Kama* 87a, where Rabbi Joseph, who was blind, had voluntarily fulfilled such commandments as he was not obligated to fulfill. See, also, the *tosefet* in *Eruvin* 96a, s.v. *Michal*, where the *tosefe*t discusses the statement in the Talmud that Michal, the daughter of Kushi (or the daughter of King Saul) used to put on *tefilin*, and the wife of Jonah used to make the festival pilgrimage to Jerusalem. Both of these were " positive commandments limited by time." Rabbenu Tam holds the opinion that women may pronounce the blessing over the fringed *talit*. But Maimonides, in *Yad, Hil. Tzitzit* 111.9, says that women may put on the fringes if they wish, yet may not say the blessing and he adds: "So with all the other positive commandments that women are free from, if they wish to fulfill them without reciting the blessings, we do not prevent them." The *Hagahot Maimuniyot* at that passage in the *Yad* says in the name of Rashi that he, too, was opposed to their reciting the blessing.

So the law is clear enough: One authority believes that a woman is actually in duty bound to wear the fringes. All agree that she may wear them if she wishes to, except for the limitation that it might look like the pride of extra piety. This solitary objection can hardly apply to the young women if we put the *talit* upon them. They would simply consider it part of the ceremony. Besides, in our Reform Movement where special emphasis is placed upon the religious equality of men and women, there can be no real objection to young women putting on the *talit* when they participate in the service.

Marriage After a Sex-Change Operation

American Reform Responsa, New York, 1983, #137

Walter Jacob

QUESTION: May a rabbi officiate at a marriage of two Jews, one of whom has undergone a surgical operation which has changed his/her sex?

ANSWER: Our responsum will deal with an individual who has undergone an operation for sexual change for physical or psychological reasons. We will presume (a) that the operation is done for valid, serious reasons, and not frivolously; (b) that the best available medical tests (chromosome analysis, etc.) will be utilized as aids; and (c) that this in no way constitutes a homosexual marriage.

There is some discussion in traditional literature about the propriety of this kind of operation. In addition, we must recall that tradition sought to avoid any operation which would seriously endanger life (*Shulhan Arukh Yoreh Dea*h 116; *Hul.*10a). The *Mishnah* dealt with the problem of individuals whose sex was undetermined. It divided them into two separate categories, *tumtum* and *androginos*. A *tumtum* is a person whose genitals are hidden or undeveloped and whose sex, therefore, is unknown. R. Ammi recorded an operation on one such individual who was found to be male and who then fathered seven children (*Yev.* 83b). Solomon B. Freehof has discussed such operations most recently; he permits such an operation for a *tumtum*, but not for an *androginos* (*Modern Reform Responsa*, pp. 128ff). The *androginos* is a hermaphrodite and clearly carries characteristics of both sexes *(M. Bik.* IV.5). The former was a condition which could be corrected and the latter, as far as the ancients were concerned, could not, so the *Mishnah* and later tradition treated the *androginos* sometimes as a male, sometimes as a female, and sometimes as a separate category. However, with regard to marriage, the *Mishnah* (*Bik.* IV.2) states unequivocally: "He can take a wife, but not be taken as a wife. If married, they were free from the obligation of bearing children (*Yad, Hil. Yibum Vahalitzah* 6.2), but some doubted the validity of their marriages (*Yev.* 81a; *Yad, Hil. Ishut* 411, also *Shulkhan Aruk Even Ha-ezer* 44.6). The Talmud has also dealt with *aillonit*, a masculine woman, who was barren (*Yad, Hil. Ishut* 2.4; *Nid.* 47b; *Yev.* 80b). If she married and her husband was aware of her condition, then this was a valid marriage (*Yad, Hil. Ishut* 4.11); although the ancient authorities felt that such a marriage would only be permitted if the prospective husband had children by a previous marriage, otherwise, he could divorce her in order to have children (*Yev.* 61a; *M. Yev.* 24.1). Later authorities would simply permit such a marriage to stand.

We, however, are dealing either with a situation in which the lack of sexual development has been corrected and the individual has been provided with a sexual identity, or with a situation in which the psychological makeup of the individual clashed with the physical characteristics, and this was corrected through surgery. In other words, our question deals with an individual who now possesses definite physical characteristics of a man or a woman, but has obtained them through surgical procedure, and whose status is recognized by the civil government. The problem before us is that such an individual is sterile, and the question is whether under such circumstances he or she may be married. Our question, therefore, must deal with the nature of marriage for such individuals. Can a Jewish marriage be conducted under these circumstances.

There is no doubt that both procreation and sexual satisfaction are basic elements of marriage as seen by Jewish tradition. Procreation was considered essential, as is already stated in the *Mishnah*: "A man may not desist from the duty of procreation unless he already has children." The *gemara* to this concluded that he may marry a barren woman if he has fulfilled this *mitzvah*; in any case, he should not remain unmarried (*Yev.* 61b). There was a difference between the Schools of Hillel and Shammai about what was required to fulfill the *mitzvah* of procreation. Tradition followed Hillel, who minimally required a son and a daughter, yet the codes all emphasize the need to produce children beyond that number (*Tos., Yev.* 8; *Yad, Hil. Ishut* 15.16, etc.). The sources also clearly indicate that this *mitzvah* is only incumbent upon the male

(*Tos., Yev.* 8), although some later authorities would include women in the obligation, perhaps in a secondary sense (*Arukh Hashulhan, Even Ha-ezer* 1.4; *Hatam Sofer, Even Ha-ezer,* #20). Abraham Hirsh (*Noam,* Vol. 16, pp. 152ff) has recently discussed the matter of granting a divorce when one spouse has had a transsexual operation. Aside from opposing the operation generally, he also states that no essential biological changes have taken place and that the operation therefore, was akin to sterilization (which is prohibited) and cosmetic surgery. Hirsh also mentions a case related to our situation. A male in the time of R. Hananel added an orifice to his body, and R. Hananel decided that a male having intercourse with this individual has committed a homosexual act. This statement is quoted by Ibn Ezra in his commentary on Lev. 18:22. We, however, are not dealing with this kind of situation, but with a complete sexual change operation.

Despite the strong emphasis on procreation, companionship and joy also played a major role in the Jewish concept of marriage. Thus, the seven marriage blessings deal with joy, companionship, the unity of family, restoration of Zion, etc., as well as with children (*Ket.* 8a). These same blessings were to be recited for those beyond child-bearing age, or those who were sterile (Abudarham, *Birkhot Erusin* 98a).

Most traditional authorities who discussed childless marriages were considering a marriage already in existence (*bediavad*) and not the entrance into such a union. Under such circumstances the marriage would be considered valid and need not result in divorce for the sake of procreation, although that possibility existed (*Shulhan Arukh Even Ha-ezer* 23; see Isserles note on 154.10). This was the only alternative solution, since bigamy was no longer even theoretically possible after the decree of Rabbenu Gershom in the 11th century in those countries where this decree was accepted (oriental Jews did not accept the *Herem* of Rabbenu Gershom). Maimonides considered such a marriage valid under any circumstances (*Yad, Hil. Ishut* 4.10), whether this individual was born sterile or was sterilized later. The commentator, Abraham di Boton, emphasized the validity of such a marriage if sterility has been caused by an accident or surgery (*Lehem Mishneh* to *Yad, Hil. Ishut* 4.10). Yair Hayyim Bacharach stated that as long as the prospective wife realized that her prospective husband was infertile though sexually potent, and had agreed to the marriage, it was valid and acceptable (*Havat Yair*, #221). Traditional *halakhah*, which makes a distinction between the obligations of men and women (a distinction not accepted by Reform Judaism) would allow a woman to marry a sterile male, since the obligation of procreation did not affect her (as mentioned earlier).

There was some difference of opinion when a change of status in the male member of a wedded couple had taken place. R. Asher discussed this, but came to no conclusion, though he felt that a male whose sexual organs had been removed could not contract a valid marriage (*Besamim Rosh*, #340—attributed to R. Asher).The contemporary Orthodox R. Waldenberg assumed that a sexual change has occurred and terminated the marriage without a divorce (*Tzitz Eli- ezer* X, 1125). Joseph Pellagi came to a similar conclusion earlier (*Ahav et Yosef* 3.5).

Perhaps the clearest statement about entering into such a marriage was made by Isaac bar Sheshet, who felt that the couple was permitted to marry and then be left alone, although they entered the marriage with full awareness of the situation (Ribash, #15; *Shulhan Arukh Even Ha-ezer*, 1.3; see Isserles note). Similarly, traditional authorities who usually oppose contraception permitted it to a couple if one partner was in ill health. The permission was granted so that the couple could remain happily married, a solution favored over abstinence (Moses Feinstein, *Igerot Mosheh, Even Ha-ezer*, #63 and #67, where he permits marriage under these circumstances).

Our discussion clearly indicates that individuals whose sex has been changed by a surgical procedure and who are now sterile may be married according to Jewish tradition. We agree with this conclusion. Both partners should be aware of each other's condition. The ceremony need not be changed in any way for the sake of these individuals.

Homosexual Convert
Contemporary American Reform Responsa,
New York, 1987, # 52

Walter Jacob

QUESTION: "In our community there is a small group of 'gay' Jews who have gathered together to form a *havurah* . (Some of them are members of my congregation). The *havurah* meets on a regular basis and holds a monthly *shabbat* service. Occasionally members of the *havurah* attend regular services at the temple or join us for special programs. We have attempted to be as open to them as possible. Recently a few non-Jews have been attracted to the *havurah*. Several of them have indicated an interest in Jewish life, and one individual in particular has approached me in regard to the possibility of studying in order to convert to Judaism. In light of the strong antipathy of Judaism to homosexuality, should we accept a known and active homosexual who desires to convert to Judaism? (Rabbi R. Safran, Ft. Wayne, IN)

ANSWER: The attitude of traditional Judaism to homosexuality is clear. The biblical prohibition against homosexuality is absolute as seen in the verses: "Do not lie with a male as one lies with a woman; it is an abhorrence" (Lev. 18.22); "if a man lies with a male as one lies with a woman, the two of them have done an abhorrent thing; they shall be put to death—their blood-guilt is upon them" (Lev. 20.13). Other statements are equally clear The Talmudic discussion of the matter makes no substantive changes and continues the prohibition. It deals with the question of rumors, duress, and various forms of the homosexual act *(San.* 53a ff; *Yeb.* 83b; *Ker.* 2a ff; *Ned.* 51a, etc.). In the subsequent codes, the matter is briefly mentioned with the same conclusions (*Yad Hil. Issurei Biah* 1.5, 22.2; *Tur* and *Shulhan Arukh Even Haezer* 24). There is very little material in the responsa literature which deals with homosexuality, as it does not seem to have been a major problem The commentators to the above mentioned section of the *Shulhan Arukh* felt that suspicion of homosexuality could not arise in their day, and so various preventive restrictions were superfluous. For example, Moses Rifkes (seventeenth-century Poland) stated that this sin did not exist in his time *(Be-er Hagolah)*. Until the most recent modern period, there has been no further discussion of this matter. The Central Conference of American Rabbis has dealt with the issue of homosexuality over a number of years. In 1977, the following resolution was adopted:

> Whereas, the Central Conference of American Rabbis consistently supported civil rights and civil liberties for all people, especially for those whom these rights and liberties have been withheld, and
>
> Whereas, homosexuals have been in our society and long endured discrimination,
>
> Be it therefore resolved, that we encourage legislation which decriminalizes homosexual acts between consenting adults, and prohibits discrimination against them as person, and
>
> Be it further resolved, that our Reform Jewish religious organizations undertake programs in cooperation with the total Jewish community to implement the above stand.

We will not discuss the modern Jewish attitude toward homosexuals which has been shaped by two factors: (a) the attitude of tradition toward homosexuality (b) our contemporary understanding of homosexuality, which sees homosexuality as an illness, a genetically based disfunction, or a sexual preference and life style. There is disagreement whether homosexuality represents a willful act or a response to which the individual is driven.

If a homosexual comes to us and seeks conversion, we should explain the attitude of traditional Judaism and that of our Reform movement to him quite clearly. After that, if he continues to show an interest in Judaism and wishes to convert, then we may accept him as any other convert.

The entire matter is somewhat complicated by the fact that this group of homosexuals has organized itself into a *havurah*. We must ask ourselves whether it is simply for the purpose of companionship, or if this is a group which will seek to attract others to a homosexual life style. In the case of the latter, we should not accept a convert who intends to influence others in that direction. Otherwise, a homosexual who wishes to convert to Judaism should be accepted as any other convert.

Lesbians and Their Children
*Contemporary American Reform Responsa,
New York, 1987, # 200*

Walter Jacob

QUESTION: Two women who are in a lesbian relationship have raised a child who has been adopted by one of them. The child has been formally converted to Judaism with *berit milah* and *mikveh*. This was done like any other conversion and posed no problems. Now, however, the child is about to be *bar mitzvah* and the two women want to participate in the service as any parents. Should they be permitted to do so? (Rabbi M. Staitman, Pittsburgh, PA)

ANSWER: Although Jewish tradition from the Bible onward strongly condemns homosexuality, it has rather little to say about lesbianism. Some of the sources indicate that it may have been treated as a temporary phenomenon, rather than as a permanent condition among women. So, the *Talmud* (*Shab.*65a; *Yeb.* 76a) and the *Sifrei* prohibit sexual intercourse between women, but do not specify any punishment. They state that such a woman was permitted to marry even into the priesthood. As lesbianism was considered obscene, later sources demanded punishment (*makot mardut*) for those involved (*Yad Hil. Issurei Biah* 21.8; *Shulhan Arukh Even Haezer* 20.2). As, however, there was no biblical basis for such punishment, there was also little further discussion in responsa literature. We should be guided by these feelings and by our tradition's strong support of normative family life. Everything we do should strengthen the family. We should, therefore, ignore the lesbian relationship and feel no need to deal with it unless the individuals involved make an issue of it. If they do not, then their lesbian relationship is irrelevant. They should be permitted, along with other individuals, both male and female, to participate in the *Torah* readings as well as other portions of the *shabbat* services. This will indicate to both the congregation and this household that we recognize the love and care given to the child and do not focus on the lesbian relationship.

CONTRIBUTORS

Rachel Adler is Joint Assistant Professor of Modern Jewish Thought and Gender at the School of Religion, University of Southern California and the Rabbinical School, Hebrew Union College-Jewish Institute of Religion, Los Angeles. She is the author of *Engendering Judaism: An Inclusive Theology and Ethics* (1998) which won the 1999 National Jewish Book Award in Jewish thought. She is the author of numerous articles.

Elliot N. Dorff is Rector and Professor of Philosophy at the University of Judaism in Los Angeles. He has been a member of the Committee on Law and Standards of the Rabbinical Assembly (Conservative) since 1985 and currently serves as Vice Chair. He is the author of *A Living Tree, the Roots and Growth of Jewish Law* (1988) along with numerous other studies.

David Ellenson is I.H. and Anna Grancell Professor of Jewish Religious Thought at the Hebrew Union College-Jewish Institute of Religion, Los Angeles. The author of *Tradition in Transition* (1989), *Esriel Hildesheimer and the Creation of Modern Jewish Orthodoxy* (1990), and more than one hundred fifty articles and reviews, Ellenson is currently completing a book-length study of Orthodox responsa on conversion in the modern world.

Solomon B. Freehof (1893-1990) was Rabbi of the Rodef Shalom Congregation, Pittsburgh, Pennsylvania; President of the Central Conference of American Rabbis, and the World Union for Progressive Judaism; Chair of the Responsa Committee of the Central Conference of American Rabbis. Author of eight volumes of responsa including *Today's Reform Responsa* (1990), as well as *Reform Jewish Practice* (1947, 1952), *The Responsa Literature* (1955), *A Treasury of Responsa* (1963) and fifteen other books.

Walter Jacob is Senior Scholar of Rodef Shalom Congregation, Pittsburgh, Pennsylvania; President of the Abraham Geiger College in Berlin/Potsdam, Past President of the Central Conference of American Rabbis, President of the Freehof Institute of Progressive *Halakhah* and the Associated American Jewish Museums. Author and editor of twenty six books including *American Reform Responsa* (1983), *Contemporary American Reform Responsa* (1987), *Liberal Judaism and Halakhah* (1988), *Questions and Reform Jewish-Answers—New Reform Responsa* (1991), *The Healing Past: Pharmaceuticals in the Biblical and Rabbinic World* (1993), *Not By Birth Alone, Conversion to Judaism* (1997).

Peter Knobel is Rabbi of Beth Emet, Evanston, Ill; Chair of the Liturgy Committee of the Central Conference of American Rabbis; past Book-review Editor, *Journal of the Central Conference of American Rabbis*. Editor of *Gates of the Season* (1983).

Jacob Z. Lauterbach (1873-1942) was Professor of Talmud and Rabbinics at the Hebrew Union College, Cincinnati. Chair of the Responsa Committee of the Central Conference of American Rabbis. Editor of *Mekhilta deRav Ishmael* (1933-49); contributor of the *Jewish Encyclopedia*.

John Rayner is Lecturer in Liturgy and Codes at the Leo Baeck College, London; rabbi emeritus of the Liberal Synagogue in London. He is the author of *Understanding Judaism* (1996), *A Jewish Understanding of the World* (1997), *Jewish Religious Law: A Progressive Perspective* (1999), and many essays.

Michael Rosen is a businessman involved in technology and the financial markets. He is president of T1Xpert.com, a company developing financial service systems for the financial industry. He has an M.A. in Religious Studies, is married to Rabbi Karen L. Fox.

Richard Rosenthal (1929-1998) was rabbi in Tacoma, Washington for forty-one years and combined his rabbinate with teaching at the University of Puget Sound, civic activities and a regular newspaper column. Past president of the Pacific Rabbinic Conference, he published a number of essays on *minhag*.

Moshe Zemer is Director of the Freehof Institute of Progressive *Halakhah*; a founder of the Movement for Progressive Judaism in Israel; founding rabbi of the Kedem Synagogue-Bet Daniel, Tel Aviv. *Av Bet Din* of the Israel Council of Progressive Rabbis, Senior Lecturer in Rabbinics at the Hebrew Union College, Jerusalem. Contributor of numerous articles on *halakhah* in the Israeli press and scientific journals; author of *The Sane Halakhah* [Hebrew], (1993) which has recently appeared in German and English translations.